EDUCATING
THE
YOUNG HORSE

The Thinking Trainer's Guide

EDUCATING
THE
YOUNG HORSE

The Thinking Trainer's Guide

by JULIAN WESTALL

Half Halt Press
Boonsboro, Maryland

EDUCATING THE YOUNG HORSE
The Thinking Trainer's Guide
© 1994 Julian Westall

Published in the United States of America by
Half Halt Press, Inc.
P.O. Box 67
Boonsboro, MD 21713

Photos © H. Mercedes Clemens
Chapter Heading Illustrations © Cathy Kelley

Book and Jacket Design by H. Mercedes Clemens
Illustrations by Patricia Naegeli
Chapter Heading Illustrations by Cathy Kelley

Library of Congress Cataloging-in-Publication Data

Westall, Julian. 1948–
    Educating the young horse : the thinking trainer's guide / by Julian Westall.
        p.   cm.
    ISBN 0-939481-39-1
    1. Horses--Training.   2. Horsemanship.   I. Title
SF287.W43   1994
636.1'088--DC20   94-35346
                                                                        CIP

Contents

14: First Mounted Work   133

15: Further Mounted Work: Off the Lunge 149

16: Work Outside the School   171

Acknowledgments

As in most endeavors, this book could not have been completed without the assistance of others.

Sincere thanks are due to the following individuals: Lyne Morgan of Fair Play Farm and Helen Francis for their patient assistance; Patricia Naegeli and Cathy Kelley for their inspiringly creative artwork; and Mercedes Clemens of Pandora Publishing & Graphics for her extraordinary patience and good humor in completing the photography and design of the book. Special thanks are also due to Beth Carnes of Half Halt Press, Inc. for her skillful editing, as well as shouldering the unenviable task of bringing the whole project to fruition.

Introduction

I have often found it interesting to note how the concept of "basics" is regarded in various disciplines. To some such as a marksman "basics" denote not only the "starter kit" of shooting but also the essence of the sport. For example, relaxation and breath control are essential whether one is a beginner or an experienced shot. Moreover, the trigger is squeezed no less delicately just because a person is a novice. With careful and progressive instruction, these and other "basics" become not merely the foundation, but also the building itself. The same can be said for making oneself a competent musician, painter, or architect, or anything else for that matter.

How does riding fit into this picture? Alas, some horse people approach their sport in a haphazard manner, which yields mediocre and sometimes dangerous results. The time-intensive aspect of our sport frequently spawns both impatience and a consuming ambition to reach one's goals. Unfortunately, learning to ride well and educating a horse to a similar standard cannot be gotten by "cramming," as one does for an exam. For the horse and rider, the process of learning is not only a time-consuming affair, but the lessons have both immediate and perpetual practical application.

Nonetheless, there is a prevalent notion that the "basics" are the equivalent to preschool for small children and that "real learning" only begins when they start reading or using the multiplication tables! But, while it is increasingly recognized that the quality of the basics affects performance at all levels, its true value is not always clearly understood.

For instance, the "basics" are all too often regarded as something a young horse initially learns and which are then superseded by more "advanced" techniques and exercises. This is an erroneous concept, because the structure of "advanced" work is made up of "basics" which, when expressed or emphasized in certain ways, give the illusion that what the horse or rider does is something "new."

It follows then, that the "basics" are not something transient, but instead are very much at the heart of everything that is labeled as "new" or advanced. Moreover, the "basics" are not limited to merely being a structure upon which experience is built, but in addition also have remedial values.

For example, one of the main reasons why many attempts at retraining horses are unsuccessful—or their effectiveness is, at best, short-lived—is because they violate two important principles.

First, the time allocated to remedying a habit or situation, that often has been manifesting for years, is telescoped into a very short time-frame. Second, the means to do this is by addressing the symptom, instead of the cause, giving the *appearance* that all is well once more.

The fact of the matter is that a band-aid treatment is no good if our horse needs reconstructive surgery! It is by doggedly using quick-fixes whose effects are impermanent that retraining often inherits its reputation of being "difficult;" because by adopting the methods most commonly used, its success rate is pretty low. Only by returning to the "basics"—whose function is both remedial and constructive—can the horse be successfully reclaimed.

Just like any good schoolteacher who aspires to make her pupils literate and equip them with skills to help them function effectively in life, so does a trainer—if worthy of that title—also bear a similar responsibility to his charges. This important task cannot be achieved simply by a lot of T.L.C. and encouragement, no more than a child could be educated solely by these means. Although these play an important role in a horse's education, the good trainer also needs to have considerable knowledge of his craft, be a keen observer, and have a logical mind.

I would hazard a guess that a large percentage of people that drive motor vehicles probably couldn't describe how a petrol engine works—nor do they care! Yet in spite of this they are perfectly capable drivers. This is fine as long as they don't have to repair a breakdown or even rebuild an engine once it's in bits.

Horses can be *ridden* quite successfully on this principle but they cannot be *trained* well with such limited knowledge. Thus it behooves the trainer not to be merely a "driver" but also a good "mechanic."

To do a really good job of educating green horses requires experience. Yet, a substantial number of horses are more or less broken to saddle each year with little or no formal schooling and are subsequently able to muddle along somehow, to the satisfaction of their owners. This phenomenon does not invalidate the more formal approaches to training the young horse, but instead merely indicates that most of those animals had very tractable dispositions! If they had been taught more methodically, they would undoubtedly have become even better equipped for their destiny.

It should be noted that there are other good ways of making young horses, often less time consuming. However, these require an expertise that is assumed the reader does not have. The methods here described are simple, efficient, and not subject to any time constraints. Although most of the work should be done on one's own to avoid confusing the horse, for reasons of safety for both horse and rider some parts are best undertaken with the cooperation of an experienced rider.

In addition, it is essential that the trainer not only understands the theory of lungeing, but is also able to apply it practically. Using the young horse as a guinea pig to learn this skill can only lead to disaster. If one doesn't know how to lunge, it's well worth spending several hours with a competent professional before attempting this task on a young horse.

I wish to further stress this point because although any practice one obtains by lungeing an obedient horse is certainly valuable, it is at best a poor apprenticeship for lungeing a green youngster who doesn't know the rules of the game, and whose reactions to one's instructions are less than measured and compliant. Although one could easily fill a book to describe this craft, it would be almost impossible to learn it from this medium without some previous practical experience.

Moreover, although there are many references to the techniques of lungeing, they number only a small portion that makes up this skill. These take the form of important reminders as well as some techniques that one may not normally learn on a made horse. In other words, the latter are peculiar to working green horses or re-schooling older ones whose proficiency in this facet of their training is lacking.

Desirable Qualities for the Trainer

Love

The first quality the trainer should have, is love for the horse he is training. I believe this to be the most important quality since it sets a cooperative tone to all our dealings with him.

As we know, like all other animals, horses are very sensitive to the attitude and moods of their handlers. If our interaction with each horse is conducted with a sense of interest in his mental and physical welfare, then he will reciprocate by trying to give of his best. When we approach his training with the attitude that we are there to *help* equip him for a strange role, one for which nature had not intended, instead of how he can be exploited, then communication between horse and man is on a superior footing.

The trainer's task is difficult in this respect, because he so often has to wear two hats. The first is one in which he would like a utopian situation, where there is perfect harmony between person and horse with both parties being on an equal footing and each willingly catering to the other's needs. Then, he has to sport the second hat, since he is confronted with the everyday realities—a playful, if not exuberant youngster who doesn't quite see the point of why he should be introduced to saddlery and lessons when he's just spent the last three or more years doing pretty much as he pleased!

Under these circumstances the trainer's attitude is far from utopian. While wearing his second hat, equality tends to take a back seat, as the trainer becomes "the master." In this guise he has many roles—teacher, mentor, provider, disciplinarian.

Understandably, it's not easy to switch quickly from one hat to another. For example, if while being lunged, a beefy youngster spooks badly and, catching you unawares, has just finished dragging you around in the dirt, unless you are a very disciplined and understanding individual, the word love is unlikely to spring immediately to mind!

As the horse becomes more experienced these provocative incidents gradually diminish (and, alas, others of a more subtle nature take their place!). So we may intimate that with time, it is easier to love the horse because our patience is not being so blatantly challenged. That is why it is often harder for the trainer of young horses to keep his temper and to realize that, unless he is mistreating his horse, the animal's pranks, misbehavior or unruliness are not a personal attack. The horse would in some measure probably behave that way whomever was handling him.

When the trainer understands this, he can begin to wear both hats at the same time—the ideal and the practical merge. The horse does not resent necessary corrections. Why? Because the way he is corrected, however sternly, and if administered in a spirit of love and detachment, takes the sting out of that admonition. The horse comes to understand there is no need to resent the correction or the corrector.

Intent

For our purposes we may define intent as the "mental game plan."

We, as the trainer, should have a clear idea of what we want our horse to do. In its general form, this intent can be simply having a goal for a particular training session. In its more specific form, it is the ability to clearly visualize something we want our horse to do at a certain time, such as an unhurried transition from trot to canter.

This is a very important point because most animals—including the human one—best receive communications in a pictorial form. So when we visualize that unhurried canter transition in a clear, detailed way, we address the horse's mind—which, with careful training becomes increasingly receptive to our suggestions. Once we start to connect with his mind, our tactile signals become less obvious, less frequent and their role becomes more suggestive than authoritative.

Many problems are caused by the trainer's lack of intent. These range from disciplinary problems to inefficient performances. For instance, the following is a typical example with which I'm sure we can identify, since we've all been guilty of such conduct at one time or another.

The horse has been halted for a while and has been standing on loose reins, then the rider decides to move off. Most riders will signal the horse to walk forward, and as he does so, shorten the reins. Meanwhile, the horse goes forward at an undetermined speed and, in all likelihood, in some undefined direction. Although many riders would find no fault with this and may even defend it by claiming that things can be taken care of pretty quickly, the good trainer on the other hand would regard it as unacceptable. Why so?

Well, it's analogous to climbing into a strange car and driving off into the traffic while adjusting the tilt of the steering wheel, the angle of the rear view mirror and the position of the driver's seat. It would be unthinkable!

Returning to our horse, if we don't want him to think that we don't care or are slapdash, then we should walk him forward in the following way:

1. The rider adjusts his seat so he is sitting squarely and with the appropriate seat for his horse's level of training.
2. As his legs gently close on the horse's sides, the reins are picked up and adjusted to a suitable length.
3. The rider decides and concentrates for a moment on the energy, rhythm and speed he will demand of the horse's walk, and what precise direction it will take. At this point the rein length may have to be readjusted.
4. A moment before he gives the aids to walk on, the rider tries to will the horse to move forward simultaneously with his (the rider's) own movements—as if one unit.
5. As the horse moves off, the rider immediately monitors and, if necessary, corrects any deviation from his own original plan in terms of energy, rhythm, speed, lateral balance and direction.

If this sounds like a ritual, you are quite correct—it is! Yet in its own way it is no different from the ritual a weight lifter adopts to focus his mind, and psyche up for the impending effort. Or from that of the tennis player, who routinely takes a deep breath and shrugs his shoulders before bouncing the ball a specified number of times. Only then will his body have been cued or triggered to serve the ball efficiently. So it is with the horse and rider. Both are prepared so as to give the transition to walk the best chance of being a good one.

One may still object, arguing that since (to most riders) walking is something one does to loosen the horse up or else give him a breather, why should the rider's attention to such detail seemingly border on the pedantic? There are at least two good reasons.

One may be described in data processing jargon, namely "garbage in—garbage out!" In short, we reap what we sow.

The other is that with a green or young pupil, "consistency" takes on added importance compared to when training a more experienced horse. The latter's knowledge and experience invariably forgives the rider's minor and sporadic inconsistencies, as well as fairly successfully deciphering what his rider *meant* to tell him, as opposed to what he was actually told! The young horse, on the other hand, has no such background. Like a child, he takes things literally. When he is allowed to make a slapdash transition from a halt to walk, he doesn't understand why, for instance, the same leniency is not accorded for a transition to trot or canter. He becomes confused by such double standards.

This is why we need to pay attention to the quality of a seemingly mundane movement, such as going from halt to walk. Start the way you mean to go. In fact, a useful thought to work by, is to ride the horse as precisely as you would drive your car in traffic; he will then feel your sense of purpose.

One last point, which is often overlooked and can account for why the use of intent is frequently ineffective, is that it is projected at the wrong time. As we've just seen, the intent that we project to the horse must precede any other type of communication, whether verbal or tactile. Then, if necessary, that intent is continued alongside the verbal or tactile signals but the intent must be broadcasted to the horse *before* all else.

Will

Where intent, if repeatedly projected to the horse's mind, can produce quite good results, its efficacy is more or less diluted without the agency of will. Intent is the game plan, but the trainer's will is what jump-starts and fuels it.

When intelligently used, our will can make a fidgety horse stand still for mounting, encourage a hesitant horse to cross or jump an obstacle, mesmerize a worried horse into being docile, and can even control a horse's behavior at a distance. These are only some of the situations where the use of will can be helpful.

The use of our will has little to do with the direct physical domination of the horse. Nor is it inflexible. Rather, it is something the trainer measures out according to the situation, the mood or receptivity of the horse. It is the mental and emotional effort needed to direct the horse's mind to our wishes when it is necessary to do so—meaning that its powers should be used selectively. Indeed, for much of the time the trainer plays a passive mental and emotional role if the young horse is doing well on its own without our assistance.

In short, using our will is not an excuse to steamroller over the horse's own volition. If wisely used, it can soothe, reassure, suggest, encourage, cajole or order.

Calmness

Quality learning involves a considerable amount of thinking and thinking is arguably the hardest work a sentient being has to do.

It is also true to say that to think and learn well, one must be able to concentrate. In turn, this concentration is best developed in an atmosphere of calmness. That is why when we start training the young horse in his first lessons in concentration, we obtain better results if those lessons are conducted in an enclosed arena of some kind, free from unnatural noises and visual distractions. In other words, in calm surroundings.

However, these idyllic condi-

tions are not always at our disposal and we have to make do with what is available. No matter. Such disadvantages can be greatly offset by the calm demeanor of the trainer. With a calm handler the horse will come to be imbued with that quality almost by osmosis.

Frequently, simply being passive with a detached attitude prevents the trainer from playing into the horse's "hands." The trainer shouldn't always react to everything his mount does, as if the horse were manipulating him.

One of my earlier experiences as a trainer was working at an establishment which imported young horses for resale. Once acquired, they were shipped on a seven to ten day journey by truck or rail to our operation. Needless to say, after travelling that long in cramped accommodations without exercise, they were always excited and very fresh. One groom was assigned to look after them for the first week in their quarantined part of the barn.

A retired bricklayer, he knew little about the care of horses apart from the basics, such as picking feet, watering, and so on. He walked slowly, with stooped posture, and had to stop periodically to catch his breath. Due to his advanced age and poor health, he did everything very slowly and his standard of workmanship would, at best, be described as barely adequate— with one exception: all his young charges would soon stand or lead quietly when he handled them.

When I first saw him, I thought the poor fellow was destined to get hurt handling all those lively youngsters. He soon dispelled my fears. He would lead a horse that was cavorting and pulling to go forward with stooped posture, and at his habitual tired but steady shuffle, occasionally admonishing his rambunctious charge with his gruff, weak voice. One got the impression he was like a log the horse was pulling, with difficulty in doing so. Nonetheless, the horse would quickly settle and allow himself to be led without making a fuss.

This "technique" (which in his case was due more to his ailing health than to equestrian expertise) worked so effectively that I decided to try it for myself. In doing so I reasoned that since there were no specific "aids" involved to be learned, my recourse was to do exactly what he was doing. To this end, I imagined myself old and feeble. I walked like such a person would walk. I even used the volume and tone of my voice in the same way.

The speed with which lively horses would calm down and lead quietly was a revelation. I also noticed that if I merely walked slowly, the results did not come as quickly, nor were they as good. When I played the "old man" role in *all* its aspects, the best results were soon obtained.

We should note that calmness does not necessarily imply inaction, such as standing around like a blob! Rather, we should be calmly active and actively calm.

Concentration

Concentration is one of the most important qualities needed by the trainer of horses. The lack of concentration triggers off so many problems for the trainer that it will in fairly short time (unless the young horse's disposition is lamb-like) allow the horse to become unruly and, in turn, inevitably subject it to unnecessary reprimands and even punishment.

Why is this the case? Because a young horse is an undisciplined force. Work is alien to him, especially after having spent three or four carefree years out at pasture. It's only natural that he should in some measure resent the restriction imposed by the tack on his body and the discipline of movement his trainer demands. Like a young child, he prefers to play. Also, his reflexes are very fast. So how can the trainer hope to cope with a horse who weighs eight times his own weight and whose reflexes are much faster than his own? By concentration. Paying attention to the horse's facial expression, bodily posture and movements gives us those important telltale signs of impending problems. If we act promptly on that information, we can forestall the inevitable manifestation of a larger problem. Consequently the horse can for the most part be corrected tactfully with a minimum of physical strength, which helps to keep him sweet.

In short, it's a lot nicer for the horse to be given an aspirin early on, instead of surgery at a later date simply because we neglected to spot the early symptoms.

Patience

Some people are naturally patient, but for those who are not so endowed, it is not merely by quelling one's impatience that one comes to attain this virtue. One may be able to dupe a person by such a facade, but not an animal, much less a horse.

Patience can be cultivated in a genuine way, but it comes not from disciplining one's impatience but, instead, through understanding. When we understand why a horse is struggling to master some exercise we have presented to him, it becomes much harder to become annoyed with his floundering efforts.

Patience is the sum of certain skills and attributes which foster that virtue, and in turn it reciprocates by further developing *them*. Some of the more important of these from an equestrian standpoint are: empathy, a keen sense of observation, a sense of logic, compassion, and ingenuity. Since we are trying to impart ideas to a being that is neither human, nor communicates in the way we do, then extraordinary patience is needed to prevent that interaction from degenerating to frustration, and eventually anger. The good trainer—like the good schoolteacher—realizes that his pupil's inability to grasp what is being imparted is, more often than not, due to the way the material is presented.

As a child, like most of my classmates I really disliked math. It was meaningless, boring, and the calculations were expected to be worked out in a long-winded way to show all the steps that led to the answer. One day we were assigned a new teacher who, after having observed the traditional struggles that budding mathematicians are heir to, calmly informed us that he deplored this "blow by blow" approach to calculating problems, and moreover stated that all good mathematicians were lazy! Well, you can imagine how we reacted to all this. We were agog with anticipation, thinking that maybe we wouldn't have to do homework anymore or some such thing!

What he meant was that many calculations, especially those involving fractions, could be done much more easily in one fell swoop at the end. Not only was this an attractive concept to us, but more importantly, he got our attention with what seemed like an outrageous promise and then showed how it could be implemented.

He was more than a math teacher, because through his ingenuity he introduced us to concepts that had practical application even outside the field of mathematics.

When such an attribute plays a leading role in training horses, it's very difficult to lose patience. If one solution doesn't work on a particular horse, our ingenuity and logic will come to the fore. In fact, it's almost addictive, in the sense that good trainers will not accept defeat—and so will be spurred to find a better solution.

Equestrian Tact

Equestrian tact may be defined as the ability to:

- Know when to do something.
- Have a sense of priority.
- Know how to ask.
- Have a sense of justice.

Know When to Do Something

This is the ability to know when (both emotionally and physically) to *ask*; when to *push* for something; when to *resist passively*; when to *yield*; and to have the good sense to *back off* when whatever you are asking the horse to do is making him unmanageable, mentally or physically.

In order to use each of these criteria effectively, our decision should be governed by three considerations: having a sense of "occasion," the mood of the horse, and his attention level.

By having a sense of occasion, we mean knowing what is appropriate or inappropriate. For instance, asking a horse to do exacting work when he is either tired or "high" is clearly going to produce poor results. An example of having a *wrong* sense of occasion would be asking your boss for a raise shortly after he had been told how unproductive his staff are by his own boss!

Taking into account *the mood of the horse* when making a request is essential at any level of training. With a young horse, because the conditioning process that solicits his unquestioning obedience still has a long way to go, it behooves us not to ask for the impossible. If the request is fair, within his abilities, and the horse *is in a cooperative mood*, we will get what we want. If he is in a stubbornly contrary mood, his attitude may be so uncompromising that we may not have the ability to persuade him—let alone coerce him—to do what we asked.

With a more experienced horse, his sense of obedience will generally override his unwillingness to comply with a request. However, this means that the horse did only what he was told—not that he put his heart into it and did it well.

Knowing when to do something is the ability to sense the most propitious moment to ask the horse a question. This sense of timing is largely dependent on whether the trainer has the animal's *attention* or not. Moreover, with an untrained horse this "window of opportunity" for getting his attention may at first be fleeting, which in turn puts a premium on the trainer's sense of observation and quick reflexes. The following scenario (which was repeated many times) may give the reader a sense of this point.

When my dog was a puppy I sometimes used to exercise him in a nearby park where a group of "doggy" people would meet each morning to let their animals exercise and socialize. Occasionally I would stop and let my dog play with the others. These games usually turned out to be "a free for all" with the dogs becoming increasingly excited, until sooner or later they had to be separated and calmed down. I would allow my fellow to play and roughhouse, but not to the point where he would become so excited that he was a slave to the frenzied activity. Whenever I felt he needed a mental respite or, indeed, needed to quit for the day, I would call him off out of the pack from quite a distance—and he would come.

The procedure so impressed some of the people, that they would periodically offer me money to teach their dogs to be equally cooperative. Unfortunately, they missed the point. It wasn't so much that their dogs needed retraining, as it was themselves. All they saw was that when I whistled, my dog would break away from the pack and come to me, giving the impression that in spite of being involved in a frenetic activity, he hadn't lost his marbles and that he was a superbly obedient dog.

They were duped!

The fact of the matter is that at the time he was probably no better trained that most of the other dogs. His "impressive" act required him to know only two things: a whistle that signalled he was expected to come to me and some arm waving to indicate where I was in the crowd, combined with some hand slapping on my knees as an encouragement. None of these signals by themselves were of the slightest use unless they were given at the appropriate time. This meant that my dog had to be in a position or state to at least acknowledge that he had heard me, even before complying with my wishes to come over. I would wait until he was either facing in my direction or had paused momentarily, even for a couple of seconds, before whistling to him. At that moment, the signal had sufficient impact to make him stop and at least look for me. The arm waving and the knee slapping, coupled with some vocal encouragement, did the rest.

Have a Sense of Priority

What I mean by this is that there are many occasions where it's advantageous to overlook a fault (one which would normally be corrected), because in doing so we feel that the horse will give or has given us something more valuable.

For example, let's say that due to the horse's one-sidedness and stiffness he has difficulty in striking off in the canter without first running at the trot. Through various exercises and corrections we eventually get a clean transition but alas, on the wrong lead. If we have equestrian tact, it behooves us to overlook the fault of the incorrect lead, since the horse finally gave us at least half of what we wanted: an unhurried strike-off. It would be both petty and confusing if we corrected the remaining

Making the horse feel proud.

fault. It's as if we were saying "Yes; it's good that you did an unhurried transition but you failed to do so on the correct lead."

The good trainer will make his horse feel like a success, with no hint of a blotch on an otherwise good performance, at least for the time being. Then, after three or four similar consecutive results, when the horse is more confident, we can interrupt the transition as if to say "hang on; not so fast; you didn't pick up the correct lead!"

As we can see, this has nothing to do with sweeping a problem under the carpet, but instead having the wisdom to know when to overlook it temporarily in favor of a coveted advantage.

Knowing How to Ask

This means, being able to judge at any given moment, the degree of emphasis given by the aids. Let's digress for a moment, to better understand what is meant by emphasis.

It does not, as is generally supposed, have much to do with giving a stronger signal with leg, whip, or rein, though it's true that sometimes this is the right thing to do. Emphasis can be given in two ways. First, for example, is when a horse that is feeling contrary is asked to go forward. However, due to his peevishness he resents the interaction of the rider's legs and hands, threatens to stop, and overcollect himself, perhaps as a prelude to rearing. One way to solve this is to use the stick sharply, but with the possible risk of provoking a worse attitude—even a dangerously combative one. The alternative is to ease the reins and shepherd the horse forward with inviting legs and soft clicks of the tongue. If this soft glove approach is scorned and there has to be a showdown, then so be it. However, it is poor horsemanship to neglect exploring more diplomatic ways of getting the horse to do what we want.

Second, the strength of a signal is governed by its clarity. The following analogy helps to illustrate this point.

Imagine you are listening to the radio to someone singing with musical accompaniment and that the singer's poor diction makes it difficult to understand the lyrics. Now there are two ways you will be able to make out the words. First is by simply raising the volume. The second is by lowering the bass and turning the tone knob to maximum treble, but without raising the volume. With this second approach the singer's words will be crisper and hence more easily understood.

It's the same with the rider's aids. When through the steady control of the rider's hands and legs, those signals are given distinctly, but without force, then they are immediately acknowledged and better understood by the horse. Furthermore, these same aids will not be sufficiently clear unless they are preceded and followed by periods of silence. This "silence" is dependent on the rider's movements being in unison with those of his mount. However, to be in perfect harmony, his "seat" must also project the appropriate feel for the situation.

It's rather like reciting poetry. One can recite the lines in a deadpan voice—which almost certainly will not project the feel the poet originally intended of his work. Alternatively, the piece can be read with passion, verve or sorrow, depending on whether the poem is about love, adventure or tragedy.

Thus, it is in this state that the rider's seat is deemed to be "quiet."

Any movement from the rider that emphasizes the status quo, or else is inharmonious, is immediately registered by the horse. The former as an aid, the latter as interference or "static." It is this "static" that confuses the horse. Many are the occasions when instructions are given at an inappropriate moment, i.e. at a time which is not synchronized with his movements. To give timely instructions on a steady, experienced horse is relatively easy; to do so on a green one is much harder. His unsteady, erratic, and sometimes unpredictable movements pose quite a challenge to even a skilled rider. Consequently the horse has a riddle to solve, namely, whether the rider's movements were accidental or whether they were instructions.

Having a Sense of Justice

This is the ability to judge, when for example, the horse makes the same mistake on two separate occasions, how and to what degree he is to be corrected. Maybe on the first occasion you deem it necessary to correct him, but on the second one you decide to let it slide.

An illustration of this is when a horse stops twice at a sizable jump. On the first stop, he might be reprimanded briefly but sharply, because the rider truly thought his horse was being lazy. But on the second occasion the rider let it be and instead soothed his mount with the voice, followed by a brief pat on the neck, before negotiating the jump again—this time successfully. To an inexperienced onlooker, the rider's differing reactions to his horse's stops may seem illogical. On the first attempt he gets after his mount, while on the second he does exactly the opposite—he pats him!

Why? What happened in the second instance?

Perhaps the rider judged that the approach was on too long a stride and without sufficient impulsion. Consequently the horse arrived at a difficult take off spot and prudently slammed on the brakes, fearing disaster if he attempted the leap. The horse's judgement was correct; the rider's was not. The rider reassured his mount that all was well between them and started over.

Regarding this subject, another factor comes into play. I refer here to the option of letting what would normally be a reproachable act, slide. For instance, a horse may nip for a tidbit when he's already eaten your supply or he may buck quite hard when he's feeling good (and being ridden). Or, he may playfully—yet frustratingly—give you the runaround when you are trying to catch him. During any one of these incidents, we may decide to play along and laugh at his mischievousness. It may seem contrary to and inconsistent with the way we would normally handle these things during training, yet even animals appreciate when we bend or even break the rules occasionally. However, this does not imply that we allow the horse run rough-shod all over us—not at all. In fact, if he is getting precocious to the point where the level of "play" becomes either an obnoxious habit or dangerous, he must be told that enough is enough.

If nothing else, it reminds us that although the bulk of the craft of interacting with another sentient being can be learnt, there is an important aspect that cannot be taught. It's a sense or form of expression that a person either does or doesn't have. Nor is it manifested by each person in the same way. For instance, depending on the trainer's personality, he may laugh at his horse's antics or else dish out some dry humor. Alternately, he may be reproachful with "tongue in cheek."

It's fortunate we have this trait, because it is one way of expressing a less formal side of ourselves, which is sometimes difficult to do when the more "serious" business of training is the agenda of the moment.

Studying the Horse

Let's now examine our youngster's makeup, so that by knowing both his strengths and weaknesses we can better interact with him.

The Senses

Timidity

Foremost, by nature the horse is a timid animal. And, nature made the horse one of the faster quadrupeds so he can flee from danger. His fighting abilities are secondary to this primary instinct of self preservation. That is why rough, threatening, or thoughtless actions will do little to inspire his confidence in the trainer.

Having said that, the clever and sensitive trainer can sometimes play on a horse's timidity in order to energize him or to move in a certain direction. This is easier to do while working from the ground, i.e. during loose schooling, lungeing and long reining. Naturally, this ploy should be used sparingly and selectively, or a horse might become scared of his trainer, or become so inured to these tactics that he becomes increasingly cold to the aids.

Sensitivity

The horse's timidity indicates that he is also sensitive, and it is this very sensitivity—to which he is often a slave—that frequently freezes his ability to think calmly and hence clearly. It is the trainer's job not to make him necessarily less sensitive, but rather to encourage him to be the master of his emotions, instead of being their slave.

Sensitivity may be likened to an energy which the trainer has little trouble in soliciting; it is easily directed, yet not quite so easily controlled. In some ways it is a two-edged sword in that it is a boon for the sensitive and skillful trainer, but becomes a nightmare for a person deficient in those qualities. Although as a general rule some breeds are more sensitive than others, the sensitivity of a more "cold blooded" horse can be improved to some degree. Getting such a horse's attention *and maintaining it* goes a long way to accomplish this.

Reasoning

The horse doesn't reason in the sophisticated way that humans can. Much (but not all) of his learning process is based on simple cause and effect and generally with the proviso that the two be closely connected, within seconds of each other. The following example may help illustrate this principle.

A groom is in a horse's stall, when suddenly the animal steps on his foot. In great pain, the groom hops outside, nursing his bruised limb, then returns a few minutes later to yell at the horse and angrily slaps him on the rib cage. Though understandable, the groom's behavior was irrational from a training standpoint, since the horse probably didn't appreciate why he was being chastised. The more logical tactic would have been to reprimand the horse immediately after the misdemeanor. The animal would then have understood that in future it must be respectful of the handler's space.

Attention Span

Getting the horse's attention is the number one priority in training. If you don't have his attention, he is not going to learn very well. This principle applies as much to gaining a horse's confidence or calming him as it does to teaching him the various exercises. To put it into context, try teaching something to a distracted human and see how far you get! At some

point if you don't actu-
ally say it, you will al-
most certainly think
"You aren't paying at-
tention!"

In some respects,
young horses are like
children: their attention
span is short, and they
are easily distracted.
Knowing this, the good
trainer makes each
schooling session short,
about thirty to forty
minutes. Also, he is

Horse paying attention.

careful to further break that period down into smaller segments. For instance, a working segment may last just a few seconds or as long as five
minutes. This is followed by a brief intermission, during which time the
horse is given a break and has a chance to reflect on what he just did.

Often, attention problems are caused by the rider not appreciating that
the criteria that govern a human's attention are quite different from those
of the horse. Let's look at the human perspective first.

Just like pedestrians, riders often tend to have a posture which lowers
their gaze. Moreover, they tend to stare at the horse's ears, which results in
limiting their range of vision to a few yards ahead. Now we come to the
horse. He, poor fellow, lives in a situation where his attention is split into
two parts. One satisfies his natural tendency to look far ahead, which is the
opposite to what most humans do, while the other is drawn in the opposite
direction, to his rider behind him.

The first tendency explains why, for instance, when the horse is taken
out on a hack, he may spook and take his rider unawares. The horse was
cognizant of something within his range of sight (far ahead) which the
rider failed to spot. In such circumstances the horse cannot be prevented
from using his eyes and ears in the way they naturally function for him, so
it behooves the rider to use his own eyes and ears in a similar way to how
the horse does. By this, the rider's awareness is on a more equal footing
with that of his mount.

A time honored way of restricting the horse's visual and auditory senses
so that he is less distracted and finds it easier to concentrate on his rider is

to school him in an indoor ring. However, this should not be overdone; otherwise, when the time comes to ride him out of doors, his senses will be assaulted by the many distractions he has been missing, thus making him a very inattentive pupil.

The other part of the horse's attention is behind him, towards his rider. The rider who is not experienced with young horses certainly appreciates the need for the more mature horse to pay attention to him, and understandably expects a high degree of attentiveness and obedience from such a horse.

Now we transfer that rider onto a green horse. Assuming that he's a reasonably sympathetic character, he will invariably excuse his young horse's inattentiveness, skittishness, or overreactions to his aids, simply as youthful inexperience. This is a laudable viewpoint but, I venture to say, is not quite the whole story. Two points have been overlooked, which his experienced horse would have compensated for, but to which his youngster would be less forgiving:

• The nervousness of knowing the rider is on his back behind him, but not being able to see him.

• His fear of not being able to use his eyes as means of figuring out his rider's next intentions and wishes.

What does all this mean in practice? With reference to the first point, the rider must appreciate how edgy a young horse can at first be when his rider is distracting him, one might say, backwards. Here is an animal who is in the habit of paying attention to things in the distance. Then within a short period, he must get used to a person being on his back—behind and above him. The more the rider shifts around, the more the horse gets worried. In this case, the rider must try and sit very quietly to gain his horse's confidence and allow him to figure out how best to carry this new-found weight without distraction.

While the first point pertains primarily to newly backed or green broke horses, the second point is relevant to horses at all levels of training. When the average rider wants his horse to do something, he simply gives the appropriate signals, and in doing so expects the horse to answer promptly and smoothly. I would venture to say that it is quite remarkable the horse replies in this manner.

Why? Because, while the rider has had plenty of time to think about what he is next going to tell his horse, the animal is rarely accorded the same advantage. In other words, the horse is expected to reply unhesitatingly and correctly. If you think this is splitting hairs, let's take two examples that illustrate the importance of this point.

Imagine for a moment the consequences of eliminating all the amber lights from traffic signals. Since drivers are no longer alerted when the lights are going to change to red, the accident rate would skyrocket. Besides, policemen would have a field day issuing tickets for running a red light!

Another example is illustrated by sprinters at the start of a race. Normally the athletes are settled in their chocks, balanced between two hands and one knee on the ground. The starter alerts the competitors with the words "On your marks," followed by the advisory signal "Get set." This cues them to raise their knees off the ground and prepare their bodies for launching. In turn, this is followed by the starting gun. Imagine what a ragged start there would be if the official simply turned up, waited for a moment, and then fired his weapon!

Our horse also needs advanced warnings. We can't always alert him as to what his next instruction will be, but we can always signal him that such an instruction is imminent. Moreover, before we can even alert him, we have to ensure that he is aware that such a signal has been given in the first place.

In order to satisfy these conditions, the rider must first try and sit as quietly as possible so that when he moves his limbs or his weight, this is done deliberately, to signify that a signal has been given to the horse. If the rider is careless on this point, his horse will find it hard to decipher whether his rider's movements were inadvertent or whether they were instructions.

As to the signals themselves, at first the horse is cued verbally. For instance, if he is trotting and we want him to walk, we prefix the instruction the reins give him with the verbal command he will have learned during his lunge training. Then, as he becomes confident that his rider will not hurt his mouth, the verbal cue can gradually be substituted by others, such as a change in the rider's posture and eventually by half-halts.

Space

Space may be defined as the "comfort zone" surrounding a horse. In human terms, it's analogous to wanting "elbow room," an aversion to being "crowded," or taking offense at someone "breathing down your neck."

All of these situations will create a resentment which is expressed either mentally, verbally or physically. So it is with the horse.

Although these illustrations suggest that it is an outside force that invades the space of the subject, it is also true that the "space" can be broached by the subject being pushed involuntarily towards such a force. It is this latter example of the horse's aversion to being crowded that the trainer can deliberately exploit in order to obtain certain results.

For instance, let's say we are lungeing a horse who is lazy and is inattentive to the urging of clicks of the tongue and the whip to send him forward. On finding that escalating these signals either in frequency or intensity doesn't have much effect, we then have to solve the problem some other way.

We begin by lungeing the horse in the ring, to a position where the wall is tangential to the lunge circle. Now, as the horse approaches the wall at an angle, we purposefully and quickly stride towards his flank so that he is "crowded" by the wall on his outside and by us advancing towards him on his inside. The result is that he will race through the bottleneck we have just created. In effect we curtailed his "space" and played on his instincts of self preservation (to flee) in order to energize him and be more respectful of our signals.

It's worth noting that although this ploy will certainly bring our horse back to life, when used by itself it has only limited benefits. The reason for this is that it does not correct his contempt for answering our voice and whip. However, if we use one or both of these signals simultaneously, while curtailing the horse's space, within two or three such repetitions the voice and whip will be effective in their own right. The horse will have learned by association.

Flight Distance

What is flight distance? It is the closest distance from the horse which an unwelcome object can approach without provoking the horse to retreat to safety. The more familiar the horse becomes with that object—be it a dog, person, farm tractor, etc.—the shorter that flight distance becomes. Similarly, a horse's flight distance will come into play if he is asked to approach an unwelcome object, as opposed to the object approaching him.

Encroaching into a horse's flight distance immediately brings into play his most powerful instinct, that of self preservation. The trainer who ignores this instinct in an untrained horse by bullying him into approaching the object he fears runs the risk of three setbacks in training.

First, the horse will generally associate the pain of strong legs and whip (which are inevitably used to urge him forward) with the object of his aversion.

Second, he learns how to ignore the rider's signals. Since he is prey to his own overriding fear, then any order that forces him to approach a frightening object will barely be considered. This is a serious training error because, when dealing with a green horse, we studiously cultivate his obedience by avoiding situations where he stubbornly refuses our requests. Once we sow the seeds of successful resistance in his mind, we will have unwittingly shown him his power to tell us to get lost! The horse isn't stupid— nor will he be slow to learn how to exploit this ruse in the future.

Third and most important, the trainer will have made a dent in his horse's trust in him. On future similar occasions, the young horse will question his trainer's wisdom and ability to make judgements that are in his (the horse's) best interest. The more trained the horse becomes, the more his sense of obedience tends to override and partially subdue his own natural instincts. However, in the young horse the opposite is true, hence our concern to not provoke our mount into an unnecessary confrontation, which will invariably have unwelcome repercussions.

The Horse's Mind

Memory

The horse has a phenomenal memory. A good trainer makes extensive use of it by soliciting certain actions from the horse and then presenting him with a rewarding experience. By association the horse remembers this and subsequently will be keener to comply with those requests in the future. In short, the horse learns more quickly.

This same approach can be used

to dissuade the horse from exhibiting unwelcome or dangerous habits. The only difference, of course, being that when the horse manifests these he is presented with an unsavory experience of some kind. Incidentally, this is not a euphemism for physical punishment directly from the trainer. Such an experience can be in this form, but it's not the only way.

For instance, the voice used scoldingly can be very effective on some horses. Another corrective measure is when the horse is put in a situation where he punishes himself. He will remember the subsequent discomfort or inconvenience, and will be less keen to repeat the misdemeanor. Moreover, this situation has the added advantage that in the horse's mind, the trainer was not involved in the process and so is not viewed as "the bad guy."

Another point to note is that because the horse makes very efficient use of his memory, whereas humans generally do so to lesser degree, it is often difficult for a human to relate to what a horse regards as noteworthy. In other words, what a horse regards as important and worth remembering, may be dismissed as of no consequence by us and so doesn't impress us enough to remember it. In view of this, the good trainer doesn't regard any incident as inconsequential. He won't make a federal case of it, but he doesn't forget it either because his horse almost certainly won't.

How do we know what the horse finds important to remember? Well, it's sometimes difficult to tell. The incidents we know will be best remembered are going to be ones to which the horse reacted physically in some way, either with pleasure or pain. However, a horse remembers a lot more than good and bad experiences or routines. How he processes these other incidents escape all but the most attentive human observer.

For instance, most people find nothing unusual in a horse intently watching something that has caught his eye. This is generally attributed to the horse being surprised, on the lookout for danger, or the fascination with something new. With this I have no quarrel, but I believe it to be only half the story.

As an example, put a human competitor in a ring, and you will nearly always see his peers standing by the rail watching like hawks—assessing, learning and remembering. We see the same characteristics in intelligent performance dogs—such as those used for police work or sheep herding. They learn and remember what they observe. Horses are no different. It's not unusual to note the intelligent ones that are lively, as opposed to being jaded or ring sour, watching a fellow horse jump a course of jumps or perform in some other way. These horses don't miss a trick, and with such a keen attention it's hard to imagine their memory would fail them.

Intelligence

It is not uncommon to hear people say that the horse is a rather simple-minded animal—much less smarter than cats or dogs—and that he is barely capable of thinking. This belief may be fashionable, but if you question people who have spent a lifetime around horses most of them would dispute that notion. Not every horse is "smart"—but neither are all people. Some horses are slow on the uptake, while others quickly catch on to an idea imparted to them.

The accusation that the horse is not very smart, I believe stems from three factors. One, his infrequent interaction with us; two, his environment; and, three his size. I mention this because to some extent we can change the first and second factors—but not the third one.

With reference to his interaction with us, we can safely assert that the time spent with our horses is considerably less than that spent in the companionship of a dog or even a cat. So, naturally these other animals are bound to learn more, even if in an informal way.

The horse is disadvantaged in this respect. He is ridden perhaps an hour a day, preceded and followed by some time for grooming, feeding, etc. and that's it! He can't travel in the passenger seat of our car. He can't sleep on our bed at night. He can't sit quietly by our table while we eat. He can't be stroked or cuddled while we read or watch television. He can't follow us for walks or be with us during our vacation, shopping trips, and so on. All of these things a dog can do. With all this interaction, no wonder the dog is regarded as the smarter animal. Heaven help us if the horse was given similar opportunities—he would probably become less thrilled at the idea of maintaining his current subservient status!

The second factor is somewhat similar to the first in that to a large extent his limited environment, especially when coupled with limited human interaction, determines the way and to what extent he can use his wits. Many a horse spends close to twenty-two hours in a stall which is not a whole lot bigger than he. Or else he is turned out for a few hours each day in a paddock whose fence line he has explored thousands of times. How bored he must be with this limited vista. His poor brain becomes addled. At best, it is stimulated by squabbling with his fellow horses, or the distraction of an occasional disturbance, such as a noisy tractor—and that's about it! If he is lucky, he's is hacked out or taken to a show on weekends. Let's face it, this regimen would stultify the mind of any intelligent being.

The third factor why the horse is so often accused of not being very smart is because of his size. Unlike other domestic animals, he is large, heavy, very strong, can panic easily, and thus able to use his superior strength against us when we try to unskillfully dominate him. If necessary, a dog can be manhandled and be cowed into submission, but doing that to a horse is not so easy. Besides, the results from such an outcome are questionable. No, the horse is not stupid, but alas, it's all too easy to atrophy his mental faculties if we don't encourage him to use his brains—especially when we are teaching him.

Using His Intelligence to Learn

There are basically two ways we can get a horse to work with us.

The first method, and the one more commonly used, is where the trainer more or less coerces the horse into giving a response. This procedure is repeated many times until the horse memorizes, by association, the correct response to a given order.

The second method, which encourages the horse to respond by using his brains, hinges on the trainer giving him the opportunity to make a choice. By this, we don't mean to say that the horse is given the choice of two alternatives which are equally attractive for him, since obviously this dilemma would produce random results for us. Instead, we skillfully set up conditions that would make it easier or more comfortable for the horse to opt for the outcome we prefer, while difficult (but not impossible) for him to choose other options.

I might add that at first the trainer needs to get into the habit of thinking creatively, otherwise it's all too easy to use the first method to the exclusion of the other. This is not to imply that the first method is invalid. Not at all. It should go hand in hand with the second one. In fact, in order to establish a frame of reference, the first method will be the predominant choice. Then, once the horse begins to understand and respect the basic aids that allow the trainer to have some effective control, both methods can be used, depending on which is the more appropriate for the kind of work that is in progress.

An example illustrating the two approaches is when a horse has a habit of backing up whenever the rider tries to mount. If all else fails one can slap his barrel with the flat of the hand, tap his buttocks with the whip or even let him run into an obstacle. All these methods work, but they dissuade the horse either by direct confrontational intervention or else are reliant on "props," i.e. an obstacle.

The other alternative is to let the horse step or even run backwards, but on the condition that he backs in a straight line, i.e. without twisting or being crooked. Since backing for the excessive number of steps that he will want to take is very hard work, he will soon decide to halt of his own accord. After a few repetitions, he will find that standing still is a lot more comfortable than stepping backwards.

I'm not suggesting that this latter approach be favored over the former on every occasion. It does, however, illustrate what can be done to help the horse come to his own conclusion about this situation. By choosing to go backwards, he was allowed to make unnecessarily hard work for himself. By exploring the alternative, he had to use his brains. On subsequent occasions, his ever-evolving habit of thinking will curtail the time needed to understand what we would like him to do. Then, little by little, he applies that knowledge to help him solve other puzzles.

Understanding & Learning

With skill, it is relatively easy to help a horse do something new. However, it takes a much longer time to teach him to the point where his *understanding is confirmed*, thereby giving the correct response to a given set of instructions, time after time. One of the main reasons for this is because when teaching something new to the horse, the explanation and the execution are one and the same. This is a very difficult approach to learning.

Imagine the following scene. A person, in answer to an advertisement for "work," turns up at the appointed time not knowing what to expect. His new boss leads him to a place where there are twenty different articles on a table which are to be pieced together to make an object. The boss gives no explanation as to what the finished product might be (the objective) nor the process needed to complete it. He merely joins each piece one by one until the object is made, after which he asks the new employee to get on with it.

Chances are that our worker will be clueless as to the identity of the object until it is at least two-thirds completed! Not only that; since no step by step instruction was given, his memory will be sorely taxed. Obviously, such an instructional approach leaves much to be desired. Perhaps now we can better appreciate the difficulty the horse experiences in understanding what we require of him, when he is taught in the same way as our hapless worker.

It is for this reason that our explanations need to be given calmly, accurately and broken down into progressive, small segments to help the horse understand and remember.

More About the Learning Process

Teaching the horse something new requires three ingredients: repetition, intensity of impression, and time.

It is certainly possible for the horse to learn by repetition alone, but we also run the risk of either confusing him or letting him "switch off" through boredom. However, when intensity of impression is added, the horse pays attention and tends to remember more easily. Finally, consistent success is assured when we teach that idea over a period of time.

This is the way of clever advertisers. During their thirty second television or radio slot, they repeat the name of their product or their phone number, generally three times (repetition). Then they craft that advertisement to be outlandish, bizarre, or humorous (intensity of impression). And finally they bombard us into submission over time, so we cannot fail to buy their product next when we visit the supermarket!

These principles are so important that they deserve a closer look.

Repetition

There is a difference in the way a human and a horse view the process of repetitive instruction. What seems logical and instructive to us is not necessarily viewed as such by the horse.

In order to effectively apply this facet of the learning process, it's important to understand how both humans and horses process this input.

If we cast our minds back to our childhood, we may recall examples of how repetition was used to teach us. One was chanting the multiplication tables over and over, until we memorized them—even if we didn't really understand what they meant! Or, we would sing out in chorus, in answer to a question posed time and again by the teacher. This classic cheerleading technique is also used by marching soldiers, because the repetitive chanting makes them pay attention to the rhythm, as well as engendering a sense of corporate spirit.

In these examples we note that by repeating the material to be learnt, through many consecutive repetitions, we tend to first remember, which then makes it easier for us to understand. The background to the horse's process is not only more involved, but also different.

When we teach a new exercise—in contrast to confirming or improving it—the horse will become confused if he gives us the correct solution (in whatever measure), and we counter by insisting he repeat it for three or four times in quick succession. Since the horse originally gave us the right reply, when asked ad nauseam, he starts to question whether his reply was correct after all. Why else would his rider repeatedly and without any respite ask for the same solution? To better understand why the horse thinks this way, we have to examine an even earlier stage in his mental process.

Although the horse is certainly capable of quite sophisticated thinking, much of the knowledge he acquires is based on the way he reacts to the different circumstances which are presented to him. Just like with humans, a good deal of this is based on whether something is pleasurable or painful, in varying degrees.

For instance, let's say we are unmounted and teaching a green horse to go forward from the whip used on his thigh.

A light tap might solicit no movement at all, even after several such signals. The horse will soon find them annoying and will then take some action to get rid of this discomfort. His solution might be to back into the whip or kick out against its action, neither of which is the required response.

With the whip still relentlessly tapping him, his next idea may be to move his quarters sideways; since he can't "squash" its action by moving towards it, he decides that moving away from it might relieve him of this nuisance. If we turn his head in the same direction his quarters are escaping, he will not be able to easily evade the angle at which he was halted.

The whip is still tapping him. His next solution is to take one step forward. The taps of the whip immediately stop, signaling that with the correct solution came a respite from the annoyance. Within two or three repetitions of the process just described, the horse will figure out that a tap on the thigh means "go forward."

Now, let's suppose that when he did finally step forward for the first time, we kept tapping him, to either ensure he did not stop or else to make him go faster. What is the horse to make of this riddle?

If the "annoyance" of the whip is still present, he naturally thinks that stepping forward is an incorrect solution—just like the others before it. Otherwise, why on earth would the trainer reproach him for doing something correctly?!

We also have to admit that once the horse takes that first step, then continuing the relentless tapping of the whip will certainly coerce him forward. It works—but have we allowed the horse to use his brain by stimulating his deductive powers? I doubt it.

In view of this, we can now appreciate why mere repetition does little to educate the horse. Instead it has to be used selectively if the objective (in this example) is not only to move him, but to develop his mental growth in the process.

Intensity of Impression

This technique is used extensively in training, both as an adjunct to repetitive instructions and as a technique in its own right. As a tool for training, it addresses all the horse's senses with the exception of the olfactory one. Unfortunately, he uses his sense of smell to work against the rider's interests; for example, when he smells the person's fear.

It's interesting to note that horses are wary of other smells on a person. For instance, when I buy a pair of goatskin gloves horses dislike their smell and will not permit me to caress them near their face without showing signs of resentment. Yet, once I dig my gloved hands into the dirt to mask the odor, they accept their smell right away.

Intensity of impression affects the horse just like it influences ourselves. For example, a person may drive a car hundreds of times each year without incident, yet if he is questioned about what happened on a particular day six months previously, he almost certainly couldn't tell us—unless it was noteworthy. However, if on that day he had totalled his car and had sustained a broken arm, then he would probably be able to quite accurately recall each detail of all the day's events.

So it is with the horse. The good trainer takes great care to make noteworthy impressions on the horse's mind. How he does this is not just limited to addressing his pupil's senses, such as feeding a tidbit, using the voice in its various roles, or using the hand to soothe him or the stick to stimulate him. Indeed, equally important as all these is his sense of timing for triggering the horse's maximum interest, acceptance, or even revulsion to these stimuli.

A commonplace example of intensity of impression in action, is when we are encouraging a horse to be more social with us. We can use a word or phrase to cue him to come to us, and use food to stimulate him to do so. Now, if we just feed him a quart of grain in a bucket, he will in all likelihood eat it up, turn round and walk away with no further interest in us, especially since his appetite is satiated. He won't have learnt much about the meaning of our verbal cue, nor will he do so in a hurry in the future. The reason is that the stimulus (the grain) was a weak one. It's true he was given a lot of it, yet, it is this very amount that made him more interested in the food—and for too long a time—instead of paying attention to its source, that is, us.

The better approach would be to call the horse and proffer a small tidbit. This is repeated two or three more times so as to pique his interest in us. Then, while still calling, we lure him by holding the tidbit just out of reach, so that he is compelled to move towards us for a step or two before receiving his reward. The smaller treats do not satiate his hunger, and moreover, by being offered frequently, they irresistibly reinforce his obedience to the voice command over a short period of time.

The next time we meet the horse (assuming we are close by), he will very likely come over when called, at which point he must of course be rewarded in the usual way. Quite soon he will come to us obediently from progressively greater distances and must always be rewarded for doing so.

At some point, we may discover that another stimulus can gradually take the place of food. For instance, the horse may adore having his chin or throat scratched and will not miss that opportunity by coming to us. In turn, we as skillful trainers will not be slow in satisfying the horse's need, while at the same time using this craving of his to teach him something specific.

Time

This third ingredient is one of the cornerstones of efficient learning. For some peculiar reason, although it's well understood and accepted that it takes time to learn a new skill or profession, the same criteria are all too often not accorded to the training of animals. It's odd and illogical to think and expect an animal to learn as fast, or faster than a human—and then get upset for his not doing so!

Time implies the use not only of repetition, but also of patience. Giving yourself plenty of time to help the horse overcome a problem is absolutely essential. Frequently it's all that is needed to convince him to get over a mental block. Two typical examples are ones that I'm sure most of us have experienced at one time or another—a horse refusing to enter a trailer or not wanting to step or jump across a ditch.

By not allowing the horse to move backward or sideways the only choice is to go forward on his own. He knows what we want him to do and, given time, it never fails. By time, I mean we should be prepared to stay there quietly for as long as it takes. You may think this is extreme and time-consuming and so it is—but it always works. In these cases our patience must be unshakable. It is like besieging a city. All you need to do is wait, and sooner or later the mental resistance of its citizens will cave in—usually without any fighting.

Horses—just like people—need time to learn anything. If we could understand and remember everything that we read, were told or did—just once—a technician could be fully trained in a couple of weeks or a doctor in two years. If we cannot do it, it is unreasonable to expect such extraordinary intellect from our horses.

Listening to the Horse

Although much of the advice in this book describes what the trainer needs to tell the horse, we should never lose sight of the fact that this information is governed to a large extent by *what the horse tells us*.

In this respect, it's not unlike a game of chess, meaning that although we have an overall strategy and have memorized all the standard opening moves, the way we shape the game is frequently influenced by the moves of the opponent. Besides, however good we are at luring our opponent into making the moves we wish him to make, the element of unpredictability is always present.

For the rider, a useful exercise in listening is to periodically ask himself "What does this horse think of me?" If the trainer is introspective and honest, the answers will inspire him to further develop his virtues or, in the case of negative or sub-quality interactions, will urge or even shame him into changing the way he interacts with his horse.

Another factor that should not be overlooked in this regard is that the ridden horse is nearly always more attentive to his rider than the rider is to his horse.

This may be a hard pill to swallow, but there is a great deal of truth in it. Most riders primarily use their sense of sight to be aware of their horse's actions, posture, and so on. But the horse uses his sense of feel to be aware of the rider and his wishes, *since he cannot see his rider*.

If, in the process of receiving information from one another, the horse uses his sense of feel while his rider uses his sense of sight, then the two parties are not really on the same wavelength. Good riding is primarily an exercise in *feel*.

Reward, Punishment & Correction

Although the word "reward" sounds friendly enough and "correction" is acceptable, the same cannot be said for "punishment." Many people have a problem with it, thinking "I'm too nice a person to do that sort of thing!" In a sense, such a viewpoint is understandable and often justified. However, if we were perfect trainers with perfect horses, I'm sure that corrections would be both mild and infrequent, and punishment would be unnecessary.

Unfortunately the situation is far from Utopian. In our human world, the day we learn to behave will be the day we disband the system of law enforcement. If that sounds inconceivable (at least in the near future), why then should we hold our horses to a higher standard? Just like people who are ambitious, energetic, or uncompliant, horses also have similar qualities. If these are not channeled into productive avenues by their trainers, they will all too easily grow into behavioral problems.

To bring this into context, we need to appreciate that such behavior in a herd of horses is both natural and even necessary. It perpetuates the system of the "pecking order," which may appear somewhat feudal to us, but is what, in a more primitive hierarchy, culls out the weak members of a species and also produces the leaders.

Be that as it may, when we attempt to domesticate the horse, our physical vulnerability leaves us exposed to his primitive emotions and his superior strength—unless we take steps to either channel it or, if the need arises, to control it.

This can be accomplished in many different ways—it's not only the wide choice of remedies which allows us to suitably tailor the corrective process, but also that such a repertoire can be considerably expanded and made more effective when used in the appropriate measure and at the right time.

Reward

The horse can be rewarded in four ways. The first addresses his sense of taste through tidbits, such as pieces of carrots, apples, or grain. The second addresses his auditory sense: we repeat a word or phrase in a pleasant tone of voice, which he has been conditioned to understand as a form of approval. The third way is by caressing, patting or scratching the appropriate places, usually on the neck, chest or withers, which creates a pleasant sensation.

The fourth is the cessation of whatever tactile signal was being used to obtain his cooperation. This is viewed as a reward, if only by virtue of the fact that any signal is to some extent an annoyance, even if only a minor one.

The method one chooses to reward a particular horse is governed by factors such as its personality and the ease with which the reward can be given. For example, regarding personality, some horses are very sensitive or shy and prefer to be caressed or spoken to softly, while others appreciate a more flamboyant approval or are more partial to being fed treats.

Rewards should be given at the precise moment the horse gives us the correct response. This sounds easy enough in theory and would be satisfactory if the horse was a willing partner and behaved impeccably. However, with a timid horse the timing of the reward and how he is rewarded is significant.

Let's take a practical example which you will almost certainly experience: teaching a timid horse to advance toward something he fears. The horse approaches the object, stops and is wary about going forward. We soothe him until he's regained some of his composure and then we ask

Rewarding the horse.

him to advance. He does so willingly enough and we estimate he's good for maybe five or six steps. We stop him, however, in four.

As he steps forward we immediately reward him with a kind word and perhaps—if it's not distracting or if he isn't on edge—with a caress or a pat. We then stop him and do nothing. Why so? Because stopping is not one of his problems. In fact, he's only too eager to do so! His hang-up is about going forward and it is for this that he should be rewarded.

Keep this distinction in mind as we go to the next scenario, again with a nervous horse. He is fairly close to the object and doesn't like what's ahead of him, so we stop him (assuming he hasn't done so of his own accord). Then, when we deem it appropriate to ask for forward movement, we sense that he will give us what we want but perhaps only one step's worth.

Now, this one step is worth four or more of the previous ones, because he was formerly quite happy to barrel on. But, this one step is given to us at great cost to himself. All his instincts of self-preservation are screaming at him to do anything except go forward towards the "danger." We in turn, have to appreciate his courage and acknowledge it by rewarding him in some way.

How can we do it?

This one's tricky because we must only reward him for doing the thing he's very reluctant to do, go forward. He must not be rewarded for stopping—something he's only too keen to do.

He's going forward for one step only, since that is all he's going to give us anyway! This step lasts about a second, after which he stops. Remember, he must not be rewarded for stopping, only for going forward. If we pat him as he stops we are, in effect, saying "Wonderful. You've stopped. Do it again!" We can appreciate how precise the timing of the reward must be. Note that often the only reward that can be given in that instant is with the voice. A pat or caress is too distracting in a tense moment and cannot be given speedily enough.

This is where one reaps dividends from having thoroughly taught our horse the meaning, through lungeing and later from the saddle, of a short but distinct list of words.

For example, when I interact with any horse, whether handling it in the stable or training him from the ground or the saddle, I begin right away in murmuring the word "good" when he does what I want, and especially if he was hesitant in following my demands. It doesn't matter whether he's just picked up one of his feet for me or whether he's yielded to my leg after some hesitation or confusion, I immediately murmur the word "good." That way, at a later date when the horse is doing other work he will instantly recognize and understand its meaning.

The word is short and murmured at a fairly high pitch. Try murmuring the same word with a low pitch. It sounds like a threat, doesn't it?

This can be advantageous because it will reward the horse, and is brief enough to do so at precisely the correct moment and not one instant later.

We should clarify the advice about *not* rewarding the horse for either stopping or having been stopped. Naturally, we don't want to miss the opportunity of soothing him. After all, in most instances we stop him because he's on the verge of "losing it," so it's essential we pet him. However, we don't do so the moment he stops or is stopped. We soothe him a few seconds *after* halting. Then, he will associate our caresses with putting him in a better frame of mind, instead of being rewarded for stopping. If the lack of interaction during the interim makes him nervous and he begins to fidget, a quiet "Whoa" will likely settle him. He stops. We wait, and only then do we interact with reassuring words and caresses.

These details may seem pedantic under normal circumstances, such as when the horse is willing to take several steps forward. However, when the time span between going forward and stopping is very brief, misguided rewards only result in confusion.

Punishment

Punishment can be an effective way to dissuade a horse from repeating a serious offense. One of the principles of good schooling is that the correction should be commensurate to the misdemeanor.

In other words, if he's under-corrected the horse will ignore this ineffective retribution and is likely to repeat the misdemeanor with impunity. If he's overcorrected, he will feel abused and harbor a sense of injustice. A punishment is perfectly legitimate if the offense is grave enough. However, this should be more the exception than the rule.

How can we tell what is grave enough to merit punishment? Well, this is a gray area. Several questions need to be answered that will determine if a punishment is needed or if that offense can be overlooked. First, did the horse do something out of malice or out of fear—and hence in self defense? The former is generally a punishable offense if only for the reason that due to his size and strength, the horse can easily hurt us. He must be unequivocally told that such behavior is not tolerated.

I said malice is "generally" a punishable offense because it's not unusual for a horse who has had a history of abuse to react violently in self defense. Then, if that abuse persists and he becomes inured to it, his fear dissipates but his violent reaction becomes so much part of his normal behavior that it manifests even when unprovoked. In this case, direct physical punishment can only perpetuate the horse's defensive behavior. Instead, the clever trainer will think of some way to help the horse to gradually abandon his violent habit. This, however, is unlikely to be the case when training our green youngster.

On the other hand, when a horse reacts out of self defense, we then have a dilemma. If it seems that in the future we can avoid exposing him to whatever made him behave nastily, then it pays to either ignore it or display a milder form of disapproval by growling with the voice. The former option is appropriate with a young horse, since it buys him some time until he becomes more experienced, or mature enough to deal with the problem more confidently. On the other hand, even though his reaction is in self defense, it may on occasion be prudent to reproach him sharply enough to make a lasting impression. It is unfair but regrettably necessary.

An example of this would be if the horse kicked a hound during a hunt meet. The horse may have been skittish and when startled by the canine, he kicked out. An understandable reaction, to be sure. However, a sharp cut on the shoulder with the crop will impress on him the idea that kicking hounds (who are nearly always well behaved in such circumstances) is a no-no. Period.

Let's not forget that a horse who is fit or who is particularly ticklish will sometimes kick out when he's being groomed. He is just feeling good and shouldn't be punished for that. Another instance where he shouldn't be punished—unless he endangers the rider—is when he bucks simply because he feels good. Two common times are during the warm up phase of work, especially on windy or cold days, and after jumping a fence or line of fences.

Correction

Correction takes many forms and is a subject that needs to be studied with care, because the way we make them determines how quickly a horse learns. The following are some of the most common methods of correction:

1. The horse corrects himself.
2. The horse is given a choice.
3. Using the voice.
4. Using the legs.
5. Using the whip.
6. Using the reins.
7. Using the spurs.

Let's look at each in turn and illustrate them with some examples.

1. The horse corrects himself.

Any time we can get a horse to correct himself, we put ourselves on a neutral footing. In other words, the horse does not see us as the administrator of the correction. The result is that he still views us as a friend and not "as the guy who 'hit' me."

An example is when a spoilt horse runs backwards as an evasion to prevent the trainer from mounting, leading him forward, or lungeing him. In this instance it is quite possible that there is one or more underlying causes to his behavior; in spite of this, though, it may be deemed important—as a first step in the remedial process—to stop his evasion. Since we don't want to give the horse any further excuses of blaming people for his evasion, we simply allow him to do what he wants, that is, back up.

It is true that as we walk forward, facing his forehead, while he goes backwards, our position and movement may to some extent provoke further backing, but that suits our purpose just fine. Our objective is to back him in a straight line until he tires or towards some obstacle. A wall will do in a pinch. Better still is to back him into two or three oil barrels. They will make a din and keel over, causing enough of a commotion—which he can hear and feel but which he cannot see—to scare him into quitting.

Having repeated this ploy a few more times, the horse should be convinced that his evasion is the precursor to unpleasant experiences. Equally important is the fact that the trainer, who is innocently walking forward near the horse's head, *appears* to be uninvolved in any way with the correction that is going on at the rear end.

2. The horse is given a choice.

When the horse is given a choice to do something, we can load the dice in *our* favor by making it easy for him to choose what *we* want and difficult (but not impossible) for him to choose anything else. This principle uses one of the horse's characteristics, his laziness. He will almost always opt for the easy way out.

For instance, let's say our horse is rooted to the ground and won't budge. If we bend his neck to one side (especially on his stiff side) and maintain a steady resistance, then sooner or later his muscles will start to ache. To obtain relief from this relentless resistance, the easiest solution for him is to shift his feet.

3. Using the voice.

The tone of voice is a more effective correction than a specific word or phrase. Short, sharp words can be powerful admonitions, as can a growl. The advantage of using the voice is that physical coercion is absent. However, on occasion, some kind of physical action may need to be used with the voice so as to impress on the horse's mind the meaning of the latter. Once the connection between the two has been made, only the voice is necessary, and so the horse is spared tactile correction.

Clicking with the tongue can be both an encouragement and an admonition to either go more forward or not slacken off the speed.

4. Using the legs.

Corrections with the legs when the rider's lower calf or heel is used, range from a pinch to a sharp tap and, if necessary, a kick. These corrections very much depend on the sensitivity of the individual horse. A kick that would get the attention of a cold blooded horse would agitate a more sensitive one.

As with a trained horse, any leg signal that is being ignored eventually must be escalated without disengaging the leg from his barrel. If necessary, this can be reinforced by the whip. The legs can admonish not only by escalating their intensity, but also by giving repeated signals one after the other. This "drumming" can be used both as a correction or as a means of getting a horse's attention.

5. Using the whip.

Using the whip on its own as a means of correction has limited benefits. A slap on the shoulder can be an attention-getter. However, the main advantage of the whip is as a reinforcer of what the rider's legs are saying to the horse. This being the case, it follows that the whip must be used at the same time as the legs or immediately after. If the whip precedes the legs, it is illogical and confuses the horse—it is somewhat like shooting first and asking questions afterwards.

Correct use of the whip requires not only good timing but also accurate placement. For example, normally it doesn't make sense to use the stick on the horse's thigh, when he is dull to the rider's leg, which is asking him to go forward. The stick must be used as close as possible to the riding boot. This way he thinks the stick is the leg.

To do otherwise is akin to persuading a child to stop putting his finger up his nose by stamping on his foot. The child's finger will leave his nose in a hurry to be sure, but if no other explanation is forthcoming, he will have learned little. A correction that is better understood, would be to grab his finger or wrist and pull it downwards.

A second way to use the whip as a correction, is to affect a lateral displacement of the horse's body. Used on the neck, shoulder, or thigh will prevent him drifting to that side. If used in a more attention-getting way, the horse moves away from it.

The third use of the whip, again used far from the rider's leg and sometimes unconnected with its use, is to touch the horse in specific spots for certain purposes. Two typical cases with our young horse follow.

One is where he habitually leaves a hind leg back when halting. In this case, a tap on the delinquent limb will bring it forward alongside its partner. Another is when the horse is somewhat deaf to the rein aids to slow down or stop: the shaft of the whip (in contrast with using its end) pressed or lightly slapped across his chest will quickly get the point across.

A fourth way of using the whip is to exploit its noisemaking properties. For instance, if we don't want to use it on the horse's body because perhaps through repeated use he has become deaf to it, we can substitute this action by slapping it on our riding boot. The noise will stimulate the horse into going forward. However, since it has no physically coercive powers—its potency being due to the element of surprise—if it is used more than two or three times consecutively, we run the risk of the horse ignoring it. He gets used to the noise through repeated or indiscriminate use and will simply disregard it. It goes without saying that the whip used in this way must be in conjunction with leg aids.

6. *Using the reins.*

Using the reins as a correction should not be indiscriminate. In fact, if we want to keep the youngster trusting our hands we shouldn't use the reins this way at all. This is the ideal the trainer must strive for. However, in practice one occasionally comes across a situation when using the rein as a correction (which is perilously close to bordering on a punishment) can bring a horse to order. It can hardly be salutary but is effective.

Unfortunately it is this effectiveness, which becomes less so with each frequent repetition, that lures the rider into the trap of using it indiscriminately. This is wrong. The trainer who adopts such tactics as a matter of course is either not using his imagination for other solutions or has lost his patience with that horse. The former problem requires fresh ideas, while in the latter case it is best to stop work for a while and take stock of the situation. If on resumption of work the young horse still frustrates the trainer it's a good idea to consider assigning his training to someone else.

Incidentally, there is no shame in this latter solution. There are horses and people who just don't "click" because the chemistry isn't there.

An example of using the reins as a correction would be if a horse is giving small bucks and won't quit when admonished either with the legs or the whip. In this case, the reins can be slackened so they are slightly loose. The rider kicks so that the horse lunges forward, taking the slack out of the rein and meets the resistance of locked hands. The ensuing jolt can have a sobering effect on the horse. We note that the rider didn't actively administer the punishment by pulling on the rein or reins; the horse punished himself. Needless to say, such corrections should be used very sparingly and with discretion.

7. Using the spurs.

Using spurs as a correction should not be considered an option when training a green unspoilt horse. Indeed, even the wearing of spurs on such a young horse is something to be avoided. The main objection is that the general unsteadiness of a young horse frequently requires the rider's legs to be used to steady himself, if only briefly. It is in this role of self-preservation that spurs can inadvertently be applied. Moreover, this accidental use of the spurs almost always generates exactly the opposite effect from what the rider wants!

A second objection is that the general dullness of response to the rider's legs from a green horse lures one into using the spurs both sharply and in a relentlessly repetitive way. This approach accomplishes one thing and one thing only—it anesthetizes the horse to the influence of the rider's leg.

This trait alone is the most dangerous of all in a horse at any level of training, since not going forward from the rider's legs allows the horse to get away with a multitude of serious problems. Among these are napping, shying, rearing, jibbing and even running away.

Although spurs can be used to reinforce the lateral influence of the rider's leg, on a green, unspoilt horse this task is better served by using a whip.

The Trainer's Safety

The trainer should be always aware of his own vulnerability when handling green, high strung, or excitable horses. This is especially so when working from the ground. The only thing that can happen in the saddle is that you may get hit in the face if the horse's head is raised sharply or you take a fall—which may or may not result in injury. However, on the ground one's chances of being injured increase considerably. One can get kicked, bitten, squashed, or simply run over.

This is not to say one should approach this work timidly—an attitude that is quickly detected and not infrequently taken advantage of by the horse—but rather that one should have eyes everywhere. What is meant by this is that one's consciousness should be all encompassing, not only on all parts of the horse but also on the surroundings, since these could be instrumental in provoking a reaction from the horse that might injure the trainer.

When working a green horse from the ground, there is one safety rule that shouldn't be forgotten: while you are within kicking range, you must constantly be aware of what the horse's hind legs are doing. Ignoring this increases your chances of being hurt. This is especially the case when you are about to use the whip since a horse may kick out even if it hasn't touched him; the mere threat can provoke this reaction. A lithe horse can kick you in the chest or head in an instant—even if you are positioned parallel to his girth—so keep your wits about you and be extra careful until he has proven himself to be reliable.

Incidentally, with regards to this danger, it is one of the reasons why the lunge line must be *firmly* grasped while working at close quarters, and especially when using the whip. A casual grip allows the horse to rip the coils out of your fist, so that his forehand is then free to swing away so that his quarters are presented towards you.

In addition to being aware of what the horse might do to endanger us, it is essential to clearly define for him what our "space" is, and that he can enter it only when invited by us. From the human standpoint, what is this "space?" Strange as it may seem, it's not a finite distance around us, but is instead a variable one. In fact, "space" has as much to do with the circumstance of the moment, or the attitude between horse and trainer, as it has to do with distance.

For example, we prefer to be physically close to our horse when we pet him, in which case the linear distance is minimal. Yet at the same time, there is a respect on his part (for us) and a trust on our part (towards him) that he will not hurt us. In other words, he is considerate of our "space," but, one might say, in an emotional or mental way.

Now let's suppose that we are in the same situation, but this time the horse disrespectfully and even belligerently pushes us around with his head. Clearly, although he is the same distance from us as in the previous example, he nevertheless has definitely invaded our "space."

From our point of view, the rules of engagement appear simple enough, but for the horse it must be confusing at first. Why? Because we generally (but not always) expect a double standard. Much of the time we both need and expect the horse to be very close to us: when catching him, leading, grooming, saddling up, and so on and moreover become irked when he doesn't allow it! *All of this occurs when we are physically at our most vulnerable.*

Yet, on other occasions, we demand the exact opposite relationship. We prod, push or lean on him if he gets too close when he is being led. Then, while on the lunge, he is forbidden to approach us at all—we prefer to have him somewhat drawing outwards, away from us. *All of this occurs at a distance where he could not possibly hurt us.*

What is he to make of all this? Probably, that we are not very logical! This is why, when we train a young horse, who is not aware of these complicated rules of the game, it's important we define each one precisely and with consistent standards.

As to equipment, there are three items the trainer should use on green horses for his own personal safety: a helmet or hard hat, preferably with a harness, gloves, and a whip. The protective head gear should always be worn when working green horses because their actions can at times be exaggerated and unpredictable and so increase the chance of an injury.

While one might opt to ride without gloves, to do so while lunging is not smart. When handling horses whose movements can be sudden and erratic, the chance of getting a rope burn is high.

As to the whip, this may seem an odd choice for a "safety instrument." Nevertheless, I would suggest making it a habit of never riding a green horse (or any other horse for that matter) without something to back up the authority of your legs—in this case the whip.

You may go quite a while without using it, but when it's needed you'll be thankful you carried it. A timely correction or, if necessary, a sharp reprimand, does wonders to nip in the bud a situation that can all too easily get out of hand and most likely spawn additional problems for the rider. When the horse feels he can ignore the idle threats of the legs because his disobedience to them wasn't backed up by some sharper retribution, then he's well on the way to thinking up some unsavory tricks that could compromise the rider's safety.

Equipment You Will Need

In undertaking the training of the young horse, it's important to have the appropriate equipment. It's advisable to obtain the tack before you need it, and to buy the best you can afford. Makeshift gear will do at a pinch if you are skillful.

One may argue that some of the equipment will be of little use once the young horse has been backed, but don't you and your horse deserve the most efficient tools for a job (hopefully well done) whose results will last a lifetime? When your youngster in his exuberance overreaches and cuts into his leg, putting him on the sick list possibly for several weeks, then that $80 investment for brushing boots will seem remarkably cheap. The following list of items is essential if you wish to lower the odds against accidents and increase your chances of accomplishing your task in the easiest way.

Halter

A comfortably fitting halter with sufficient room on the noseband so it can be slipped on and off easily. A halter which is too big can be dangerous because the horse could get a foot caught in it. If your youngster is very shy of humans, you may opt to leave the halter on in order to catch him more easily. In that case, a halter with a leather headpiece which will break in emergency is preferable, as opposed to a nylon one which won't. A long *lead rope* which doesn't fall apart on the first sharp tug is essential.

Brushing Boots

Next come brushing boots, one pair for his front legs and a pair for the hind ones. The former will help guard against knocks causing splints and give protection to his tendons and fetlocks. The latter will protect his fetlocks from knocks against each other. This can occur when you lunge him on circles.

Lungeing Cavesson

As important as the boots is a good quality lungeing cavesson. The only worthwhile type, to my mind, is an all-leather model with heavy-duty metal fittings on the outside of the padded noseband. It will have three rings, one on each side of the center ring. Lungeing cavessons can be bought in different sizes: pony, cob, and horse. However, most tack shops will only carry a "one size fits all" cavesson. For ponies or horses with small heads, the fit is unsatisfactory, so the equipment requires some doctoring. In contrast with the cheaper nylon versions, the leather cavesson is designed to stay in place on the horse's head without twisting when the lunge line is tugging at it sideways, thus endangering the horse's eye on the outside. The designs of cavessons on the market are generally poor, primarily due to the jowl strap being stitched too high up on the cheek pieces. Moreover, the jowl strap is often designed so it's attached at right angles to each cheek piece *(Fig. A)*. When fastened tightly, it acts like a throat latch and throttles the horse, instead of the strap lying on the jowl so to prevent the cavesson from moving. For instance, when the lunge line is pulled, it causes the cheek piece on the opposite side to ride up against the horse's eye. A better design is one having the jowl strap stitched so as to hang at a downward angle, thus tightening in the middle or lower portion of the jowl *(Fig. B)*.

In the event your cavesson resembles *Fig. A*, a simple adaptation is to fasten a thin strap on the cheek pieces, level with the middle or lower part of the horse's jowl. Attach it with sufficient tension that it will pull the cheek pieces down from the horse's eye *(Fig. C)*. To do this, attach the strap on one cheek piece, run it under the horse's jaw and fasten it to the other cheek piece.

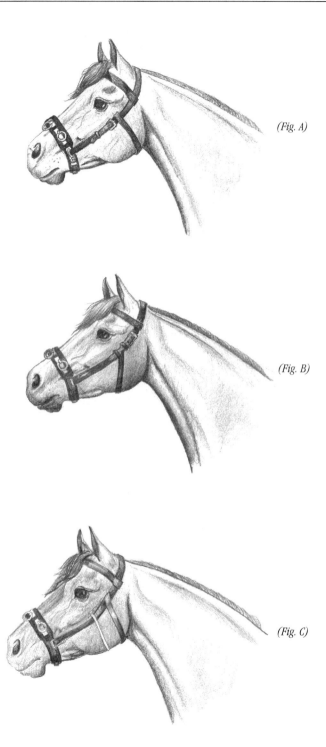

(Fig. A)

(Fig. B)

(Fig. C)

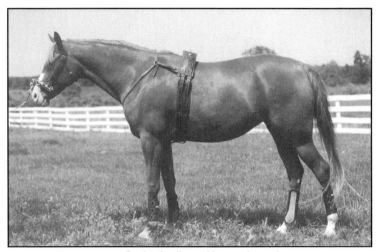

Horse outfitted with roller and hunting breastplate.

Breastplate

A worthwhile investment is a hunting breastplate, which will be invaluable when you are backing the young horse and also during cross-country work later. It not only prevents the saddle from sliding too far backwards or sideways, but also gives the rider something to hang onto if the need arises.

Roller

A stable roller can be a good substitute for the specialized training rollers. At a pinch, a cotton web surcingle will do, as long as you stitch D rings in the approximate positions where they would be on your saddle. This use will be explained later on.

Side Reins

A set of side reins for a horse at this level of training should have some kind of elastic inset. Buckles make it easy to adjust their length. My personal preference for the clip that attaches the side rein to the bit is the sliding hasp type, since these can be easily opened and released in an emergency.

Lunge Line

The lunge line should be chosen with care because if made of the wrong material, too short, or with stiff, cumbersome fittings, it can make life difficult. The ideal is one of sturdy cotton webbing with a snap hook attached to a swivel. Avoid ones with a chain between the snap hook and the web line, since any signal (except the most violent) will be absorbed by the chain and will not reach the horse's nose.

Incidentally, the heavy cotton tubular lines are somewhat cumbersome and until they've seen a lot of mileage, they don't hang limply enough to coil properly when wet. Shun nylon lines, since the nature of the material makes it twist and then snag in your fist. Worst of all, it will surely give you rope burns. Again, it's wise to wear a pair of leather gloves when working with the lunge line.

As to the length, you will bless the day you acquired a 30-foot line. The more common 25-footers really cramp the trainer's ability to play the horse on the end of the line if he's off balance or simply feeling full of himself.

A useful feature is a hand loop at the end of the line which lessens the chances of losing the horse. However, *never* put your wrist through the loop—only the fingers should grip it, otherwise your wrist could be severely damaged if a horse should drag you and you find you can't let go of the line.

Lunge Whip

A lunge whip is an indispensable part of your lungeing equipment. It need not be expensive or made of fancy materials, but it does need to be in perfect working order. The shaft should be fairly stiff, otherwise it bends too much when the lash gets heavy with mud and water. When this occurs, it's impossible to use the whip with any speed or adroitness. A few dollars will buy a nylon model with a five-and-a-half foot shaft and six-foot lash. A silk "snapper" attached to the lash is essential because without it your whip becomes impotent, since it cannot be cracked or used with finesse.

Bridle

The bridle we use may require a drop noseband. For general purposes, or unless your youngster has a physical or educational problem, a fairly thick loose-ring or full-cheek snaffle are ideal hardware. An egg-butt snaffle could also serve our purpose, especially with a horse who plays with the bit excessively.

Saddle & Fittings

As to the saddle and fittings, naturally, the saddle must fit the horse comfortably. If you are backing your youngster in the cold months, a fleece saddle pad is a useful addition. When your horse is eventually saddled, ensure that the saddle fits him even with this additional bulk underneath it. Check the area on each side of the withers for possible pinching. The gullet must be sufficiently wide so the panels don't press on his spine and cause him discomfort. Nor must the pommel be so low that it presses on the spine, especially when the stirrups are weighted.

If you have an old saddle, check that the stuffing is both even and in sufficient amount to cushion your weight. The balance of a saddle in poor shape can be significantly altered, often lowering the cantle so that the deepest part of the seat is too far back. When the saddle forces you to sit on the horse's kidneys, he will spare no effort to try to relieve himself of your weight.

The *billet straps* should be in perfect condition. If the holes are running or the leather is splitting or thinning, replace them. If a defective billet breaks, you could be in for an unpleasant fall. The chances of a breakage when riding young or green horses are significantly greater than when handling their older, more staid counterparts.

The *girth* should be chosen for pliability, elasticity, and fit. Leather girths are a good choice, foremost among these being either the Balding girth or a shaped (Atherstone) girth. Both are cut away slightly where the elbow meets the belly, thus allowing unrestricted movement without pinching the skin at those points. However, leather is expensive and if not well maintained becomes stiff and abrasive.

An excellent substitute at half the price are the heavy cotton or nylon cord girths, popular with dressage enthusiasts. The strands are much thicker than the more commonly used string girth, and unlike its poorer relative, the girth is wide enough to keep the cords from bunching up like a piece of rope. They are one of the easier pieces of equipment to maintain since you can put them in the washing machine.

Familiarization

When your horse arrives at his new home, take the precaution of leading him off the trailer with a lunge line instead of a lead rope. If he's excited and backs out hurriedly, you might lose him—an inauspicious start to your relationship! Once in his stall, look him over to make sure he hasn't sustained an injury during the journey.

Understandably, your friends will want to visit the new arrival; however, it's wise to let the horse settle in for the first few days with a minimum of fuss. The new views, smells and sounds will keep him on his mettle, so peace and quiet are essential to help him adjust to his new surroundings. If he is very upset, it's often useful (if the construction of the stall allows it) to shut the top door so he rests in the dark, since the gloom has a settling effect.

For the next week or so, it's best if your youngster is handled only by you or at most one other person of similar disposition to help him relax. It goes without saying that yelling and abrupt gestures within the vicinity of the horse should be discouraged. During this period, you should try to visit him frequently. These interactions encourage the horse to trust you and, for a short while at least, show him his dependency on you for both his creature comforts and emotional support. Your quiet, unhurried attitude instills in his mind that you are his friend.

If Difficult to Catch

If your horse is difficult to catch, at the first opportunity tie a piece of twine (with a short tail) snugly around the top part of his neck. This will give you something to catch when you entice him to you. His box stall is a good place to teach him to be caught without fuss, since the restricted space doesn't allow him to escape from you.

One of the easiest techniques is to appeal to both his hunger and his inquisitiveness. Instead of walking up to him while he dances around the box stall evading you, rattle a handful of grain in a bucket and *wait for him to come to you.* Unless he is facing you and unless you are convinced he won't wheel around and kick you, avoid approaching or speaking to him. Above all, don't allow yourself to be trapped in a spot from which you cannot escape. Speech distracts him from the rattle of food in the bucket. Tilt the bucket to show him the contents, all the while rattling it at intervals.

You may have to wait a few minutes, but if you stand quietly he will start to show interest and step over to you. If he is particularly shy, you can edge up to him a little at a time, with frequent and long pauses. However, when you are close, the final initiative to make contact should be his. He must be the one to come to you and not vice-versa. While he eats the grain, you may speak the same reassuring phrase repeatedly ("good boy"). Do not attempt to catch him on this or the next two or three occasions, because he must not associate your visiting him with always being caught.

When he comes promptly and willingly to you, then is the time to catch him, lead him around, or tie him up. After a while you will notice he will face you as you enter his stall and will likely stand still while being approached. At this point you can dispense with grain as a "come on."

Tying

Before we familiarize our horse with the routines that are often necessary to do outside the confines of the stall, such as grooming, saddling and shoeing, we must accustom him to being tied up. Teaching him to stand quietly while being tied is a simple procedure and often best introduced in his stall, a place in which he feels safe and where he can't escape if he breaks loose.

First, tie a small loop of baling twine around the ring on the stall wall. The lead rope is then tied to this loop, using a slip knot. If your horse pulls back sharply, the twine will snap, leaving the halter and rope intact. Once this occurs, nearly all horses will run back a few steps and then stop of their own accord, having found that being tied up is not as restrictive as they had imagined. Besides, if they are introduced to being tied while in their stall, they cannot escape if they break free.

Teaching the horse to be tied using a tree or snubbing post, objects which are unyielding and in an area that is not closely confined by a fence line, should be done with great care and only by experienced trainers. Otherwise, it can result in nerve damage, dislocated vertebrae, and a thoroughly frightened horse.

If you let him feed from a hay net (and, if necessary, give him a handful of grain in his feed bucket), he will soon associate being tied with the pleasure and distraction of food. However, on the first few occasions, don't leave your horse tied while unattended. If he's startled, your presence and reassuring touch will dispel his fears.

Only after he's in the habit of standing quietly, tied by a single line, both in and out of his stall, should he be accustomed to standing on cross-ties. To avoid making him feel claustrophobic, initially have the cross-ties longer than normal so that he's not "locked" in place.

Touching

Accustoming your youngster to being touched all over is an important aspect of horse training, so he learns to tolerate being touched and grasped in places which are either ticklish or instinctively threatening to him. Untrained horses tend to have an innate fear of falling or lying helpless, so nature has endowed them with limbs that can both kick powerfully in self defense and allow them to flee rapidly from danger. That is why in some systems of training, the green horse is compelled to feel helpless against the power of his handler, by being thrown to the ground and kept there. In this position he is forced to come to terms with his fear of various things to which the trainer subjects him, such as touching (and even thumping) him with a sack, blanket or lariat.

In contrast, our approach will encourage the horse to confront his fears—

but without coercion. In other words, unlike the aforementioned system, the horse's fears are of his own making since the trainer carefully avoids provoking such a state of mind. Then—if and when appropriate—he will take steps to allay the horse's fears with voice and touch. However, sometimes a studious indifference to the horse's mental turmoil will be the greatest help of all. As in any aspect of training, the trick is knowing what to do and when to do it.

When handling his feet, at first only lift them for brief periods, maybe only a few seconds at a time. Otherwise, it can both worry the horse and cause him discomfort from standing in this unaccustomed position. This is especially important when handling the hind legs, which are often lifted too high. Tall people need to be particularly aware of this.

When handling the horse's head, the four points that are of interest to us are his eyes, nostrils, ears and mouth. His eyes alert him to danger faster than any of his other senses and especially if you abruptly move your hands within eyeshot. As soon as he tolerates your hand in that area, cup one hand, hold it over his eye for a few seconds and then lightly stroke it outwards towards the side of his face. Repeat this several times periodically until he tolerates your hands without tossing his head. Once he knows you're not going to hurt him, he will be less spooky to your movements near his head during other situations. Incidentally, when this cupping is done with a certain amount of pressure (once the horse is used to it), many horses will be almost mesmerized into standing quietly if they were jittery to begin with.

The nostrils are the horse's breathing apparatus, so if you pinch them, he might get panicky. Gently stroke his muzzle and let him sniff your hands.

His ears are sensitive not only from an auditory standpoint but also physically. Handle them gently at first and then more firmly. If he repeatedly tosses his head or if his ears feel stiff, tense or unmalleable, be more gentle and, if necessary, return to them when he is more relaxed.

Lastly, being able to open his mouth without a fuss is essential for when he is bridled. Place your left thumb into the corner of his mouth on the near side and play it up and down until he starts to chew and open his mouth slightly. If you do this routinely, in a short while he will soon cooperate; after which you can slip a soft, nonabrasive lead rope in his mouth for half a minute or so. This way when you introduce him to the bit, it won't seem so strange.

Getting Started

We begin formal schooling by working the horse from the ground, first by teaching him to lead correctly and subsequently by lungeing. My personal preference is to teach the horse to lunge without the aid of an assistant because he should learn to respect our wishes even when we are in a disadvantageous position to make him go forward (because we are to his side). So, since having no assistant to help us lead or shoo him onwards may cause the horse to think that the dice are loaded in his favor and that he can disobey us, how do we solve the problem?

A short time invested in teaching him to lead properly, walking on and stopping upon voice command with whip and lunge line will instill our authority over him, initially at close quarters. This is an important point because the closer we are to him, the greater our influence. The farther away he is, the less influence we have—unless he is first trained well at close quarters.

The horse should be tacked up with brushing boots on all four legs so that he can be led or lunged without injury to them *(Fig. 2)*. If those on the hind legs are too tight, the horse may kick out repeatedly. In addition, the lungeing cavesson should be fitted firmly enough so it won't twist when

(Fig. 2) Correct attire for initial stage of lungeing.

you use the lunge line. At this stage, the line is best hooked onto the near side ring of the cavesson since a tug on this ring (as opposed to the center one) is more forgiving.

Teaching Him to Lead

Now that he is ready for his first schooling session, take him to the working area, preferably at a time when there are no other horses to distract your pupil. The horse is halted alongside a wall or fence so that it is to his immediate right, while we stand at his shoulder on the near side *(Fig. 3)*. We adopt the same stance as when leading a horse and hold the lunge in a corresponding way. The spare part of the line is neatly coiled in the left hand, which also holds the butt of the whip (so that the whip points to the rear). Sometimes I prefer to hold the lunge line in my right hand with the same grip as when holding the reins, since this affords greater security.

At this point, the lash of the whip is best wrapped around the shaft, with the tail or snapper knotted onto the butt, so the horse is not spooked by the lash flying around when the whip touches his body. Also, for the inexperienced trainer, it's all too easy to angle the whip in such a way that the

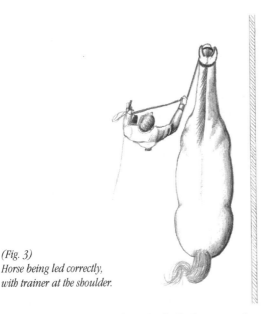

(Fig. 3)
Horse being led correctly,
with trainer at the shoulder.

horse's hind feet repeatedly tread on the lash that is trailing on the ground. When this happens, the whip is pulled out of the hand or the arm is yanked backwards.

The left hand, holding coiled line and whip, should lie just below the trainer's left hip, so that a twist of the wrist will engage the whip on his lower barrel, if you use a dressage whip, or even the hips and buttocks. However, at this stage be careful to avoid using the whip on his flank, since this is a ticklish spot and will likely provoke the horse to kick or give a small buck. If you are not well versed in this procedure, look back over your right shoulder as you use the whip to see where it's tapping him.

At first, we teach him to "walk on," using only the lunge whip and a click of the tongue. The click of the tongue will be his first verbal instruction to *go forward* as opposed to the verbal command "Walk on" (which will come later). The easily learned stimulus of the click of the tongue will instill, right from the start, the habit of going forward when told. This click of the tongue has an all-encompassing use. Firstly, as an *order* to walk and trot on, and later as a *stimulus* both at walk, trot and canter whenever the horse's energy or speed tends to wane at those paces.

We begin by giving an audible click of the tongue and a second later a tap with the whip. However, be ready to yield with your right arm and step forward promptly, especially if you feel he is about to jump forward. This avoids jabbing him on the nose—an action calculated to stop forward progress and confuse the horse. If he does not move on, immediately repeat the click and the tap, with a bit more emphasis on the latter this time. Repeat this procedure until he moves on.

Never allow the horse to become complacent about answering the click of the tongue. Until he understands its meaning, it must be backed up by the action of the whip. Thereafter, every time he appears to fade on it (which as a rule is quite frequently), the whip reminds him not to do so.

Please note that I refer to the horse as *moving* forward—not necessarily walking—because at this stage, *any* forward movement, great or small, is the objective. It is to be instantly rewarded by desisting with the aids. Reward is also given by the voice, always using the congratulatory phrase he now knows well ("good boy") with quiet approval.

If he moves only for a step or two and stops, do *not* congratulate him for stopping—only for moving on. His reward must be given the moment he moves forward, and not when he stops of his own accord. Then, wait quietly for 10 seconds or so before repeating the exercise.

When he walks on without thought of stopping, allow him to walk for, say, 20 yards, then gently bring him to a halt as follows: with right fist and elbow close to his neck, keep the arm bent and stiffened and simply walk slower than he does, so he feels you as a somewhat dead weight. At the same time (or a moment before), say "whoa-a-a" in a drawn-out, steady tone of voice. He will presently stop, whereupon the *resistance* you set up on the lunge line is automatically released and, at the same time, the horse is rewarded verbally and with a caress.

However, if when trying to stop him, you find yourself leaning back while he continues to drag you forward with no diminution of speed, it indicates that you could be pulling instead of resisting. If he continues to pull, even though you are resisting correctly, slacken the line *very slightly* and give a gentle tug in conjunction with your verbal signal. Continue to give this series of aids, with slightly increased intensity on the line (but not in your voice) until he shows signs of *slowing*. Then resist once more as previously explained until he stops. Again, as with moving on, any sign of compliance is instantly rewarded by desisting with the aids and then reapplying them until the desired result is achieved.

It should be noted that the tugs only point out to the horse that you will not put up with being dragged around when you want him to slow down. Once he acknowledges—which could be after one or more corrections— you revert to resisting in order to stop him. Little by little, he will better understand what resistance means, so that after a while a mere squeeze of your fist in conjunction with your voice will slow or stop him.

During this introduction, it helps to not allow the horse to barrel on at the walk so he is on his forehand and pulling. Short walks of twenty yards or less make it easier to maintain a slower pace. In this state, his longitudinal balance is better; he's not on his forehand, and consequently is more easily influenced by our lunge signals to slow down almost immediately when we resist.

Also, since many horses are only comfortable with being led from the near side and will often move hesitantly if led from the off side, I suggest that you initially teach him to lead correctly up to a satisfactory level of obedience only from the near side. Then, once your authority has been established, leading from the off side should provoke little or no resistance. Repeat this frequently without being in a hurry to move on to lungeing.

If your horse replies to these aids by moving forward unhesitatingly and boldly from a mere soft click of your tongue, and stops the moment you ask him to verbally, he will have learned two of the most useful aids which are essential for your control of him—both on the ground and from the saddle.

Turn on the Forehand

Once the horse has learned to go forward and stop with the verbal aids, in conjunction with the whip and lunge line, the next step is to teach him the rudiments of moving sideways from the whip by a turn on the forehand. Briefly, the turn on the forehand is movement where the horse's front legs more or less pivot around a point, while his hind legs move sideways on a large arc *(Fig. 4)*.

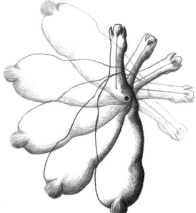

(Fig. 4) The turn on the forehand.

Although this lesson has several benefits, there are two which are of immediate interest. First, he is discouraged from barging over us when sending him out on the lunge circle, and second, we are able to maintain his distance from us on the end of a taut lunge line. If the horse should suddenly veer towards the center of the circle (where the trainer is positioned), the lunge will quickly become slack and may drag dangerously on the ground, allowing the horse to tread on it. Moreover, in such a situation the horse is out of control until the slack has been taken out of the lunge and the contact restored so as to steer or regulate the speed.

The turn on the forehand will not, of itself, prevent these evasions. It is the preliminary exercise in teaching the horse to move his whole body sideways instead of just one end of it.

The horse sports the usual equipment—brushing boots all around to guard against accidental knocks and scrapes, cavesson and lunge line. However, the lunge whip is replaced by a fairly long, thick riding whip, about 2 1/2 feet. At this stage, a dressage whip may not be the best choice (unless it is very stiff), due to its lack of rigidity and a tendency to sting if used firmly. A whip with a fishtail end is quite a good substitute.

In an open space, halt your horse as squarely as you can, while you stand near his left shoulder facing sideways to him. The lunge is coiled in the left hand, and the left elbow is bent and flexible so that when the signal is given to move the quarters sideways, it allows the horse a little forward motion as well as the sideways one.

Hold the whip in the right hand like a sword and tap the horse halfway down the thigh *(Fig. 5)*. As you do so, give the command "over." He may well hesitate, because earlier he learned to go briskly forward from a tap on his barrel and sometimes on his thigh, yet now the lunge is stopping him from doing so. Wait for one or two seconds to see if he shows signs of stepping, or even shuffling over to the right with his hind legs, and if not, repeat the aids with a slightly firmer tap of the whip. Within two or three requests, he will almost certainly offer to step sideways. Any sidesteps, however small, should be immediately rewarded with the voice and a caress.

If the left arm is slightly yielded as you tap him, the whole horse will move forward. The lunge then elastically but firmly resists further forward movement. The result of the first action is to allow the left hind to go forward so as to surpass its partner. Then the second action curtails the forward progress of the left hind and, coupled with the sideways influence of the whip, compels it to step sideways.

If the resistance on the lunge is abrupt instead of elastic, the shock re-

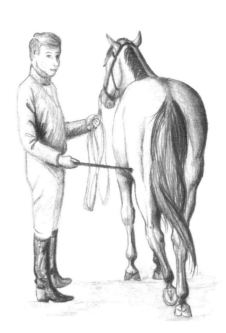

(Fig. 5)
The correct stance for the trainer
in the turn on the forehand.

ceived on the horse's nose will make his quarters run or hop sideways away for two or more steps. This may temporarily be useful for one or two attempts—if only to compel the horse in a rather crude way to do what we want. Subsequently, however, this should be avoided for three reasons.

First, because any sock on the nose (unless it is a deliberate punishment) is not going to promote much confidence in the hands; remember that the lunge is equivalent to the reins on a bridle. Second, the possible loss of confidence just described, can all too easily turn into fear of not moving forward for that important half step. This will result in his left leg shuffling sideways and probably treading on the coronet of the right foot, or he will step back to cross his left leg *behind* its partner.

Third, when he scampers sideways as mentioned above, he is unwittingly being taught to *run* from an aid, instead of *moving* from it in an orderly way. Bear in mind that any signal, whether given on the ground or from the saddle must have *one* reply—not several. Ideally one tap of the whip should solicit one side step. Halt. Another tap solicits the next step and so on. At first, with an oversensitive green horse it is more difficult to obtain such a measured response because, unlike when we are astride, there is nothing on his off side to prevent the quarters from running sideways. However, the point is that we don't want to make matters worse by provoking the horse through careless or insensitive handling.

Returning to our horse, any side steps, however small, should be immediately rewarded with the voice and a pat. We pause for a few seconds to let
the horse assimilate this new lesson, then repeat it. After a successful attempt, he is walked straight forward by giving a click of the tongue and a
tap of the whip on the barrel; then circled, and returned to the original spot
before asking for another turn on the forehand *(Fig. 6)*. Confirm his willingness to step away from a slight tap on the thigh and the verbal command, in both directions.

(Fig. 6)
The sequence for first training
of the turn on the forehand.

The next phase is to walk him forward slowly while using the butt of the
whip to prod him gently in mid-barrel. As you do this, you will notice that
he attempts to step sideways away from you with the whole of his body,
instead of just with the hind end. However, he will almost certainly react by
moving his quarters sideways faster than his forehand, and so doing a kind
of turn around the forehand (for details see Chapter Nineteen). Therefore,
in order to move his whole body uniformly sideways, we need to prod him
further and further forward until the spot that most effectively accomplishes
this is found *(Fig. 7)*. In addition, the sideways movement can be further

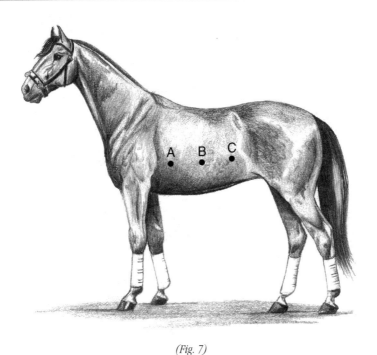

(Fig. 7)
The various prod points.
(A) leg-yielding away from the trainer; (B) Turn around the forehand; (C) Turn on the forehand.

encouraged by the hand (which holds the lunge) being pushed under the horse's throat towards the opposite side, so as to invite the forehand to move over with more dispatch.

Once you arrive at the stage where he steps sideways uniformly and willingly when you prod him lightly on the girth groove, then you can progress to lungeing him.

First Work
on the Lunge

Before describing the horse's first work on the lunge, we should address the advantages of lungeing, and why it so often has a poor reputation as a training technique. Let's begin with the latter.

The most popular accusation against lungeing is that it lames horses. That *it can do so* is undisputed—yet no more so than water can drown people or fire can burn them! Anything that is used incorrectly or to excess is eventually going to be harmful. As with most endeavors, it's not what we do that brings the desired goal, but rather *how we do it.* Lungeing is no different.

For example, lungeing on a circle that is too small for the horse's level of training will strain him. Even if he tries to evade the exercise, the evasion itself—which invariably takes the form of throwing his quarters out—will probably injure him as he smacks his hind legs against each other, as well as twisting the front ones.

Even if the size of the circle is within tolerable limits, it soon loses that status if the trainer doesn't let up by either limiting the number of turns, increasing the size of the circle (making it less demanding), or by changing the rein.

In addition, it's fairly safe to say that the majority of people that lunge, have at best, had limited instruction on how to lunge. Many instructors regard lungeing as an unglamorous aspect of horsemanship, and a time-consuming skill to teach, so they invariably bypass this important part of a pupil's education.

Many books are not immune from culpability. Neat diagrams showing the trainer standing on the spot, pointing a whip at the horse while the animal revolves on a perfect circle, are highly misleading. They are correct only in the sense that they illustrate how the horse ought to go. They do not hint at the problems that are encountered on the way. If the diagrams are to be believed, all one needs to do is revolve on a spot, point a whip or shake the lunge line in order to make the horse lunge impeccably!

The reality of the situation is that with an unmade horse the trainer's role is very dynamic. The green horse will not stay on the designated circle for long. He will pull outwards or swerve inwards. His speed and rhythm will vary. He will be highly influenced by the way his body is positioned relative to the walls of the arena. The position of the trainer in relation to various parts of the horse's body will have a similar effect. The manner in which the whip and lunge are manipulated all have an effect on the horse. It's a complicated juggling act which becomes a nightmare for the initiate learning this craft in the absence of appropriate guidance. It's no wonder that without a certain degree of competence from the trainer, many horses perform in a way that do indeed injure them. But lungeing is an excellent method of training the horse because it can prep him for mounted work.

Lungeing should not be used as a means to allow the horse to let off steam (which can be injurious) but should be an instructive exercise in paying attention, self-control, rhythm, and balance. The horse doesn't learn these things by merely being spun around on the end of a line until he is too tired to run. Rather, these are explained slowly and methodically many times over, often at the pace of walk if necessary. In this regard, we have already made a useful start by teaching our horse to lead correctly and by giving him some idea about respecting the trainer's space. We did this by making him move away from us, first through the turn on the forehand exercise, then by the turn *around* the forehand, and finally by moving the whole horse uniformly sideways.

The trainer also benefits from lungeing, but not in the way one might at first suppose. We are not referring to the person being lunged on the horse, but rather to the skills he gains while working on the ground that will make him a better rider.

On the face of it, the two roles seem unrelated. Not so. The reason is that while lungeing the trainer never has total control of the horse through physical means, by virtue of the fact that the lunge line has a predominantly turning influence. By comparison, its ability to slow the horse or to stop him is negligible. If the lunge line could be drawn backwards, parallel to the horse's sides instead of being limited to a more or less sideways action, then the trainer would have the increased advantage that is afforded to a rider with reins. With this, we can appreciate how the trainer is compelled to meet the horse halfway, so to speak. This is not to say that the animal is then half out of control! Rather, the situation demands above average levels of sensitivity, observation, tact and ingenuity from the trainer.

Moreover, this is especially the case in the initial stages when he is not afforded the luxury of lungeing the horse with side reins. In the absence of these, the skill required to keep a green horse straight in his neck and body, while luring him onto the desired trajectory, requires so much sensitivity and awareness that these attributes will stay with the trainer in whatever role he plays. Simply, it will make him a much better rider.

Bearing this in mind, let's begin the lunge work. First, the riding whip is replaced with the lunge whip. Position yourself as when you asked for the turn on the forehand. Then, with your horse standing on the track with the wall on his right, ask him to go forward. Walk parallel to him and then, while paying out the lunge line, let him draw ahead so you are positioned a few feet to the side of his flank.

While he slowly draws ahead, if he attempts to crowd you or veer leftward, then move forward (but not nearer to him) until you are parallel to his girth or shoulder. At the same time, point the whip at him and if necessary prod him behind the shoulder to remind him to keep his distance *(Fig. 8A)*. If this is ineffective, shorten the distance between you taking the slack out of the lunge. Smoothly slide your hand near the middle of the whip, then quickly raise it to the height of the withers and towards him, so it lies parallel to both the horse's side and the ground *(Fig. 8B)*. This will act as a visual barrier which, if used correctly, will instantly stop him from drifting towards you. The whip is carefully lowered the instant the drifting has ceased. This can always be repeated.

However, if you raise the whip as recommended but simply hold it at the handle, it will have little or no effect. Most of its length will be too far back along the horse's side for the horse to see it clearly and he will be a little fearful of it. When handled as described, the handle-end of the whip will be almost alongside his head, so his reaction will be instantaneous and one of

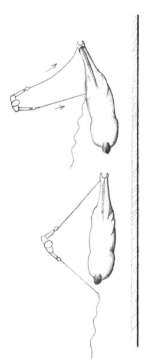

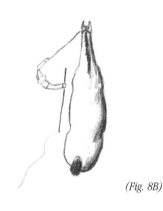

(Fig. 8A)
The horse is veering from the track. The lunge is eased while the whip encourages him to return to the track.

(Fig. 8B)

self-preservation; he will not move towards this warning gesture.

Lest this action be misconstrued, let me say that we are not talking about hitting the horse in any way, nor making the gesture so violent the horse thinks he is going to be struck. He may well raise his head quickly if he is taken by surprise, but we should not provoke the horse to shy away from us with his head.

Once he travels on a straight line while you are somewhat distant, the next phase is to walk slower than he does without playing out the lunge line. By doing so, he will start to turn so that eventually you both walk on concentric circles. You are now positioned parallel to his left hip so your body will have the effect of persuading him to keep walking forward *(Fig. 9)*.

A word on handling your whip: So far, your horse knows that he must move away from it, but if it is permanently poked in his direction he may become too used to its presence—familiarity breeds contempt! Instead, angle the whip so the shaft trails somewhat to the side and rearwards. When you need to send him on, raise the lash-end of the whip from a few inches to five feet off the ground. If you have conditioned him to instantly step forward from a click of the tongue, this, coupled with the whip raised a few inches off the ground, should make him move forward energetically as

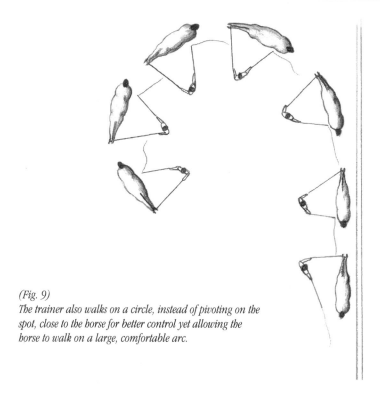

(Fig. 9)
The trainer also walks on a circle, instead of pivoting on the spot, close to the horse for better control yet allowing the horse to walk on a large, comfortable arc.

well. The higher it is raised, the more abrupt its action should be, which becomes a more emphatic order.

Occasionally, you may have to crack the whip if the horse is really not paying attention to its movements. Practice doing this well away from animals so you can do it adroitly without necessarily touching your target. Only in special circumstances should the horse be hit with the end of the lash. It takes many hours of practice to master the use of a lunge whip so that in either hand you can deftly nick the horse with the tail of the snapper anywhere you choose. If you are unpracticed in this skill, cruder but acceptable results can be had by sweeping the whip in an extended arc close to the ground rapidly enough to make the lash sing. Unless your horse is a hard-boiled offender, this should instantly have the desired effect. However, if the horse is on a short radius from you, this will cause the lash to hit him hard at the end of the sweep, something that is normally unnecessary.

Walk-Halt Transitions

Once the horse circles quietly around you, stop him by using your voice and raise the lunge line smoothly and fairly quickly to the height of his head. This will nearly always surprise him enough to make him stop. The horse will also tend to react by raising his head and neck as if coming "above the bit," incorrectly but nevertheless effectively rocking his weight towards his quarters, a redistribution of weight that suggests he should slow down and stop. When the raised lunge signal is given he might stop for only a second or two and then walk on again. If so, lower the lunge and raise it once more, while the "whoa-a-a" command is given a little more emphatically.

After several repetitions, this raising of the lunge line will become accepted as a cue to halt. Then as the horse becomes increasingly familiar with it, the vertical action of the hand is progressively diminished to the point where raising the line a few inches will create the desired response. Incidentally, this isn't something that takes months, or even weeks of practice. The horse can be conditioned to respond to such small signals quite soon, provided that the hands work methodically and precisely.

For instance, after each signal or series of signals (if these are given in quick succession), the hand should return to the "neutral" position, or almost so. Thus, any deviation from that position will of course be interpreted as an instruction of some kind. The "neutral" position is very similar to the one used by the rider. The only difference is that, for the most part, the hand is held slightly higher, so that the forearm is parallel to the ground.

Returning to our horse, let's assume for a moment that in spite of his training in being led, he's still reluctant or sluggish about stopping when we work him from a distance on the lunge. The following solutions will solicit the desired response. They should be attempted in the order in which they are listed.

Solutions for Halting

1. Draw the horse to the wall, lunge him along it (we will assume a counterclockwise direction) and shorten the line so you are no more than ten feet away from him. Then, while giving the verbal signal, raise the lunge as previously described and *quickly* step to your left so you are still the same distance from him but a point opposite about two feet ahead of his

nose. He will immediately stop *(Fig. 10A)*. This ploy can be used to stop him at trot and even at the canter. However, since it requires the handler to be very adroit in handling the line and whip, be quick on his feet, have fast reflexes and sensitivity, I would not advise using your young horse as a guinea pig at the latter paces if you are unfamiliar with this work.

Once our horse stops, we should move sideways to resume the normal position opposite his girth. At that point, we should walk up to him to reward him for complying with our wishes.

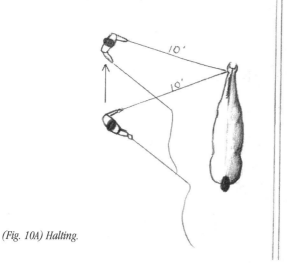

(Fig. 10A) Halting.

2. Give a tactile signal by flicking your left wrist so it sends a ripple down the line, felt as a mild jerk on his nose *(Fig. 10B)*. This needs a certain care, because if these ripples are continuously repeated without a break, a horse will often run sideways or even accelerate forward through discomfort or fear. So, give the verbal signal, coupled with one flick of the wrist, pause, and if necessary repeat the sequence but preferably no more than three times consecutively.

3. Lead the horse off the circle and onto a straight line of travel next to the wall of the ring. Then, with the help of the "whip hand" if necessary, angle the lunge backwards so it is more parallel to his body instead of being at right angles to him. This predominantly backward resistance or slight pull instead of the sideways one will help the horse understand its meaning.

However, be careful not to position yourself too far back, i.e. near his tail, or to move too energetically. He might mistake your body position and movements as a chasing signal. In addition, the lunge signals must be

(Fig. 10B) Sending a ripple down the line.

elastically hinting. Any abruptness will almost certainly force the horse to swerve inwards off the outside track and start to circle. This is something to be avoided because it's harder to stop the horse on a circle using this technique; that is why we first put him on a straight line next to the wall.

4. This next technique is more tricky because it requires swift, but silky-smooth and accurate manipulation of the lunge whip; otherwise the results will be the opposite to those intended. Shorten the lunge to eight or nine feet and stretch the left arm momentarily. Meanwhile, bring the whip carefully and smoothly forward, almost having the tip of the shaft on the ground. Keep sweeping it so it comes in front of you and as far to the left as it will go. To do this, your right arm will have to go under your left arm (whose hand holds the lunge). Once in this position the whip can be raised so that it's in front of the horse's chest, where it may be tapped sharply once or twice while giving the verbal signal *(Fig. 10C)*. If he ignores this, lower it momentarily in order to sweep it even further forward so it can then be raised directly in front of his face. This is guaranteed to halt him.

The whip must not strike his face. Moreover, it should be immediately lowered when the horse gives an *indication* that he is about to slow down or stop. This point should be carefully followed, otherwise there's a real risk that he will stop and immediately either shy or run backwards. It might be considered a salutary lesson for a hard-boiled offender, but not for the type of horse we are usually dealing with here.

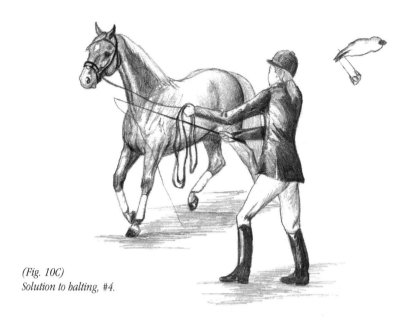

(Fig. 10C)
Solution to halting, #4.

Many of these solutions, here and in other sections of the book, usually won't be needed, but they've been included on the assumption that "Murphy's Law" is alive and well!

Do this "stop-walk on" routine on one side until he understands it fairly well, then change direction and lunge him clockwise around you.

Little by little, you can make your circle smaller until you are standing on the spot, acting like a hub of a wheel while your horse revolves around you. Bear in mind that in doing so, if you don't lengthen the lunge, you will be making his circle smaller, and perhaps uncomfortably tight for him.

At this point, even if the circle is a comfortable size, he may be tempted to swerve and cut across the circle. This must be discouraged. It can be easily countered by flicking your whip up and down behind him every couple of seconds, as well as stimulating him with clicks of the tongue to send him forward. As you do this, stride towards his tail, so you are positioned more to his rear while urging him on.

Preventing Veering When Halting

Practicing the walk-stop transitions can provoke your horse to veer and face you when he is asked to stop. For reasons of safety and to maintain his straightness, this habit should be discouraged.

To avoid this veering, handle the lunge gently and avoid having it too long. When he turns, the horse will either swing his quarters out or bring his forehand inwards. Counter this tendency by halting alongside the arena wall, so he cannot swing his quarters away from you.

In addition, if you change your position so that you are parallel to his shoulder, it will further dissuade him from turning in with his forehand. If necessary, you can also raise the whip parallel to his body as described at the beginning of the lungeing section to prevent him from drifting towards you. Once he is doing the walk-halt transitions quietly and obediently (they don't have to be perfect), he's now ready for trot work.

Trotting on the Lunge

Before describing the trot work on the lunge, the importance of mental communication with our young horse must be noted. Although this rapport is always important, it has special significance at trot and canter. The reason is that the closer the trainer is to the horse, the easier it will be to control him, because he can instantly be touched by the whip. However, the further away the trainer is, the more difficult it will be to influence him. This is the situation most of the time when lungeing on the larger circles that the paces of trot and canter require.

Once the horse is beyond the range where the whip can instantly touch him repeatedly or where the whip's action is merely a threatening one, the trainer's influence tends to be dissipated. An analogy would be that if someone threatens to shoot you, you might not be overly concerned, and might even tell him to get lost. But if he backs up the threat by pulling out a firearm and poking it at your chest, I've no doubt you would be convinced of his sincerity and anxious to be most cooperative!

To offset the handicap that distance presents, obedience to the voice takes on an increasingly important role. In addition, we have one more arrow in our quiver: mental communication. This can be used in two ways: by mentally giving word commands, or by projecting pictorial suggestions to him. The former is simple in theory. In practice it requires the sender to be mentally calm and at the same time be able to pointedly and repeatedly send the appropriate instruction. The sending of pictorial suggestions is done in the same way. However, whereas the broadcasting of word commands is sent directly, pictorial suggestions are not so literal. They are best projected in a form that would unmistakably tell the story, maybe even in a bizarre way.

For instance, to halt you might imagine a brick wall in front of your horse. Or, if he dances around when he should stand still, you might imagine him screwed to the ground. If he won't slow down, picture him

pulling a log which is so heavy that it quickly tires him.

This all may sound strange at first, particularly if one isn't familiar with these concepts. However, to dismiss them out of hand robs the trainer of the opportunity of using the oldest and not ineffective method of communication between beings. With practice, it can become an invaluable aid which will bring you and your horse much closer together on more than one level.

Returning to our horse, first circle him around you at a walk and then ask him to trot as follows: ease the lunge a little followed immediately by a sharp click of the tongue. This is followed by a brisk raising of the whip, just high enough so the horse is aware of it. If he only walks faster, then repeat the verbal command but this time raise the whip two or three feet off the ground and, if necessary, sweep it towards his rear end. He will almost certainly scurry forward.

Once he is trotting, avoid distracting him with verbal praise just yet since its soothing tone may encourage him to return to the walk. Instead, let his reward be the immediate cessation of your aids: lower the whip and return it to the original position, trailing it behind you. Finally, play out the lunge line so he is some 20 feet away from you.

If he doesn't trot at the speed of your choice, and instead moves hesitantly, animate him with the whip and a click of the tongue. Again, make sure the lunge is yielded slightly as you do so.

It's also quite possible that he will accelerate to a fast trot, and here your voice used in a soothing way can reassure the horse that there's nothing to get excited about. If he doesn't slow down within four or five rounds, trotting on a smaller circle will curtail his speed. If the horse is leaning on the lunge, drawing him towards you will generally be met with resistance. Instead, walk slowly toward him while coiling the lunge for a foot or two.

Then stop to let him circle around you on the smaller circle. This is repeated until the circle is effective in slowing him down.

If he still doesn't slow down, once the size of the circle is diminished the trainer is able to more effectively give "knocks" on the lunge. These knocks are distinct but small tugs. If given too rapidly in succession, they can have the opposite effect and send him on faster still. Experience, intuition, and trial and error are your only guides since each horse reacts somewhat differently. Be sure to praise him for each diminution of speed, so he clearly understands that you approve of his correct response. Once he is cooperating while still trotting pay the lunge out again so he describes the original sized circle.

Trot to Walk Transitions

Once your horse is trotting and requiring only an occasional encouragement from your voice and whip, he may tire after a few rounds and lapse into walk of his own accord. Allow him to do so, and simultaneously give him the command "Wa-a-a-lk." Since he is slowing down to a walk anyway, we can exploit the situation so he learns the new verbal aid by association.

Furthermore, the trot-walk transition without the use of physical aids without coercion, impresses your authority in the horse's mind. Shaking the lunge and sending ripples to his nose may be a needless aid in this instance. When training any horse, it is better to give the smallest and least number of aids to accomplish an objective.

Note also that this is the first time the horse has been introduced to the word "Walk." We didn't use it for the upward transition from halt to the walk; only the click of the tongue told him that. This goes against conventional form, but I believe that for this level of learning it has a special advantage, as follows.

Since the young horse, unless he has a very phlegmatic temperament, is likely at times to become excited—even for reasons beyond our control—we need to use the walk as a pace which will wind him down, while at the same time enabling us to continue working him. We could of course halt. This is useful and sometimes necessary to calm him but it doesn't allow the horse to continue working. With this in mind, it suits us to have the word "Walk" associated in the horse's mind with calmness and down transitions.

It may be argued that we could use the command "walk on," given in crisp tones, to go from halt to walk to differentiate it from the request "walk," soothingly given for a downward transition to that pace. In this way the horse would not be confused. This is true a little later in his training, but I think that the risk of misunderstanding is still there at this elementary level.

In fact, there may be times when in correcting an unruly horse, the word "walk" needs to be uttered in a drawn out way, yet quite authoritatively. How then is the inexperienced horse to interpret this signal? That's why it's wise to teach the horse that the word "walk" uttered in whatever tone means reduce to that pace or de-energize.

Besides, the walk is too useful a pace to squander. Although it's an excellent training pace, it is also the most difficult of the three paces to execute correctly in its varying forms. So at this stage we use it mostly for its calming influence; later we will see how useful it is as an explanatory tool.

With regard to the way the voice aids are given, the following is a general rule: aids for up transitions are given in a crisp, clipped tone of voice, though not necessarily loudly, while aids for down transitions are spoken in a soothing, drawn-out, low tone of voice. However, there are exceptions to this rule.

The Walk & Trot Commands

So far, only the click of the tongue has been used to ask for upward transitions to the walk and the trot. Now, once the horse is settled into the routine of lungeing and clearly understands the meaning of the click of the tongue, we can introduce the verbal signals to "walk-on" and "trot." From here on, the click of the tongue is to be used only as a stimulus to go forward at any of the three paces.

Again, verbal commands for up transitions are given in a purposeful tone of voice, as if you are *telling* the horse what to do instead of asking. If the command "walk on" is uttered without conviction, your horse is almost guaranteed to stay put! In addition, we prepare the horse for impending commands by prefixing each one with the word "And," drawled as "A-a-a-nd." For example, the instruction to walk forward would be: "A-a-a-nd walk on."

The verbal aid "walk on", briskly uttered, is immediately followed by raising and lowering the whip abruptly as a reinforcement. If the horse ignores you, repeat these aids, but raise your whip end three feet or so before dropping it again. If he seems confused (he should not be if you've carefully taught him the meaning of the whip aids), help him understand by giving the following aids one after the other in quick succession: "walk on," click of the tongue, whip aid. If more reinforcement of the verbal signals is needed, the whip can be rapidly, but not bombastically, swept towards his rear end.

For making an up transition into trot, we pronounce the command as "Terr-r-ot." Ease the lunge and sing out the command "A-a-a-nd Terr-r-ot." This is immediately followed by using the whip in a stimulating but not aggressive way. If he needs an additional incentive, the click of the tongue can be added.

One final note concerning the use of these two signals: they merely order the horse to make the transition from one pace to another—*and that is all*. For instance, if the horse doesn't trot at the speed you prefer but moves hesitantly or lazily, avoid telling him to "trot." As far as he's concerned he is already trotting! Instead, encourage or stimulate him with the click of the tongue and the whip.

Further Considerations

Each of the principles we've explored so far may be assimilated, though not necessarily confirmed, in a time span ranging from a few minutes to several sessions, depending on the skill of the trainer and the intelligence and disposition of the horse.

Introduction to training can be overwhelming for your youngster if not conducted carefully and sympathetically. For instance, avoid making one request after another in quick succession. Instead, allow him to try and carry out your demands as best he can. Be somewhat indulgent, allowing him to make minor mistakes, and then correct them.

You will have to use your judgement as to when and if to make an immediate correction following a mistake or what appears to be a disobedience. An example of justifiable indulgence would be when you have halted him for a long time and he has become somewhat sleepy. When he's told to walk on, he doesn't react. In such a case, I would let him off the hook and repeat precisely the same aids instead of escalating them and jolting him into action. Cultivate equestrian tact so you get a *feeling* for knowing when to bend the rules to make your horse a happier, and not ungrateful partner.

Another factor is that he needs to feel his efforts are appreciated. Praise him frequently without necessarily always being effusive. Your tone of voice and the way you caress or pat him should make him feel good about himself, even proud. When he is halted, stand calmly by his side without fussing with him too much and let him absorb your composed demeanor. If you make a habit of conducting yourself as an unruffled mentor, in time he will acquire the same poise.

The current work should concentrate mainly on trotting him on a circle of about 15 meters to help him find regularity of rhythm and with it, a better balance. If the speed of the trot keeps fluctuating and causing a loss of balance, it may be that the circle is too tight for the speed at which he's trotting. Play out the line and increase the circle's size.

On the other hand, if he's going faster than his natural trot speed and the stride becomes short, he must be slowed down. Only when the trot becomes somewhat lazy should he be encouraged to increase the amplitude of his strides.

As you work your horse, be careful you don't get so far away from him that the influence of line and whip is diminished. If necessary, keep the same distance between you but temporarily walk on a circle concentric with his. Otherwise, as circumstances allow, try to stay put in one spot so that the horse is describing a true circle. It is all too easy for the trainer, whose position should act as a hub, to wander around aimlessly so that the horse's trajectory results in a potato-shaped affair, which is hardly conducive to helping him find a steady rhythm, speed and balance.

For the first few lungeing sessions, the frequent transitions up and down should be done with two separate purposes in mind. First, walking and halting are used to give him a breather after trotting. Second, to increasingly familiarize him with each of the commands he has been taught through the agency of voice, lunge whip, and your body movements.

However, be sure that in your zeal for obedience, the transitions from one pace to another do not become jerky or abrupt. Smooth accelerations and decelerations into the required paces, even if executed somewhat lazily, are the order of the day at this stage of his training.

As for cantering, until the young horse has been taught the rudiments of obeying the requests to walk, trot, and halt, it suits us to avoid asking for it for two reasons. First, it is likely to excite him. You place yourself in a position where control of his calmness, speed of pace, and obedience may be eroded, factors which you will have been studiously cultivating. Second, the asymmetrical pace of canter is not conducive to developing his balance, given the imposition of the limiting size of the lunge circle. The symmetry of the trot pace is far more appropriate for this purpose.

However, if he offers a canter, allow him to continue for a couple of rounds before asking him to trot. Vibrate or gently "knock" the lunge while at the same time uttering the command "trot," in a low draw-out tone of voice, repeating the verbal command with each manual aid.

A common error is using the word "whoa" to make this transition, or to calm a horse that is cantering or trotting excitedly. This is quite wrong and illogical. "Whoa" means stop. The more one uses it on an excited horse that is not cooperating, the more he learns how to ignore that command. Even if he wasn't excited, and you really wanted him to stop, he couldn't go from canter directly to halt. The logical sequence of orders should be: trot, walk, whoa.

If we wish to steady such a horse, then a variation on the word "Whoa" can be used. Although there are several ways of doing this, I personally utter a series of brief "grunts"—being an amalgamation of the word "ho" and "ha." Naturally, the horse must be conditioned to respond to this signal with the aid of the lunge line. However, due to the resemblance with the command to stop, the horse soon understands their association while still appreciating the distinction between the two.

Two further considerations may help. First, avoid overfeeding him, at least for the time being while he is doing slowish work. Small amounts of grain, as little as four to five pounds a day depending on the horse, supplemented with good quality hay, will make your youngster more tractable. Many horses, young and older ones, are in fat condition. Your horse is a worker who has to carry his weight as well as yours, and as such his legs, heart and lungs should be spared the effort imposed on them through having to cope with unnecessary weight.

Also, make the schooling sessions short, while not forgetting to change direction frequently. Twenty to thirty minutes, twice a day, at this stage are worth far more than marathon sessions of an hour apiece. Besides, more than half an hour's lungeing can be strenuous for horses at this stage. Circling is hard work.

Progress carefully through each step. Confirm your horse's understanding of his current lessons, while not omitting reviewing the past ones, before teaching him something new. Ask precisely and intelligently. Praise often and avoid putting pressure on him by making your expectations beyond his reach. If he is helped along, you will add momentum to his understanding.

Introducing the Saddle & Bridle

Stroking with the Lunge Whip

Before introducing the horse to the tack he will eventually wear when he is being ridden, specifically the saddle, it's prudent to inure him to its feel. To this end, we begin by touching him all over his body with the lunge whip. The reader may find it odd that this exercise should be mentioned only now, at this relatively late stage, when traditionally the young horse is introduced to it prior to his first lungeing experience.

The rationale behind this is twofold. First, if the horse is nervous or high strung by nature, he should be familiarized with the whip very early on in the manner to be described. This way he is assured that the whip is nothing to fear.

On the other hand, if he doesn't fall into this category, acquainting him with the whip earlier often works against the trainer because the slight leeriness the horse may have of this "strange" tool of ours engenders a healthy respect for it. Since we want him to go away from the whip, it suits us to have him use his instinct of self-preservation to escape from it. Besides, if the horse has a healthy regard for the whip (but not frightened to death), it sensitizes the trainer to use it discreetly and with feeling. Otherwise, the horse will overreact, which in turn creates problems for the trainer.

Also, at this stage we are not interested in introducing the whip so that the horse becomes friends with it. However, we couldn't have gotten this far if the horse had been petrified of it! Instead, our purpose is to accustom him to being touched all over by something other than our hands or grooming equipment. So, in order to develop his courage, if only in a minor way, what better than to use the one thing of which he is somewhat wary—the whip?

In a small way this is a test. Does his trust in you prevail over his cautionary attitude towards the whip? You should find out now. If trust is lacking, it's important you work on it as soon as possible or it will create problems later on, when he will be presented with things which might be more frightening than a whip stroking his body. At this stage it is unlikely that his familiarization with the whip will make him lose respect for it, but if this should happen, use one of the ways mentioned throughout the book to sharpen his response to it.

To accustom the horse to the whip, lazily stroke all of his body with the end of the shaft, taking care not to poke or spook him. Then, draw the lash over his neck, back and sides slowly and gently, all the while reassuring him with your voice. Praise him with a pat and a kind word and repeat the procedure. Practice this a couple of times at each session until your youngster accepts it with equanimity.

Introducing the Roller

Once the horse tolerates the lunge whip being stroked over his body without flinching or quivering, the next step is to introduce him to the lungeing roller or surcingle. This will be his first experience of having a piece of tack on his back and will accustom him to having a saddle with a tightened girth later on.

First show him the roller and let him sniff it. If he's wary about the equipment, lay a tidbit on it and let him nibble the food. Next, very carefully slide the roller over his back, reassuring him as you do so. *Never let go of the roller.* If you find this awkward, have someone competent do it while you control and reassure the horse. Then gently take the roller off. Again, reassure him. Repeat the process a few times until he doesn't mind what is being done to him.

At this point he is ready to have the roller fastened around his barrel. This task should be done in a series of steps which should be followed *exactly* in this sequence to avoid accidents:

1. Fit a hunting breastplate on him so that it is comfortably loose and unconstraining. If it's fitted snugly, he may resist its restriction once he begins moving.
2. Carefully put the roller on his back as before, but do not fasten it. If you do so and he panics at the unaccustomed feel, the roller will slip back on his barrel towards his genitals, provoking him to buck.
3. Fasten the nearside strap at the upper side of the breastplate to the "D" rings of the roller.
4. Carefully reach under his belly for the buckle end of the roller and thread it through the girth loop of the breastplate. You should make sure this is wide enough for the roller before you put it on the horse. Fasten the roller loosely so it is slightly floppy. When you reach under his belly, do not put your head on the girth groove near his elbows; if he should cow-kick on feeling the roller wrapping around his barrel, your doctor will be hearing from you. Also, keep the front edge of the roller back away from the front legs when you pull it towards you, or it might startle the horse. If you have thoroughly handled his body, he should show no surprise at accidental knocks—don't take the chance.
5. Then fasten the offside strap on the breastplate to the offside "D" ring on the roller. Let him stand like this for a minute or so, and then gently shift the roller a few inches left and right, all the while reassuring him or feeding him some snack. Then, take everything off *in the reverse order:* unbuckle the roller from itself, unthread it from the breastplate girth loop, undo the straps from the "D" rings on the roller, and take the roller off, followed by the breastplate. This is enough for the first session, so praise him and quit for the day.

During the next session, familiarize him with the routine several times. Once he is unconcerned we can ask him to move forward at a walk. This is better done while you walk next to his shoulder in the conventional lungeing position with the horse on the lunge line. By being close you not only reassure him, but are better able to control any sudden forward spurts which he might make when the breastplate and roller rub on his body as he moves.

After 20 yards or so, stop and praise him. Then continue the stop-walk routine until he walks calmly, and little by little, send him away from you until he is moving on a 10-meter circle. When you ask him to trot he may react by darting forward or suddenly stopping. With this smaller circle you are nearer to him and better able to control any erratic movements. Once he settles at the trot, increase the circle to 15 meters.

Now, each time you halt him, play with the roller by shifting it from side to side, pressing down on the top and gently tugging its sides. Do this from both sides of the horse. When he's unconcerned, repeat this more purpose-fully. In addition, tap the top padded part of the roller to create both noise and pressure.

Once he's unbothered by the equipment at the walk and trot, begin tight-ening the roller one hole at a time over the span of a few schooling ses-sions. The first hole should make the roller just tight enough to prevent it from slipping. Always begin each session with a slightly loose roller. Then, after a few rounds, tighten to the next hole and continue lungeing. If he is accustomed progressively, you will avoid the commotion so beloved by some horse breakers; bucking will rarely occur—at least because of this prob-lem!

Introducing the Saddle

Having progressively accustomed the horse to the roller firmly girthed around his barrel and without him showing signs of discomfort, he is ready to be saddled. This will be the first time it is prudent to enlist the help of an assistant, unless you are truly confident that the horse will be unruffled by this procedure.

Initially, the saddle is stripped of irons and leathers, since we don't want these to bang around and unnecessarily frighten our youngster. The saddle pad should also be removed. The other tack consists of the hunting breast-plate and the girth. First show the saddle to your horse and when he is calm, have a competent helper gently place it on his back without the girth. *Do not let go of the saddle;* if he spooks it will crash by his feet and prob-ably scare him to death. Gently lift the saddle off and repeat the process several times until he ignores it.

I advise against feeding him while putting the saddle on because he can become so distracted that once he stops feeding and realizes what's going on, he might react violently. He should be fully aware of what is being done; let his reactions to your actions be your barometer as to when to stop what you are doing. In this way you will avoid accidents that will rattle your horse and which could set back his training program. If he shows signs of nervousness, suspend the operation and soothe him before continuing.

When he is used to the saddle being lifted on and off his back, wiggle it left and right while holding on to it. Then tap it all over with the palm of your hand until he ignores the noise. After that, gently raise and lower the flap on the near side until he shows no fear, and then let the flap fall from an increasingly raised position until he is indifferent to this as well. Always praise his good behavior.

Next, remove the saddle and put the hunting breastplate on the horse. Buckle the girth onto the off side of the saddle, and slide the girth over his back and position the saddle as before. Proceed as you did with the roller: first attach the nearside strap of the breastplate to the "D" ring of the saddle. Then thread the girth through the girth loop of the breastplate, fasten the girth to the near side billets lightly but not loosely, and lastly, attach the offside strap of the breastplate to its "D" ring on the saddle.

I would like to repeat a cautionary note concerning this procedure, because ignoring it can be disastrous. If you are doing this on your own, it's very important to *buckle only the nearside strap of the breastplate* to the nearside "D" ring of the saddle before the horse is girthed up. Only then should you go to the offside of the horse and attach the other breastplate strap. The reason is that if the horse moved around or shied as you were in the process of going to his offside, the ungirthed saddle would slide and crash violently against his forelegs. Since it is hanging from the breastplate, unless the horse freezes, any subsequent movement he makes will repeatedly make the saddle bang against his legs. I'm not going to describe the consequences of such carelessness—just avoid it!

One last note concerning this point: once lightly girthed up, a timid horse may lose his nerve and start to move around and possibly rush off. In this case he won't allow you the luxury of attaching the offside breastplate strap to the saddle. However, as long as the nearside one is buckled, and if your equipment is sturdy, the saddle will be prevented from sliding around excessively, even if the horse's movements are lively. If you take extra time in familiarizing such a horse with the saddling routines as described, including that of the roller, this scenario is unlikely to occur. However, as you can never be absolutely sure, don't take that chance.

The purpose of the breastplate in this instance is not to lock the saddle in place to prevent it slipping sideways or backward. Rather, it is there to prevent these things happening to excess since some slippage will occur due to the girth being only lightly tightened.

To this end, the breastplate needs to be somewhat loose for the first session or two. The slippage will be so gradual that the breastplate will progressively strain against the horse's chest and shoulders in a way that he will barely be aware of it. However, if it is tight to begin with the horse will *feel* as if it's restricting his shoulder movements. That, coupled with the strange saddle bumping on his back, can give him a feeling of being attached to one piece of equipment while being restrained by the other. As a result he may be very reluctant to trot and perhaps even walk forward. This is an unwelcome situation because when invited or coerced forward, he may rebel by bucking on the spot, half-rearing, or turning on the forehand to face the trainer.

Now, take up the lungeing position and with a short length of lunge lead the horse forward. He may give one or two spurts forward and stop due to the strange feeling of the saddle. Go with him and encourage him to walk on in the normal way. Frequently stop and praise him. Then move the saddle from side to side and pat it gently again. When he becomes indifferent to these actions the saddle can be slapped with increasing force.

If he appears reasonably calm, begin walking and halting on a 10-meter circle. Then, still on the circle, ask him to jog on. If he goes too fast, the saddle flaps will bang and create unnecessary commotion. The small size of the circle enables the trainer to control the speed more easily than if the circle was larger.

If he is spooked by the noise of the flaps and accelerates, gain his attention with a few gentle tugs on the lunge and reassure him with your voice. Then walk him again to recover his composure. When the trot is resumed, you may find he won't be as bothered by the flaps or of the saddle lightly bumping on his back.

The procedure of introducing the saddle to the horse for the first time is a crucial affair—nothing must go wrong. This can be accomplished in one schooling session if you feel confident about your horse's placidity. If in doubt, take a couple of sessions or more to accustom him to this routine. One cannot afford to make mistakes on this issue. Confirm each step before going on to the next, regardless of how long it takes. If the trainer avoids accidentally provoking the horse into rebelling, the horse will see no need to misbehave. Moreover, due to foresight and good judgement, the less you have to correct or reprimand him the better your relationship with him will be.

Once he's unperturbed by being saddled and having his girth tightened,

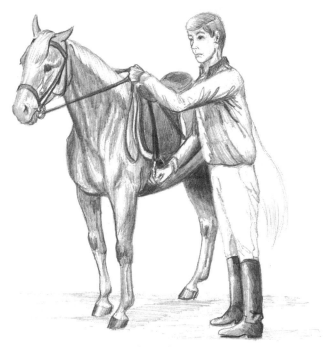

(Fig. 11)
The trainer applies pressure to the stirrup iron.

the stirrups can then be attached. At first hang them close to the stirrup bars; in this position they will barely bump against the saddle at the trot, even if he should be excited and starts cantering. Little by little they are lowered until they hang about six inches shorter than normal riding length to prevent them from banging his elbows. At times they will bump quite energetically on his barrel, but since you've taken the precaution of lowering them progressively he shouldn't be worried by this.

During this period the horse is given his first taste of pressure on his back. At a halt, ensure the girth is reasonably tight, then lean down on the near side stirrup *(Fig. 11)*. The pressure should be made progressively stronger until you are leaning most of your weight on the iron. The purpose of this is to simulate mounting, for which he should stand quite still. However, if you lean on it too abruptly, it will make the horse stagger sideways towards you. This is especially the case with narrow chested horses, whose lateral base of support is shorter and more unstable.

When he is unperturbed by this routine done from each side, get a helper to lean on the offside stirrup at the same time, and in the same degree that the near side one is weighted. This will somewhat simulate the pressure he will feel when we eventually mount him. Again, the pressure is initially soft and progressively increased—but never to a level of discomfort. If the horse hollows his back, squirms, or starts to fidget, it signals that the exercise was done too fast, the pressure was too strong, or the routine was too long and he is getting sore. Little and often is the way to go.

Introducing the Bridle

Once our young horse is used to working with the saddle, we can accustom him to the bridle. This needs to be undertaken with care to avoid problems such as head tossing and other resistances. It's wise to have his teeth checked periodically by a vet or dentist to ensure that the action of the bit and the subsequent movement of the lower jaw does not cause discomfort or injury, as will happen if the teeth are sharp and lacerating his cheeks.

Choose a bit which is appropriate for the shape of his bars, depth of palate, and thickness of tongue. The subject of correct bitting is too extensive to cover here but generally speaking, the jointed snaffle is a good choice, with the severity of the bit being governed by its thickness. The thinner the bit, the stronger its effect. Bear in mind that thickest is not necessarily the best; it depends on the shape of his mouth and tongue.

It is essential that one avoids forcing the bit into his mouth. Instead, the horse's mouth should be opened by putting the left thumb into it at the corner of his nearside lips and gently prying his bars open.

Pay particular attention to two points. First, the bit should hang at the correct height, with the corners of his lip just wrinkled. If you notice your young horse starts to play with the bit and looks like he's getting his tongue over it, raise it immediately. If he persists, let him wear the bridle when he eats his grain for the next two or three days. It will dissuade him from this bad habit since he can't do that and eat at the same time. Also, the brow band should be sufficiently roomy so it doesn't pinch his ears where it meets the headpiece. Carelessness with these details can lead to head tossing and nervousness.

It's a good idea to introduce the bridle to your horse in his stall so he can't escape if you accidentally let go of him. Besides, it's home for him so he's more at ease there. On the first two or three occasions you bridle him, leave it on for 10 minutes or so, but don't leave the horse alone in his stall. The bit or cheek pieces may irritate him initially, and he may try to rub the bridle off his head. If you've chosen a full cheek snaffle, the cheeks could snag in a crack in the kicking boards or catch underneath a manger or hayrack, badly bruising his mouth and frightening him.

One sometimes sees young horses being bitted with mouthpieces that have keys hanging from the center. Although such bits may temporarily serve a useful purpose in special cases, I would advise against their use. The horse's penchant for playing with the keys teaches his tongue to "snake," which invariably leads to him putting it over the bit.

Using a drop noseband to close the mouth should be a last option. If it is used, avoid overtightening it. It should be just loose enough for him to chew a tidbit comfortably.

Introducing Side Reins

After he has worn his bridle for a few sessions, we introduce the side reins. These are not, as one might suppose, used to control the forward motion of an unruly horse. They can be used for that, but if we've schooled our horse carefully to this point, he should be cooperative enough to make the side reins redundant for this purpose. Instead we will use them for two specific tasks:

1. To accustom him to the feel of the bit being drawn in his mouth—and accepting this with equanimity.

2. The side reins receive some of the horse's forward energy without letting it spill forward wastefully. As soon as he discovers this and willingly accepts the "barrier" action of the side reins, that energy is channeled back to be reused. Later, the horse doesn't wastefully send the energy forward to lean on the reins, but instead uses it selectively. He does so to improve the quality of the engagement of the hind legs, to supple his back, and to harness his energy so as to direct it more upward instead of flat and forward.

The process may be likened to boiling water in a pot. Without a lid, the water may never come to a rolling boil. The energy generated, the steam, escapes unbridled and becomes lost energy. However, with a lid on the pot that steam is contained and can be harnessed to do many things.

At first, adjust the side reins loosely so they sag somewhat—except when the horse's neck is in the natural position. As the horse moves, they will slightly sway and even flop around. By accustoming his mouth to this mild treatment, he will be more forgiving when you ride him and inadvertently pull on the reins. This can happen if the rider is caught off balance due to a young horse's erratic movements. Alternately, the horse can lose his own balance and raise his head and neck rapidly, altering the contact with the rider's hands. When he regains it, which could be a moment later, he will lightly jab himself in the mouth as the contact is resumed from slackened reins. The side reins will accustom him to the feel of normal reins, and as progressively shortened, still keeping them at a comfortable length, they will simulate the contact the rider expects from the horse.

If we want a happy horse, we must be clear about the final objective: mounted or otherwise, the horse is encouraged to look for and accept contact with the bit. If the trainer tightens the side reins indiscriminately to "shape" the horse, it will surely lead to difficulties. He will buckle up into a shortened outline and when his muscles start aching from the strain, he will seek release by hollowing his back, pulling or worse. Before we know it, our rapport has regressed.

Introduce the side reins in the schooling arena and not in his stall. You can never know for certain how the horse will react. If he feels the contact once he moves on, he could suddenly stop, run back, rear, and maybe even throw himself to the ground. While this is unlikely if the side reins are long, don't take the chance.

You can attach the side reins to each side of the girth or through the front billet at varying heights, depending on what you are trying to achieve. However, for our purpose, it's more important to ensure the side reins do not slide further and further down the girth. They should lock into the chosen position.

Next, assuming you begin lungeing on the left rein (counterclockwise), snap the offside rein to the bit ring on that side, then fasten the nearside one to its corresponding bit ring. Walk your horse and halt him a few times, then, with a shortened lunge, trot him slowly. At this pace, he should be undeterred by the swaying of the reins. Once he is settled, lengthen the lunge. If he speeds up or starts to canter, the reins may jump around and worry him. Soothe him with the voice and lunge him on a 10-meter circle till he regains his composure. When you stop for a breather, unsnap the reins from the bit, fasten them to the "D" rings of the saddle, then back again to the bit. The more you "play" with him, the quicker he will accept all this interaction as normal.

Once he accepts the side reins and is unaffected by their movement, lunge him with side reins over a ground pole. The way the horse is introduced to this will be described in the next chapter. When he stretches down to look at it, he will take up some slack on them. Soon he will extend his neck more confidently and, in an exploratory way, make brief contacts with the bit. Finding that it doesn't hurt him to do so, he'll take courage to feel for the bit for more sustained periods.

Eventually, the side reins are shortened, one hole at a time, to help him make a more prolonged contact while in his normal working posture, and also to caution him not to be too much on his forehand. When he proves himself to be consistent by comfortably taking up contact most of the time, the inside rein can be shortened one or two holes to help him bend according to the degree of the circle he is describing. Being bent in the same direction of progress on the circle will help refine his balance. However, this may be counterproductive with some horses since it encourages them to bend only in the neck, as well as allowing them to escape sideways in the direction of the outside shoulder.

Before adjusting a side rein, always unclip it from the bit ring. The tongue of the buckle may get stuck in holes which are too snug, so that on freeing the buckle the sudden jolt jabs the horse in the mouth. It won't if the side rein is temporarily unclipped from the bit.

At first, lunge him only on larger circles; a 15 meter circle is appropriate. The bend in this neck and body will be slight and thus comfortable to him. As he settles down, evenly stretching both side reins, you may notice that his hind feet don't always track in the same line as his front feet. He will sometimes (but not always) swing his quarters out, so his back feet describe a larger circle than his front feet. This will be more evident when he circles in one direction than the other. This is because, at their current adjustment, the side reins suggest the correct bend the horse makes with his forepart, but have relatively little influence to control the path the rest of the body takes.

One way to prevent him swinging outwards is to temporarily shorten the outside rein to give him a counterbend. The adjustment should be slight, a hole or two, or an excessive bend might encourage him to drift inwards with his shoulders. It helps to lunge him in an enclosed area. If you are in an indoor school with the conventional width of 20 meters, lunge your horse in the corner at one end so he will be framed at least on two sides of his circle by the school walls.

Remember that a circle has no straight lines. In other words, your 15 meter circle touches the walls (real or imagined) only four times, once on each wall and exactly half way along each one. To obtain this accuracy, keep checking that your position is central. If you are lungeing him on the left rein, dig your left heel into the dirt and pivot around it. Then, as long as your lunge line is held at the same length and gently stretched, your horse will be describing a circle instead of some potato-shaped affair.

This of course is the ideal. There may be moments when we have to walk on a circle concentric to his, so our position is either more towards his rear (in order to urge him on) or towards his front (to prevent turning in).

Any tendency to spiral inward towards you can be countered by pointing the whip at his neck. If he ignores this, take a couple of brisk stomping steps towards him as you do so, in order to "shoo" him outwards. As a last resort, you can shake the lunge so it snakes towards the side of his face, thus encouraging him to move away from it. However, be careful not to overdo it, or he will quickly equate the raising of your arm, the action needed to snake the line towards the side of his face, with shying away. Since the raised arm is also used as a cue to halt, indiscriminate use of this tactic can create problems when halting.

Once he takes a steady and even contact with slightly shortened side reins, he can then be lunged over single ground poles spaced far apart on the circle and eventually over multiple ground poles on a straight line of travel.

Cavaletti Work

Up to this point we've been lungeing our horse at the trot, without requiring any special physical effort from this gait. He's been allowed to work at his "natural" trot. Moreover, he has found his lateral balance within the confines of the lunge circle, no easy task when he's compelled to go round and round with very little straight-line travel. In addition, his longitudinal balance has been further improved by the frequent transitions from one pace to another.

The principles behind these two approaches are good and valid for training at any level. However, unless the trainer is very skilled in the craft of lungeing, they won't by themselves easily bring out the best in the horse's trot or his balance in general.

A good vehicle to this improvement is the use of cavaletti, which encourage the horse to:

- Place his feet between the poles so that the length of his steps and strides are uniform.
- Raise and lower his feet in a purposeful way, instead of sweeping his legs forward in a lazy manner.

- Spring from one diagonal to another (at the trot).
- Learn how to do all the above without losing his balance.

Further advantages are:

- It teaches the horse to think.
- It makes him pay attention to where he's putting he feet.
- It teaches him judgement—something that will be useful when he starts to jump.
- It builds his muscles so he can better carry a rider, as well as being able to more easily do the various tasks required of him.

Lungeing over One Ground Pole

In the beginning, place one ground pole at a right angle to his lungeing circle. But, don't lunge him over it immediately because he will almost certainly run out. Horses don't see the reason why they should go over the pole when it's much easier to go around it; that is how your youngster thinks. Instead, lead him up to it and stop. On a long rein let him look and sniff at it, and even touch it with his hoof. Turn away and then return, leading him over it. After a second or third pass, he can be lunged over it at a walk.

At first, he may be hesitant just before stepping over it. This is not necessarily a display of fear; he is probably confused as to how to step over it in stride. Let him sort it out for a few passes and then trot him over the pole.

I recommend that for at least two schooling sessions you not increase the number of poles. Chances are he will trip over multiple poles. Just because he performs well after a few passes doesn't necessarily mean he is ready for a different lesson. He needs time first to be introduced to something new, and then become comfortable with it. Remember; *confirm* the current work before attempting anything new.

Objectives of Using Multiple Ground Poles

- The first objective in working your young horse over more than one ground pole is to encourage him to step over them without fear.
- The second objective is to negotiate them unhurriedly and rhythmically.

- The third objective is to encourage him to stretch forward and down with his head and neck. This will help round his back and make his gait more elastic.
- The fourth objective is to develop his ability to increase the flexion of the hind legs and to gradually develop a more powerful upward thrust, instead of allowing them to merely push the horse's mass forward.

I would like to emphasize the importance of the sequence of work about to be described. To many people it may seem pedantic and overly cautious but I don't believe this to be the case. Admittedly there are many horses who are quite happy to cross over multiple poles spaced close together on the very first pass without any introductory work. However, there are many more that balk at the idea and for this reason I urge avoiding shortcuts. With experience the trainer will intuitively know when the horse is ready to go on to the next phase. Usually it's not the sequence of steps that is skipped, but the time spent at the various steps that is curtailed.

Introducing Multiple Poles

Introducing multiple poles must be done only once your youngster walks and trots quietly over single ground poles. These poles will not be laid on the lungeing circle as were the single poles. Instead they are placed on a straight line near our lunge circle.

When we lay two or more poles on the ground, they are configured so that the horse takes one step in between each pole. The distance between each pole for walking is shorter than for trotting.

There is a lot of confusion as to what the distance between each pole should be. Most sources dealing with this give specific distances for walk, trot and canter. Understandably, one needs some rule of thumb as a guide, but in practice such advice is often confusing. Why? Because horses don't all have the same length of stride. In addition, if a horse walks calmly, his stride will tend to be fairly long. But if he is excited, even though he is still walking, his stride tends to become shorter and more elevated. In this instance he could easily take two steps in the space between poles, instead of the intended single step.

Our first objective is to encourage him to step over each pole confidently. To do this, first observe the shortened length of strides when your horse is walking slowly and lazily. These will be shorter than his normal vigorous steps when actively working.

We choose this short distance because the horse will probably hesitate and shorten his stride when confronted with more than one pole, especially if the gap between them seems to require a greater effort in order to clear them. If the spacing between poles allows for this reaction, then he will step more willingly over the poles. Besides, if the spacing was uncomfortably wide, he might at some point tread on the poles, which could roll under his hooves and rattle him.

To begin, we lunge him over a single pole at walk to which he is accustomed. Next, place a pole two steps away from the first pole so that he has to step over the first pole, then take another step on the flat and finally step over the second pole. You should lunge him at a slow walk over this configuration.

As you do this, keep the lunge line short, about eight feet. If he tries to run out away from you he won't have enough line to do so. If he tries on the other side, you are close enough for your body and lunge whip to act as a barrier. Since the poles are laid parallel to each other, and to be negotiated in a straight line of travel, then you must walk parallel to him as he crosses them in order to avoid pulling him off course.

After three or four passes he should be confident enough to go on to the next phase. Roll pole #2 back towards pole #1 so that he steps over each pole without an intervening "non-pole stride" *(Fig. 12)*. Repeat as before. When he goes over without hesitation, go to the next phase.

Place pole #3 two steps beyond pole #2. He now steps over pole #1, then over pole #2, followed by a step on the flat and finally over pole #3. Whenever we add another pole, it never immediately follows the preceding one but is placed two steps beyond it. This way, the young horse is not discouraged and frightened by a cluster of poles. If they were all presented close together at one go, they might seem too complicated to negotiate.

This problem would be magnified if the horse is required to trot them, as he might be surprised by this strange problem that he's forced to solve at speed. Since he cannot do so, unless he's an exceptional horse, he does the best he can. If he's not allowed to stop or run out, then his only options are to rush—almost certainly knocking or treading on the poles in the process—or jump the grid. All this can be avoided by our careful, progressive introductions.

The point is not whether or not he can physically step between those closely spaced poles. Of course he can—he's not a klutz! No, the real question is whether he *thinks* he can do it. It's not his body we have to take care

(Fig. 12)
Trotting over two ground poles.

of here—*it's his mind.*

This point is so important that it's worth reemphasizing, and indeed, remembering it as a general principle of training. If at all possible, *never show a horse what he can't do.* In other words, avoid exposing him to the *idea* of limitations. If through thoughtful and skillful training you don't sow seeds of doubt in his mind, he will develop the confidence and then the courage to do all that you ask of him.

Returning to our horse, after he is comfortable we now roll pole #3 back towards #2 so he has to step over all three poles in three consecutive steps. When he is walking calmly over these, a fourth (and last) pole may be added, two steps beyond pole #3. Eventually #4 is rolled back one step towards #3, so our horse crosses four poles in four steps.

During the process of adding poles, if you note the horse's confidence is on the rise and he tries to take slightly longer steps, stop, and increase the distances between the poles in small increments so he isn't forced to cramp his steps. Once the young horse is confident with this exercise, the whole thing is repeated at trot starting from the first phase: first a single pole, then two poles spaced two comfortable strides apart, and so on. At the trot, the distances between the poles will be longer than for walking.

When he trots the grid, if you encourage him to jog into it instead of a hurried trot or one that is too energetic, he will nearly always pick his way through unhurriedly. After a few passes, he might become elastic, almost dancing over the poles with hints that he wants to stretch his neck forward and down. It's at this point, when all three or four poles are down, that the spacing may be carefully increased by small increments of two to three inches. He now has to work a little harder.

However, be vigilant and conservative when increasing the distances. Too much, too soon will tax him, with the result that he stops rounding his back and stretching forward and down. Instead he might prance through the grid, excitedly hovering at each stride with a hollow back. Alternately he might start rushing to get enough momentum "to make" the newly increased distances.

If anything like this happens, calmness must first be restored. Stop all work for a minute or two, then resume with walk and trot work well away from the poles. When this is accomplished without any trace of excitement, bring him back to the poles at the walk. To make life easier you can have one set of poles spaced correctly for walking and another set for trotting, in another part of the ring.

Once he is calm walking the grid, we can reattempt the trotting grid. This time, remove two poles from the trotting grid and decrease the distance between the remaining two poles. Jog him over these until he is calm, then add the third pole and finally the fourth. When he goes over these quietly, again increase the distances between them very carefully, avoiding the previous mistake.

As he develops in this work, more effort can be solicited from him by raising the poles. This is most safely accomplished by using the lowest setting on cavaletti. These are preferable to raised jump poles because they are more stable. They won't roll under the feet it trodden upon and they will stay put if knocked.

Using these tools will make your horse more attentive to both you and to where he is putting his feet; it will develop his coordination, build his muscles and make him better balanced. Let's remember that any horse can go across a bunch of poles willy nilly. But to cross them at a given speed, rhythmically and with poise, requires muscle control. This is what the horse learns by doing this type of work.

A final reminder is that this exercise is very taxing for a youngster. Walking and trotting over the grids make him pick his feet up and flex his joints. If overdone, it will make him sore and disgust him with this work.

Introduction to Small Jumps on the Lunge

Once your horse is confident about going over three or four ground poles, he can be introduced to jumping a small obstacle, about 12 to 18 inches high, while under tack. The main purpose of this is to promote rounding his back as he jumps so that he feels the saddle more keenly and learns to ignore it. Moreover, after jumping, he will canter. He can also be taught to land on the inside lead, both valuable assets, which in some horses might prove difficult to obtain by other means.

As always, brushing boots must be worn to avoid knocks. Side reins must not be worn. At first he is jumped without the saddle since we don't want the noise of the flaps to rattle him during an experience that might get him excited. Take care not to jump on hard, unyielding surfaces which jar the legs, making the exercise distasteful to him as well as running the risk of developing a splint.

Place three ground poles on the outside track spaced for trotting, with their outside ends against the wall. The spacings should encourage the horse to produce fairly energetic and forward-going trot strides.

Beyond the third pole, and at a distance of about nine feet from it, put a fourth pole on the track. On the outside of this pole, next to the wall, put a jump standard. On the inside, place a barrel either upright or on its side. When we convert this last pole into a small cross rail, the lunge line won't become snagged on the barrel as it would be with the conventional shape of most jump standards.

The first exercise is to simply trot our horse over all four ground rails so that he is familiar with the configuration. Once he trots the grid rhythmically and without hesitating, either by slowing up or snaking, then he's ready to be presented to a jump.

We build a cross rail where the barrel and jump standard are, about 12 to 18 inches in height at the center. The horse is led at a walk up to the approach side of the jump and allowed to thoroughly inspect it. Then turn away and lunge him at trot on a 10-meter circle in front of and a few yards away from the jump. Establish a steady but not an overenergetic trot; then take him at a tangent off the circle so he trots parallel to the wall and faces the jump. Make sure you walk briskly and parallel to him so not to inadvertently pull on the lunge line and turn him towards you.

If he hesitates on the approach, gently raise your whip and encourage him with a click of the tongue so he strides purposefully over the trotting poles. As he jumps, open your left fist and let the spare coils of the lunge line be drawn out of your hand so he doesn't receive an accidental jab on the nose.

On landing he will almost certainly canter. Gently turn him, shifting your own position away from the jump so that if he should be excited and keep cantering, the jump will not be in his line of travel. Then, gather in your lunge line and ask for a trot, walk, and halt. Quietly praise him as he stands calmly for a minute or two.

If, on the first one or two passes, he bucks on landing, don't punish him. Chances are it will be a single innocuous buck or just "baby capers." Ignore this for the first couple of times, since he must not associate punishment with jumping. If this habit continues, quickly but without roughness tug on the lunge and simultaneously show your disapproval by using your voice. A short, sharp "No!" will startle him into reasonable behavior.

During the first session, jump him only five or six times, with no purpose other than encouraging him to negotiate the jump as quietly and steadily as possible, with minimum interference from the lunge line, especially during the flight and landing. If he lowers his head as he peers at the jump, avoid snagging the line on the drum or jump pole by raising the

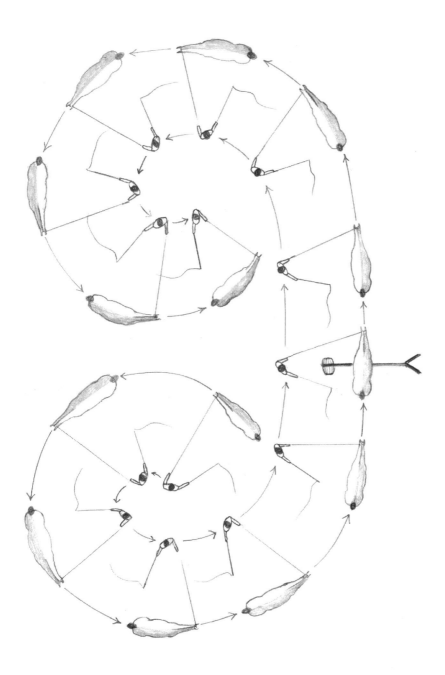

(Fig. 13)
The first presentation to a jump.

lunge without abruptness about two feet, so the lunge clears the obstruction.

After each pass, stop your horse to reassure and settle him. This work may excite him at first if he isn't given a chance to calm down. It's not necessary to be all over him during these intermissions. Stand quietly by his side, caressing him and perhaps offering a tidbit. If you remain calm, your demeanor will go a long way to help him regain his poise until eventually it becomes a habit with him.

As time goes on, if his trot is unhurried, rhythmic and reasonably energetic each time he approaches the jump, then all the trotting poles—with the exception of the one nearest the jump—can be removed. This placing pole will continue to train the horse's eye as to the ideal take off spot. It also compels him to jump that fence from the same spot successfully nearly every time. In so doing he will learn more quickly instead of fumbling his way to competence through trial and error.

However, this is not to say that everything our horse jumps must be carefully set up in such a way he becomes cosseted and we prevent him from using his brains. Not at all. At first it's important we instill confidence by making each jump easy for him to leap successfully. Then, when this has been established to some degree, he should be asked to negotiate jumps in less ideal circumstances.

To this end, the outdoors is an unparalleled training ground. Here we can expose him to fallen logs, ditches, coops, and the like with approach distances and footing that are less than ideal. In short, the horse is taught to think on his feet. He becomes clever, handy and quickly learns to mentally and calmly switch gears from relative inaction to action, at short notice.

It's advisable to delay cantering on the approach to a jump for a while. Trotting promotes rhythmic striding, calmness, ease of judgement due to its slowness of speed compared to the canter and, when a bigger jumping effort is demanded, the horse has to work that much harder to propel himself over the obstacle. At the canter that effort is diminished. First, because the pace itself is a series of small leaps and so gives the horse a certain elevation and bounce in his stride. Second, the faster pace of the canter gives him impetus to clear the jump. At the trot, that impetus is reduced so he is compelled to develop his muscles to propel him up and over the fence.

Returning to one of the main purposes of this exercise: if all has gone well, we can now saddle the horse and jump him (riderless, of course).

At first we remove the irons and leathers since the saddle flaps will often create enough noise on their own, to make our horse wonder what on earth is going on! Once this commotion doesn't rattle him anymore, the stirrups can be attached again. Initially they are configured so they don't hang below half way down the flaps. Then, if the irons are not too heavy, they can be lowered to below the flaps—yet not so low that they swing forward to bruise his elbows.

These free-swinging stirrups gradually accustom him to accept distracting noises and movements on his barrel. However, we don't want to anesthetize our pupil's sides, otherwise when he graduates to being ridden he will likely be stone cold to our leg! So, as soon as we notice he isn't distracted by the stirrup's movements, it is time to run them up and secure them.

One important point: slacken the girth one hole or so the first two or three jumping sessions. The reason for this is that the effort of jumping will make the normal tension on the girth feel tighter then usual. The horse will often show his annoyance by bucking once he lands and is on the getaway. This precaution is especially important with girths that are solid, and have no elastic at one end that yields to a sudden expansion in the horse's barrel. No harm is done by this practice; the saddle won't slip exaggeratedly (if at all) out of place since the hunting breastplate prevents it.

By paying attention to such small details, we spare our pupil the reprimand that we must inevitably give him for bucking, especially since in this case it's likely to be an ongoing habit unless the cause is either removed or if, by chance, he learns to put up with this new-found discomfort.

Rushing after the Jump

What happens *after* the jump is almost as important as the way the horse approaches and jumps the obstacle. Once our young horse has jumped the fence, he may become excited. If he starts rushing after landing, first try humoring him with a cheery voice, showing him how pleased you are with his effort. At the same time, walk in a sideways direction away from the jump so that as he comes around again he won't be near it.

This change of position may not have sufficient impact to slow him up but it's better than disciplining him—with the risk of him thinking that jumping brings some kind of retribution. The next thing to do is to ensure you are more relaxed. Do this by making the movements of your steps and the tension in your arms very phlegmatic. Become a dead weight instead of a combative one.

Another tactic is the way we use our eyes. When a horse is tearing around, it is natural that we fix our gaze on him to pay attention to what he is doing or likely to do. Alas, it is this very instinct that provokes many horses to remain excited. If we lower our gaze to the ground, with brief but laconic glances to see how things are progressing, a horse will generally quiet down more quickly. This can be interspersed with low, soothing verbal signals inviting him to trot.

As for using the lunge line, it's a judgement call whether to give exploratory, gentle "knocks" right away or to delay these until the horse becomes responsive to the previous suggestions. Done too early, these may have the effect of exciting him more. If you have difficulty in gauging intuitively how the horse will react to the lunge at this time, then the only recourse is to use it and see what happens.

When he starts to settle, shorten the distance between you so he makes a set of progressively smaller circles which will help to curtail his speed. How this is done is worth describing.

First, avoid the obvious tactic of pulling or drawing the horse inward to you by shortening the lunge line. When the horse is going fast, out of balance and probably leaning against you, this approach is going to make him lean on you even more. Instead, slowly walk towards him while shortening the lunge, a foot at a time, all the while walking on a circle concentric to his own. After one or two rounds, slow your walk and gradually make your own circle smaller until you are rotating on one spot. Let him go another round or two on this new-sized circle and then repeat the procedure until the circle is small enough to encourage him to cooperate.

In this way you are not antagonizing him to pull because you yourself are not pulling. As you walk on a concentric circle, your body and its motions are used more as deadweight, which the horse feels he can drag around (since you aren't locked into one spot), but one which makes this choice of his very hard work. Remember that earlier we saw that since horses have an element of laziness in their makeup, they will nearly always opt for easier solutions.

There are two pointers that will help in these situations. First, avoid holding the lunge with one hand. This is fine when the horse is going quietly and well balanced but useless in this case. Each time he spurts forward or veers away, he will simply straighten your arm and probably either have you running after him or yank you off your feet. Moreover, when the horse is able to brazenly yank the trainer's arm straight, this accidental yielding condones the horse's behavior and encourages him to repeat the process.

Instead hold on with two hands with elbows well bent. The hands should be separated by at least 12 to 18 inches, with both taking the strain on the line evenly. Avoid having an upright posture with straight legs or the horse easily will upset your balance. Instead, tilt the hips backwards while keeping the knees slightly bent. If the horse becomes very strong, increase the distance between the two hands so that the hand that normally holds the lunge is jammed behind and slightly below your hip on the same side. In this way, your body is used as a resistance that the horse finds great difficulty in making yield. As soon as possible, return to the more elastic way of manipulating the lunge.

The second point is to avoid, insofar as is practical, handling the line with such roughness that the horse's quarters repeatedly swing out, causing him to knock his back legs together or strain his joints. Similar effects can be provoked if the horse is racing round on a circle that is too small for that speed. Observation will warn you when this is happening.

Teaching the Horse to Land on the Inside Lead

Within a few lessons, after he jumps and quietly returns to trot, walk, and halt, your youngster can then be taught (if he isn't already doing so) how to land on the inside lead. One of the simplest ways is to rest one end of a pole high up on the outside jump standard. The pole will be on the landing side of the jump. Bringing the end that is on the ground away from the wall so it is angled towards the inside of the trajectory, will invite the horse to veer towards the trainer as he lands. In doing so, his instinct of self-preservation will compel him to land on the inside lead.

It is also possible to use the lunge to do the same job if the trainer draws the horse towards him during its flight. However, unless one is practiced at this I would recommend adopting the first option. To avoid ruining a young horse's confidence in jumping, it's best to allow complete freedom of his head and neck during the flight, without any interference from the lunge. This latter procedure requires perfect timing, quick reflexes and an instinct of whether to "feel" the line, resist, draw, or perhaps even tug on it. These corrections may not bother a more experienced horse that's being retrained, but a young one may well object and become confused with such methods just when he's learning the ropes.

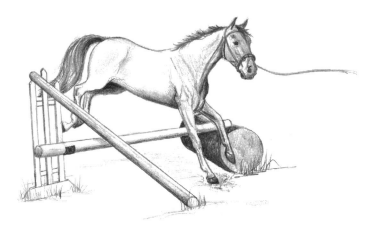

(Fig. 14)
Training to land on the inside lead.

If the horse has landed on the inside lead, with both front and back legs, allow him to canter for a few rounds, making sure you change your position so he circles well away from the jump. If he canters disunited, help him to pick up the inside hind lead by keeping him close to the wall or fence as he approaches the jump. The wall discourages his quarters from swinging outwards, so he is better positioned to make the inside hind leg reach more forward.

At first, canter only a few rounds after each jump. Remember, he is unused to faster work on reduced rations and so he will easily tire. If he proves himself to be obedient and calm, gradually increase his grain ration to give him sufficient energy for this work.

Jumping is better done after about fifteen minutes into each lesson for the first two or three sessions and thereafter occasionally interspersed throughout the lesson. When he lands on the correct lead almost every time, he is ready to canter without the aid of the cross rail.

Cantering on the Lunge

Difficulties in Understanding the Cantering Commands

Before looking at how we give the aids to teach our young horse to canter on voice command, we need to consider the complexities of the exercise as far as the *horse* is concerned. What are these?

Let's begin by asking ourselves this question: since the whip, click of the tongue and some stimulating or threatening body movement are our only means of urging the horse forward, how will he distinguish these signals to mean canter, as opposed to trotting faster? The answer is that it will be difficult.

When he accelerates the trot instead of cantering, and we in turn decelerate the trot to correct him, with this sequence probably repeated several times, we begin to appreciate how hard it is for him to understand our wishes.

It is true that the energizing aids alone will eventually succeed in making him canter, but only by virtue of the fact that they push his trot to the point where he can't sustain it and, through loss of forward balance, has no other option but to canter. This is an effective way of initiating the canter but may be unsuitable with a sensitive or spirited horse.

A great help is to visualize what we want and then broadcast it to the horse. The more skilled the trainer is in sending these mental pictures, the more receptive the horse will be to following their directions. Also, the more frequently this means of communication is used on a particular animal, the more likely he is to be receptive to it.

Although we have already made reference to this skill, we should note that it is particularly useful in the case where one set of tactile signals are used to indicate two different responses. Our scenario here is a good example; should the horse trot faster or canter? Apart from the strange new verbal signal to canter, the tactile signals for the two tasks are sufficiently similar for the horse to find them indistinguishable at first.

While he is being taught the code for cantering, visualization will help him see the difference. Once he understands the meaning of the verbal command to canter visualization can be dispensed with, if that is the trainer's choice.

Preparing the Canter

Before we ask the horse to canter, it's well to define the most important ingredients for a good canter strike-off, including the canter itself.

Just as when we learn a new skill, our youngster's efforts will be tentative and the results will be erratic, ranging from something bordering on confusion to quite respectable performances. The better he is trained at this point to obey the voice, whip, and the lunge to control his speed and energy, the closer he will come to attaining the ideal.

A good strike-off should be unhurried, smooth, and well defined. However, the more likely outcome is that he will speed up, either through misunderstanding or in an effort to gain momentum. In addition, he might leap into canter instead of almost "gliding" into it. Then, it is more likely to be a mixture of trotting interspersed with the canter strides that often resemble scampering and scrabbling. The canter should be crisp, energetic but unhurried, the foot falls even and rhythmic, and the horse balanced both laterally and longitudinally.

At first, the canter will certainly be energetic, but this energy will tend to be flat and converted into speed. As he becomes stronger, it will become somewhat slower and more upward. The rhythm and evenness of footfalls will improve as the other transitions improve, and when he becomes strong enough to balance himself on an accurate circle. In the meantime, it can be regulated to some extent by judicious squeezes on the lunge and timely use of voice and whip.

As to his lateral and longitudinal balance, they are largely a product of these factors. Special attention, however, needs to be paid to the lateral balance because when this is lost, his longitudinal balance suffers also. This point is so important both on the lunge and in ridden work, it's worth examining the mechanics behind it.

Let's say I'm walking alongside a friend, traveling a straight line, when suddenly my companion playfully shoves my right arm hard enough to unbalance me. At this point two things will happen. First, I will have been pushed forward and sideways off my original course.

Second, unless I am indifferent about falling over, I will instinctively break the regularity of my original stride and take longer and faster steps to stay on my feet. Not only will I have to change the rhythm and length of footfalls, but also to modify my longitudinal balance. This has changed from walking upright one moment to pitching forward at an increased rate the next. All this occurred because of a disruption of my lateral balance.

Our young horse has the same problem. He doesn't, of course, have anybody shoving his shoulder sideways, but there are several things we impose on him which end up having the same effect. The three factors most likely to have a similar influence at this stage are: (1) disruptive pulls on the lunge which upset his lateral balance, (2) his difficulty in describing a perfect circle, especially if the trainer insists on habitually making it smaller than the horse's natural balance can cope with, and (3) the horse's innate tendency to crookedness.

We'll look at the solution to the first factor in a short while. That of the second, the circle being too small, is self evident. The lateral balance upset by crookedness is much more difficult to correct on the lunge unless the trainer is very experienced in this facet of lungeing. The work is outside the scope of this book and can be more easily addressed from the saddle.

Cantering on the Lunge

Our first objective is to familiarize our youngster with cantering on voice command—only that. To this end, we choose the canter lead which he favors, which you have noted in previous unscheduled forays into this pace. We lunge him only in that direction during this specific exercise until he understands the new signals, after which he is cantered in the opposite direction.

The horse is tacked up with his usual equipment, including the side reins.

Let's look at two different approaches to this exercise. The first one requires the horse to be fairly well balanced on the circle, while calmly and willingly accepting the aids of the lunge and whip. Moreover, the trainer needs to be deft in coordinating lunge and whip signals in quick succession. On paper, it appears simple enough—in practice it can be frustrating!

The second method is simpler but more crude and uses tactics that may well excite the horse—something we've been careful to guard against so far. Usually this is only a temporary setback with most horses. However, the trainer has to be vigilant that in his zeal to obtain the canter, he recognizes that this approach may be counterproductive for some horses. Although this tactic will invariably excite most horses, there are others that may *remain* excited, while understanding little of what is required of them. The more the trainer tries "one more time," the more these horses lose their poise. With such horses the first method is recommended.

First Method

The horse is lunged at an energetic but steady trot. We draw him towards us as if to ask for a smaller circle and as soon as he responds, the line is yielded. At that moment we send him forward with voice and whip. He should canter and on the correct lead.

As usual, we prefix the verbal command by saying "a-a-a-nd." This is followed by the new command, sung out as "CANTA", in a clipped tone of voice. If we repeat this process the same way for each strike-off, after a while the verbal signal coupled with merely a hint from the whip will be all that's needed to make a successful transition.

Once he is cantering, it's prudent to position ourselves opposite his hip to suggest that he must go forward at the new pace instead of breaking into a trot again. With a "sticky" horse this cannot be done by keeping a stationary position. Instead, we walk on a circle concentric to his until he canters steadily with no hint of quitting and maintains his lateral balance on the circle. We can then progressively diminish the size of our own circle until we are revolving more or less on the spot.

The way we walk should suggest to the horse that he maintain a rhythmic three beat pace. So, instead of walking any old how, we adopt a marching pace, each footstep synchronized with, for instance, the footfall of his leading leg. It doesn't have to be too vigorous; indeed, at times if the horse is getting quick, our steps should be distinct but soft, as if we are stepping on a creaky floor and don't want to wake up the household. An attentive or a sensitive horse will easily be cued by the emphasis of the trainer's footsteps as to whether the canter needs more or less energy.

During this process the whip should be used very carefully to avoid sending the horse forward wildly and disrupting his rhythm. We do this by raising and lowering the whip anywhere from a few inches to a couple of feet either with each step or every other step we take. This keeps him "on simmer." An extra stimulus but one that mustn't be overused lest it loses its effectiveness is the click of the tongue given in rhythm with the whip.

This is not to say that the whip or voice must be used repetitively and almost continuously. If this is the case, it means the horse is in danger of fading off the whip and voice and consequently needs to be reminded to be more respectful of them. To this end, the best procedure is to check if this reluctance to maintain his forwardness is also apparent at the trot. In addition, the promptness with which he makes his upward transitions will indicate if he's getting cold to our signals. If this is the case, then his responses to walk, trot and halt need to be tuned up before resuming canter work.

However, let's assume that when we tested our horse, he was sluggish only while cantering. In this instance, unless there is something physically wrong with him, he should be sent forward energetically with the whip. Using it suggestively would not only be ineffective but also invite disobedience. Instead, the whip should be angled upward and shaken so the lash snakes. If this doesn't get his attention, it should be swept from back to front vigorously enough to make the lash sing. The effect can be augmented by the trainer taking three stomping steps quickly towards the horse's rear end in a threatening manner.

Two more points worth noting:

First, the trainer must try to walk on a concentric circle which really is a circle instead of some potato shaped affair, or the horse will have difficulty in finding his balance. Second, the lunge should for the most part be used in a suggestive manner to keep the horse on the circle. If we create the feeling for ourselves that the line will snap if we resist antagonistically or if we allow the horse to continuously lean against us, he will try and balance himself instead of using us as a crutch.

In the event this doesn't work, it indicates the circle may have been too small for the speed of the canter, and his balance first needs improving on different sized circles at the trot.

Lungeing horses at the canter who have problems of balance and obedience requires so much skill that these few sentences barely touch on complexities of the subject. Unless the reader deems it necessary to pursue the subject in more depth on the lunge, the problems are more easily addressed from the saddle.

Second Method

We begin by trotting our horse on a 10 meter circle in the corner at the end of the long side of the ring. Once he is steady, test that he is listening to your clicks of the tongue by accelerating, and to your voice and lunge by slowing down. Do this a few times until he is sensitive to your signals.

Next, visualize him making a prompt and smooth transition into canter when you raise your whip. Hold this picture in your mind, and with your will calmly project it to the horse.

As his circle approaches the wall on the long side, walk a couple of steps towards it while moving in the direction of the horse's tail. By doing this you slacken the lunge and, because you've curtailed his space, he will accelerate through the gap. At the same time give him the verbal cue, the word *"a-a-a-nd"* followed by the new command to canter. A split second later raise the whip briskly to urge him on more energetically. With luck, he will canter.

Having said that, it's quite possible he will simply race on faster at the trot. If this is the case, slow him down carefully. Once his trot is settled, attempt the transition again in precisely the same spot.

If again unsuccessful, repeat the procedure but encourage him to slow down quickly, just before the point where you originally gave the canter signals. This slowing down will be enough to suggest that something other than an acceleration in the trot is what you want. Also, it momentarily rocks his balance rearward so he is not so much on his forehand.

This is only one way of teaching the strike-off. It's not necessarily the best in all cases and, admittedly, it has some disadvantages as well as merit. The main disadvantage is that the curtailing of the horse's "space" produces an acceleration—maybe even to excess. This is what we wanted to avoid. Yes, we are gambling he won't race through too quickly, but we have no option here.

The advantages are:

1. As he goes through the gap, the slackening of the lunge increases his chances of cantering because the trainer is not trying to pull him in towards him, as might otherwise happen if the horse was lunged unskillfully in an open area away from the wall. In this instance, the horse often reacts to such signals by accelerating and pulling outwards. The subsequent resisting or even pulling of the lunge by the trainer would simply hamper the horse's efforts to strike off. Even if he did so, it would likely be on the wrong lead. However, with the horse sandwiched between the trainer and the wall, these problems are minimized.

   Having said this, it should be noted that if the lunge is *yielded* instead of resisting, in the sequence described in the first method, it is possible to achieve our objective. Nevertheless, even this requires skill in order to obtain good results.

2. When we walk towards the wall and to the rear of the horse, we allow him to slightly drift outward from his circle and meet the wall, not with his body parallel to it, but rather at a slight, head-on angle. At this point he has to "bounce" inwards off the wall. In doing so, he increases his chances of instinctively striking off on the inside lead out of self-preservation. Moreover, at the moment his forehand meets the wall, he is angled in a "quarters-in" position. This informal version of the real thing, which would almost qualify as "crookedness," does have one merit. It helps the horse strike off on the inside lead with both the front and hind legs. If at this instant he does not "bounce off" and canter, he will meet the oncoming 90 degree turn in the corner at the end of the long side. The

speed at which he meets this will almost certainly force him to canter.

At this point we should not be unduly bothered by these accelerations into canter because quiet, balanced strike-offs are not immediately or easily attained with this method. Instead, our first goal is to teach him to canter on the verbal signal, in whatever way he can. Subsequently, when he remembers what this command means and becomes thoroughly familiar with the process, it will it be much easier to quiet the transitions.

Remember the success of any method lies not so much in what one does but *how* one does it. Referring to some of the pros and cons will help tailor the method to the individual's needs.

Also, it cannot be emphasized enough that regaining the horse's calmness is the top priority if he should become too quick or excited. A certain zest will not be a bad thing—but not indulged to the point where the horse becomes inattentive to the signals that steady him after each unsuccessful attempt. If he has to be stopped for a brief period to regain his composure, that is what must be done, however many times it takes.

Once the horse canters, it is best *not* to use your voice at all to praise him because he could mistake it for a steadying signal and might break back into trot. Instead, let him canter on, and after a round or two praise him with some enthusiasm. If your praise is too "silky" he might trot. Your cheeriness will be better understood and is likely to encourage him to repeat the exercise successfully in subsequent attempts.

At that point, if this successful transition has been preceded by several unsuccessful ones, it's best to stop work for this session. This way, the last impression he goes away with will be a positive one. However, if he catches on quickly, he may be worked a little longer to obtain one or two additional strike-offs. Also, if he has been struggling, then in between each correct transition it's prudent to work on something else for a short while. Any exercises that calm and remind him of being attentive to voice or whip will be beneficial.

There is also the possibility that he might canter on the wrong lead. If this is the case, at first do not correct him because at this stage any canter he offers without too much fuss is acceptable. Then, once his strike-offs are calm, he can be corrected for that mistake.

First Mounted Work

Our young horse should now be well acquainted with the commands to make transitions between halt, walk, trot, and canter through the voice and whip, which will help us control him when ridden. He is also familiar with the saddle, bridle and side reins, as well as being touched all over by hand or whip. You have slapped the saddle and gradually put some weight on it. If he accepts all this, he is now ready to be ridden.

Before Mounting

For this exercise you need the assistance of a capable, lightweight rider who can sit still in a two-point position, can follow your instructions to the letter, and remain unruffled if the horse should behave in an unexpected way. Bypass any candidates who might squeal or yell in fright since this would send the horse into a frenzy of buck-jumping or an uncontrolled gallop. Such an incident can set your training back and put a big dent into your youngster's confidence.

In the first session or two, it helps if you have a second assistant to give your rider a "leg-up." Both people should know this routine well. The second assistant must know how to deftly throw the rider up, who clears the horse's back and quarters without accidental kicks before landing lightly into the stirrups, not on the horse's back. Having done so, the rider must avoid squeezing or pinching the horse's sides with the riding boots. Neglect of this detail can panic young horses.

It is helpful to put a stirrup leather round the horse's neck for the rider to hold onto; this is preferable to the mane. Although the horse is wearing a hunting breastplate, the strap over the withers is often too near the pommel, so when grasped it forces the rider into a vertical position with the risk of being left behind the movement. The horse's reactions to this increase in weight on the back of the saddle will range from rapidly accelerating, abruptly halting, to bucking. Since the rider should adopt a more forward position for the first few rides, she needs a strap that is further up the neck.

The Passive Rider

The purpose of the next few sessions will be to accustom the horse to a passive rider on his back in the three basic gaits. During this time, the horse is entirely under the control of the trainer who lunges him. Little by little, the rider uses legs and hands to introduce the tactile aids to the youngster. These are given in conjunction with the trainer's voice and whip aids with which the horse is already conversant.

As the horse becomes familiar with the rider's aids, he is gradually weaned from the trainer's control until the rider is able to guide and control the horse on her own. At that point, the horse may be ridden free, off the lunge.

Depending on the skill of the trainer and the degree of training, placidity, and temperament of the horse, this introductory phase may take as little as two or three sessions or, more likely, a longer program. In any case, caution is advised. Plan on several lessons to accomplish this task, even if the horse is seemingly compliant. Hurrying this phase can cause horses to overreact for several reasons.

One is that a young horse can easily become sore through the unaccustomed weight of the rider. Another is that the strangeness of the new aids will often cause him to be sluggish in his responses, leading the rider to think his horse is uncooperative, and perhaps mistakenly meeting out punishment. This will not be accepted stoically by most horses. Also, the horse may be apprehensive about carrying a rider without the reassuring presence of his trainer. These and other factors should not be underestimated especially with more sensitive horses.

Mounting

We begin by lungeing the horse as usual. Towards the end of the lesson, when he is somewhat tired, halt him in the middle of the ring, well away from walls, fences, or obstacles.

Remove the side reins and attach the reins to the bridle, knot them so they don't flop but can still be used by the rider in an emergency. Recap with your assistants their respective tasks. It is best to have no spectators who may distract and frighten the horse with movements or noise since this can be a very tense moment for him.

Stand by the horse's head holding the lunge line short to ensure he stands still. The rider holds onto the pommel and cantle of the saddle while the other assistant gives her a leg up, so the rider lands *lightly* across the saddle with her chest. The assistant has hold of the rider's bent left leg, ready to ease her back down to the ground after three or four seconds *(Fig. 15)*. The rider should never jump to the ground on her own since the abrupt and unfamiliar movement can scare the horse.

(Fig. 15)
Using the leg-up procedure.

This procedure is repeated five or six times, while the trainer quietly reassures the horse during and after each leg-up. If the horse moves, the rider must "freeze" while the trainer tells the horse to stop with the conventional "whoa-a-a-a!" If all has gone well, praise your horse and take him back to his stall. Unless he is hot, untack him and leave him alone to ponder this new experience.

In the following schooling session, follow exactly the same routine towards the end of the lesson. Your youngster will likely show less apprehension than on the first occasion.

After half a dozen leg-ups, the rider should be lifted so she lands lightly on her stomach *(Fig. 16)*. Once there, she caresses the horse, first on the off shoulder, then the neck, followed by caresses on the side, where her right leg will be when she sits astride. During this, the trainer reassures the horse in a measured tone of voice and by caressing him. The second assistant never lets go of the rider's left leg, which could result in the rider somersaulting head first onto the ground on the off side if the horse starts to buck. If you've thoroughly done your homework, though, there is little reason why he should behave violently. However, never compromise your rider's safety through careless or thoughtless actions.

After the rider has been legged up on her stomach three or four times, have her dismount while you lunge your horse at a walk and trot for a couple of minutes to distract him with a familiar routine in case he feels pressured. It gives him the chance to relax his muscles if he tensed them to brace himself against the rider's weight.

Collect your assistants again and have the rider legged up on her stomach, but this time have her gently lift herself about six inches up and down above the saddle so the horse feels the rider's soft bounces. If the horse moves or shows displeasure, the rider stays still while calmness is restored by the trainer. If after a few of these leg ups the horse stands patiently, it's best to quit for that day. These may be repeated in as many sessions as needed, especially if he is showing signs of uneasiness.

Astride

Once the horse allows the rider to lie on him, the rider should be legged up so she is astride the horse. However, do not let the rider scramble astride from her former position when she lay across the saddle. The wriggling movement needed to straddle the horse from this position and the risk of

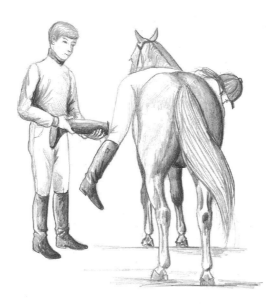

(Fig. 16)
Next, the rider is lifted so she lands lightly on her stomach.

booting him on the quarters as she swings her right leg over is likely to make the horse react adversely.

To land lightly on the horse the rider should hold the mane and pommel, not the seat or cantle of the saddle, with the left and right hand respectively. The rider takes her weight on the thighs and knees while she is helped to put her feet in the stirrups. Sitting in the saddle is to be avoided since it puts pressure on the weakest part of the horse's back. The rider should rest close to it in a two point position, staying quietly in balance and holding the neck strap.

She should avoid distracting the horse by speaking or patting him until the trainer says so, as the horse should be fully attentive to the trainer. Once the horse is reassured, the trainer leads him at a slow walk in a 15-meter circle. Every time a half circle is completed, stop the horse briefly to praise him, and continue walking. After three circles, the rider dismounts carefully and slowly on her own, making sure both feet are out of the stirrups before dismounting.

Once your youngster is unconcerned about the rider while walking and halting, the rider can caress his neck and reassure him with the voice, by using the now familiar phrase "Good boy!" This is a first and important step in which the rider begins to communicate with the horse.

Sometimes the horse will stop and start in a jerky fashion as he reacts to the unaccustomed weight of the rider. If he does so, encourage him to walk on with your voice and soft clicks of the tongue. Avoid touching him with the whip since he is somewhat tense and may jump forward. Should this occur, the rider sits as still as possible, with her torso inclined slightly forward to not get left behind, and momentarily grips more firmly with the thighs and knees.

In the first couple of sessions, the rider should keep her boots away from the horse's sides to avoid the temptation of gripping. This could frighten the horse into running away or bucking, especially if he suddenly stops or jerks forward unexpectedly. As soon as the horse seems unbothered by the rider's weight, she can progressively ease herself into the saddle at the halt and then at the walk. At this point the legs can be hung at his sides, but without tension.

An important point on how the trainer leads the horse during this initiation: it is best done as if one is lungeing with a short rein, with the lunge in the left hand and the whip in the right. This is safer and one is in more control than if the horse was being led in the conventional way with lunge in the right hand and spare coils and whip in the left. If the horse is led in the conventional way and he suddenly moves forward, rears or plunges, you may be pulled off your feet or dragged forward. You could avoid this by letting the line run out, but then your rider is in the unenviable position of sitting on an out of control horse.

Leading the horse in the lungeing configuration has advantages over the other method.

First, while it is true you can't easily stop the horse from racing forward, this is offset by your ability to turn him. The effort to do this is considerably less than the one used to control him with the other method. Since you are using less strength, his energy is squandered in turning as opposed to dragging or fighting you, which provokes the horse much less. In addition, his familiarity with your "lungeing stance" is reassuring. He should equate it with something authoritative, and be less likely to fool around.

If he should spin on his forehand to face you or sidle away, the whip in your right hand can be used to shepherd him forward. This is not possible if he is being led the conventional way because the whip would be in the left hand and impotent to do anything.

We now look at how the rider will mount without being legged up by a helper. We first prep the horse by grasping the nearside stirrup, leaning on it more and more heavily so it simulates the weight the mounting rider will put on it. When the horse is unconcerned by these activities, not staggering on his feet or shifting around, he is ready to be mounted.

The trainer stays by the horse's head so that the rider can mount with slightly loose reins. A second helper leans on the offside stirrup while the rider mounts. If the horse is very quiet, the trainer can do this. To avoid mounting in an ungainly way, especially on tall horses, it might be prudent to lower the stirrup a couple of holes until the horse gets used to the routine.

How one mounts is very important. Once the rider is standing on the left stirrup, before swinging the right leg over the horse's back, she shifts her right hand onto the upper part of the offside knee roll. Then, with braced arm, she can support the weight of her body as she swings her right leg over. She must get the right stirrup so both stirrups support her weight before settling gently into the saddle. If all goes well after a few times the trainer can stand aside and let the rider pick up a light contact with the horse's mouth before mounting on her own.

Trotting on the Lunge

If the horse is not tired and calmly accepts the rider's weight at walk and during the halt-walk transitions, five or six rounds of trot can be attempted. During this phase, the horse may wobble or stagger a bit, so keep the lunge circle as large as possible, keeping control and safety in mind. This may require you to walk on a circle concentric to that of the horse, to increase its size while still having the advantage of being a short distance from him. This way, the horse is under control on a shortened lunge and your rider is safer for it.

The rider stays quietly in the two point position without posting, or distracting the horse with hands or voice until the horse is walked once again. In this phase, as during any new exercise or experience, it is best that the horse gives the trainer his undivided attention to avoid confusion.

During subsequent schooling sessions the routine is repeated. The horse is warmed up on the lunge, the rider is legged up a few times, and then ridden work commences. At the trot, once the youngster proves unconcerned by the weight on his back, the rider can post gently. She should rise out of the saddle the minimum amount needed in order to be synchronized with the trot. The economy of the rider's posting helps in landing softly into the saddle.

This point is important because its oversight is one of the foremost causes of bucking. What happens is that due to the novelty of being ridden at the trot, the horse will stiffen his body with his movements reflecting this, or he will move forward in a hesitant, jerky fashion. He may hump or roach his back with the unaccustomed weight. The result is that the panels at the rear end of the saddle come off the horse's back as the rider rises and touch his back once more when the rider sits. This can make a horse tuck his tail and scurry forward, hence the necessity of sitting softly.

The worse—and not uncommon scenario—is when the rider is out of synch with this saddle movement and starts to sit as the cantle is rising. The subsequent unexpected clout the horse feels on his back invariably makes him very jumpy.

It is the horse's stiff, jerky and uneven movement that are responsible for this, since they make it difficult for the rider to stay synchronized with her mount. However, matters are not helped if the rider posts in such a way that increases the likelihood of such an occurrence.

Depending on the horse, this posting can be implemented almost immediately or certainly within two or three sessions. Sitting at the trot or canter should be avoided to keep the horse's back unburdened and to avoid creating muscular tension. At every other stride the seat should come off the saddle no more than is necessary. The more the seat is raised and especially if done energetically, the more the horse will be excited.

Introducing Leg Aids

The next step is for the rider to take a more active role by introducing the horse to the leg aids that invite him to go forward. Your horse should now be accustomed to the feel of the rider's lower legs hanging passively against his barrel.

Halt the horse and have the rider give a firm, progressive squeeze on the girth with both legs simultaneously. The trainer instantly follows this aid by asking the horse to walk on and, if necessary, augment it by the click of the tongue and the lunge whip. The reins are still loose and knotted on the neck, so if the horse should spring forward, startled by the unfamiliar closing of the rider's legs on his sides, he will meet no opposition from the reins. The rider must be attentive to going with the movement of the horse and of holding onto the neckstrap.

If the horse does not react, the aids from the rider and trainer are ceased momentarily and then reapplied, with the rider's leg aids escalating to a firmer squeeze or even a tap (but not a kick, which would almost certainly make the horse explode). This is backed up by the trainer's aids, which are also slightly escalated.

It's only during the brief initial period of familiarizing the horse with the meaning of the leg that we indulge him by ceasing the leg signal when he doesn't respond, then repeating it more firmly, coupled with the trainer's aids. Later in his training this would be wrong. If our horse ignores the legs, their pressure should increase without disengaging, and the stick and voice reinforce the correct response. At this first stage, though, equestrian tact suggests that the horse be helped to feel the contrast between the legs clinging passively to his sides; a signal and then an escalated one.

The slightest compliance in moving forward should be instantly rewarded by ceasing all tactile aids and praising the horse. Stop him, and after a brief rest so he can think about what happened, invite him to walk on again. Hesitant at first but with growing confidence, your youngster will react more promptly to the rider's legs once he understands what is required of him.

The trainer's aids take a decreasing role and eventually only come into play when the rider's legs are ineffective in creating the desired degree of response from the horse. Later, once the rider takes more control from the trainer, while still on the lunge, she can use a short stick to tap the horse on the shoulder to get the horse's attention if he is tardy in his response to the legs. If the horse ignores both aids, the trainer must quickly intervene with the voice and whip to back up the rider's request.

Next, the leg aids are used to invite the horse to trot. The rider uses both legs simultaneously, first with a squeeze. If no reply is forthcoming, the aid is escalated up to a tap with the heels. The trainer simultaneously orders the horse to trot with the voice and the lunge whip.

Once the horse becomes acquainted with these combinations of aids from the trainer and rider, the latter can take over the verbal commands which so far have been given by the trainer. However, the trainer carefully monitors the horse's response to the rider's verbal and tactile aids and intervenes with a judicious use of the lunge or stimulation by the whip when appropriate. At this point the trainer is still responsible for steering the horse on the circle with the lunge.

It's worth noting the advantage of the lunge line being hooked onto the cavesson instead of the bit. If the lunge was attached to the bit (and there are different ways of doing so) its action would draw the bit sideways to steer the horse on the circle. The rider's action on the reins when adjusting the speed or making a downward transition would have a backward action on the bit. The confusing pulls in two directions would cause the horse to stiffen his neck, twist his head or open his mouth. However, when the lunge line speaks to his nose and the reins speak to his mouth, the one-directional action on the bit is unmistakable in its meaning.

At first the young horse may be tardy in answering the rider's verbal command because the tone of voice and diction can vary considerably from person to person. The horse must adjust to this, hence the initial hesitancy, for which he shouldn't be penalized. Instead, the aids are repeated with the verbal aids mimicked in the form the horse has been accustomed to hearing.

Introducing Rein Aids

From the halt to walk, the rider eases the reins from a light contact, forward, so they actually droop, and asks the horse to walk on in the established way. When going from the walk to a halt, the rider gently picks up the slack in the reins and resists (without pulling) while the trainer verbally tells the horse to stop.

For instance, to halt from a walk (the same broad principles apply for all downward transitions), the rider resists with the reins until the horse offers a slowing down. The rein aid is immediately abandoned for a second or two, then reapplied until a further slowing down is evident. Even if the horse only decelerates a little bit, he is instantly rewarded for his understanding by the cessation of the aids and by verbal praise. It may take several such signals to halt him. Be patient, because in a short while a mere gentle closing of the fists will be sufficient to slow and eventually stop the horse. If the rider starts pulling, this is likely to provoke an equal or stronger pull from the horse. The same principles apply when making a transition from the trot to walk.

After a short while, the rider takes over by giving the verbal commands as well as the tactile aids. The horse is then encouraged to stand still on a loose rein. This is important because by following this approach, your horse will quiet faster than with other aids, especially if he fidgets when asked to stand still.

Introducing the Riding Whip

At this point, it's preferable for the rider to carry a riding stick instead of a dressage whip. It should be at least two feet long with a thick shaft. A fishtail or something similar is useful, since it makes a noise when applied. This auditory stimulation spares the horse being hit by a more energetic stroke of the whip.

The guidelines in this section apply to the use of the whip in general. Some of the corrective measures described are difficult to implement while the horse is still on the lunge. However, to avoid readdressing this topic once the horse is off the lunge (as he very soon will be), the basics of this subject have been described in this section.

Initially the rider takes the precaution of gently stroking the horse with the whip while mounted: first the shoulder and lower neck, then the barrel and even the croup. Once the horse is unperturbed by this, he is introduced to the whip's effect, as a substitute for that of the lunge whip. It must always be used on the shoulder, with a mild tap at first and in conjunction with the rider's legs. If no reaction to the legs is evident, a firmer tap is in order. At the same time a click of the tongue helps the horse understand the meaning of the whip. It's interesting to note that this is one of the rare times when the click of the tongue is used to back up the horse's tardiness in replying to the whip. Normally, as we have seen, it is the whip that reinforces the voice signal, not the other way around.

Once the horse is off the lunge and has been ridden free for a while, if he becomes cold to the leg and barely acknowledges the taps of the whip, he can be taught to go forward from it as follows. To ensure he goes forward, instead of moving sideways, halt the horse parallel to a fence or wall; let's say it's to your right. Bridge both of the slackened reins in the right hand, and hold onto the neck strap or mane with the same hand. The left hand holds the whip and the left rein.

The horse is asked to go forward with a mild squeeze of the legs. At the same time disengage your left hand from the left rein and use the whip firmly behind your riding boot—an instant after the legs start squeezing. The horse will react with a brisk walk, trot, or by leaping forward. Allow him to go on for 30 yards or so, praise him, and gently bring him back to a halt. Thereafter, if you need to reinforce your leg aids, the effect of the whip will not be unfamiliar to him.

Use the whip with the minimum of force required to obtain the necessary reaction. A milder introductory tap prior to the corrective tap is a good idea so he is forewarned and not ambushed in a heart-stopping way. After a few corrections, this warning can be dispensed with.

This procedure is effective for any stage of training, particularly for more experienced horses that are blatantly ignoring the rider's aids to go forward. In this case, a sharp stroke of the whip is appropriate. To be fair to the horse, however, one should try to deduce why the horse is cold to the aids. Since the fault often lies with the rider, one should appraise one's riding and rectify the problem.

The most common problems when using the whip are that the horse may kick out or even give a small hop or buck. Another is that he might raise his head, tuck his tail between his legs, lower his quarters and scamper forward. Both reactions are nearly always caused by the incorrect use of the whip.

Bucking in this instance is often due to the rider using his stick, which is only two feet or so in length, like a much longer dressage whip, while (incorrectly) still holding one rein in each hand. This practice will upset a young horse because to touch his barrel with the shorter stick, the hand has to pull back. If the stick hand is still holding the rein on that side, it will jerk on that same rein *(Fig. 17)*. The result is the poor horse simultaneously receives a "go forward" signal from the stick and legs, while at the same time the rein inadvertently and abruptly blocks his forward progress.

It doesn't take more than a couple of such signals given consecutively to incite a sensitive horse to blow up. Thus, until the time comes when it's safe to use the longer dressage whip, the rule should be to always take the whip hand off the rein before using the whip *(Fig. 18)*. The one exception to this is if the whip is used on the horse's shoulder. This method is a way to get his attention rather than possessing any major coercive influence. As such, the two ways are not interchangeable, at least not on a regular basis, and each should be used to obtain their respective goals.

Another reason why the horse reacts by bucking is because he is struck too far back, near the stifle (a ticklish spot) instead of just behind the rider's leg.

Even after three or four incidents, if the rider applies the stick in the correct place the horse will often continue to react the same way. Usually this happens because the stick is held only in the favorite hand; the horse doesn't immediately make the distinction between being hit in a ticklish spot or in the correct place. As far as he's concerned, the stick is on that side and it's uncomfortably ticklish—period.

In this instance, the best solution is to apply the stick a little more lightly near the riding boot or even slapped against it while giving a loud click of

(Fig. 17)
Incorrect handling of the whip.

(Fig. 18)
Correct handling of the whip.

the tongue. Even more important is changing the stick to the other hand every couple of corrections. In this way he is disassociated from his fear of it on any one side.

It's essential that he be instantly praised for going forward without cringing, hopping or kicking out. However, do so with a cheery voice and by petting him with the hand that is not holding the stick. If you are overzealous in your praise while using the stick hand, the poor fellow will take fright, thinking he's being punished instead of rewarded!

While we're on the subject of misuse of the stick, we should mention why the stick is invariably used too far back. In most situations, the stick is held in the fist just as one would hold a dagger (in contrast to how a sword or tennis racket is held). The stick is approximately 90 degrees to the rider's forearm. The natural sweep of the arm will make the end of the stick land far back on the flank every time. Try it both on and off the horse; when mounted, do it in slow motion and pretend you're going to use the stick.

The only way the end of the stick will land close behind the rider's boot is either to spread the last three fingers slightly, or to swivel the forearm away from a fore and aft line of travel, as when using an opening rein, before sweeping it down to the barrel.

The way the stick is transferred from hand to hand should be with great care, or the horse can easily become frightened, thinking that he is about to be hit. The quietest and most efficient way to do this (dressage whips excluded) is by (assuming the stick is in the left hand), transferring the right rein into the left hand, so it holds both reins and the stick. The right hand grasps the top of the stick and slowly draws its entire length through the left fist, just like unsheathing a dagger from its scabbard. The stick is then positioned on the rider's right thigh.

Throughout, the left fist is kept closed to maintain a positive contact with the horse's mouth, in case he tries to accelerate when he sees the stick being lifted. The only time it is loosened is if the stick has a wide, fishtail end.

Overcoming Excitement

Standing Still to Overcome Excitement

This is one of the most important exercises you can teach any young horse. We are talking here about standing still, with slack reins, for several minutes. The calmness that the horse attains through inaction, not to mention the mental mastery the rider gains over his horse, makes this exercise the simplest yet one of the most effective. If the horse moves, correct him by smoothly taking up the slack in the reins and releasing them when he stops. After a few such attempts, he will probably give a deep sigh and resign himself to standing calmly.

Later when he is taught to halt "square," he learns to balance himself on all four legs in a more uniform way. The merit of this current exercise lies in not allowing him to use the reins as a crutch, or standing on three legs with one hind leg cocked.

Excitement Through Being Sore

In this case, where the session may have been over-tiring, or simply because he is not yet sufficiently muscled to bear the rider's weight for very long, the solution is obvious: make the riding periods shorter. He should be dismounted now and then for a minute or so to relieve him of the rider's weight.

Rough rein aids can also excite a young horse. Since his mouth is easily bruised, the fear of impending pain will make him anxious. Appraise their quality, frequently and critically always trying for a response to progressively lighter aids.

Excitement Through Misunderstanding

Misunderstanding the rider's requirements will invariably upset a young horse. The fault nearly always lies with the rider, who mistakenly rides his mount as if it were older and more educated. The rider has not lowered his own mental process to the elementary level of the youngster's understanding.

An example of this would be when practicing halt-to-walk transitions. The horse is halted, and a second later he is asked to walk on. Having repeated this exercise three or four times, you notice the horse becomes uncharacteristically excited, despite the demands being simple and the pace unstimulating. Why?

Because he was "machine-gunned" with two different requests, over and over. He halted when asked, and was immediately told to walk on. In his mind he started to question whether he made a mistake in halting since he was barely allowed to do so before being ordered forward again. Maybe the rider meant him to slow down instead of stopping? After all, stop means stop, for an extended period. When this pattern is repeated several times, the horse becomes confused and then anxious, because the stop-go signals received so close together appear contradictory. We can avoid this confusion by halting and going forward, for sufficiently long periods each time so that he unequivocally recognizes the request.

Remember, the horse must always be praised for his correct interpretation of the rider's requirements with a caress or a kind word. The importance of this cannot be overemphasized, especially when he has been struggling for the correct solution and then suddenly shows signs of beginning to understand.

Checking the Horse's Welfare

Now that your horse is being ridden, reappraise his diet to ensure it is sufficiently energy-producing. For some time the work will be slow, so avoid overfeeding grain; it may make him too lively. Good grooming and also wisping of his thighs, quarters, neck, and shoulders will promote muscle tone.

Depending on the amount of work to date, check that the saddle still fits him. Without a saddle pad, see that the panels bear evenly on either side of his spine. When mounted, if you put two fingers under the pommel and stand in the stirrups, you should feel no pinching of the fingers. In addition, try putting two fingers under the front of the panels where they meet the horse's shoulder.

If the horse has lost flesh on his withers, he may need protection from the saddle sinking onto them. Use a wither pad or check if the saddle needs re-stuffing. Physical and psychological problems can often be traced to poorly-fitting tack that causes discomfort and even pain.

Daily turnout for your youngster will help him unwind both physically and mentally from the burden and impositions of mounted work. When turnout isn't available, put his boots on and lunge him for a short period, then loose-school him for 10–15 minutes in an enclosed arena. If he just stands around, *gently* encourage him to trot and canter around the perimeter.

Lungeing him prior to loose schooling is a wise precaution because it takes the edge off him. With the limitations the ring imposes on the horse, limited lengths of straight track, followed by sharp corners, a horse that is "high" can easily injure himself when loose.

Further Mounted Work: Off the Lunge

When the rider is able to walk, trot, and halt the horse without the trainer's help, the horse may be ridden loose off the lunge.

For the next few schooling sessions, begin by lungeing the horse. Then the rider mounts up, working the horse briefly while still on the lunge. Then let the horse and rider free. In this way, the trainer is able to monitor any kinks generated by overwork, discomfort, or psychological pressure on his horse during the previous lesson.

If you've done your homework, letting the young horse off the lunge should be a very quiet affair. Be sure to ride alongside the fence or wall initially since your horse needs these as a psychological prop. If you ask him to go in a straight line in an open space, he will simply weave around out of control. He still doesn't know much about the reins as steering aids, and if he is ridden alongside the wall he will follow it without deviating.

When he meets the first corner, the walls will help turn him. As he approaches it, urge him on with your legs and slightly open the inside rein. Reward the horse for his understanding, and progress to the next corner. Do no more than walk quietly, turning in the same direction, and halt periodically.

When you feel your youngster understands the basic turning aid, test him by turning before you reach the corner. Repeat this a few times. If all is well, ride across the diagonal to reverse direction.

If there's a problem in stopping, turn his head to the wall reaffirming your intention with a "whoa-a-a" command. Should this fail, wait until you meet the wall at the next corner and halt him there, without letting him swerve.

Once he is familiar with the turning aids at the walk, repeat them at the trot. At this pace, he may find it difficult to negotiate the sharp corners, so think ahead and turn well in advance, without abruptness.

While trotting alongside the fence, you may find a somewhat erratic quality in his trot , as if he has difficulty in balancing. This is a common occurrence because so far he has only carried the rider on a circle at the walk and trot while being lunged. With practice, he will become accustomed to going straight with even rhythm and speed.

The first few times the horse is ridden free of the lunge he will feel wobbly, unsteerable, and surprisingly sluggish in answering the aids. This isn't cause for concern because it's a new experience for him. He must cope not only with carrying an unfamiliar weight, but also with keeping his balance during the simple transitions between walk and trot. Moreover, the newly-learned aids of the rider's legs may not always be clearly understood. The rider sometimes grips with them to prevent being unbalanced by the green horse's erratic or sudden movements. Consequently, the horse may find difficulty in deciphering what is a signal and what is "static."

In short, this isn't exactly a fun period for either the horse or the rider! However, if we sit quietly and interfere as little as possible, within a few sessions the horse finds his "sea legs" and learns to carry us in a more balanced way. He won't stagger from one footfall to another; and will give the feeling of being more solid on his feet.

Unfortunately, the same cannot be said for his steering and his response to legs and hands. For some time he will tend to drift to one side, slightly out of control. He behaves like a car that veers to one side of the road. Once the wheels are realigned, tires swapped, etc., the car stays on course. Our horse also needs a realignment. The only difference is that a thirty minute job will fix the car, where only a long course of exercises will improve our horse.

These first few ridden sessions off the lunge have been a kind of honeymoon period. As long as the horse was more or less under control by going where we pointed his nose, stopped, and started, while allowing some license in his response time, we were satisfied. Now, however, the way he replies to our requests to halt, walk, trot and change direction need to improve in quality if we are to do meaningful work as opposed to just being carried around by him.

One is often tempted to hurry things along in order for the green horse to catch up with what his more experienced peers know. This is the wrong approach because pushing this phase of training can lead to psychological problems, and physical wear and tear. The trainer thinks the horse "can take it" because lameness problems are not always immediately apparent. This is a sad state of affairs because the useful working life of a horse can be curtailed by several years.

Admittedly, there are horses, just like people, that are subjected to excesses and still seem to be none the worse for wear. Such animals are relatively few and these examples should not be used as the justification to push their less resilient peers to unreasonable limits.

So instead of hastily forging ahead with more difficult exercises and movements, this time is better spent in paying attention to the details of the simple points. These often appear so elementary when riding a more experienced horse that it's all too easy to take them for granted. It's worth noting that the mark of a well trained horse is not the number of advanced movements he is able to do, but how well he performs the basics at the walk, trot and canter.

Walking on Long & Loose Reins

Contrary to what some may think, there is a distinct difference between "long" and "loose" reins, and what they suggest to the horse.

Riding on loose reins means the reins are sagging; there is no physical contact with the horse's mouth apart from the weight of the leather. The rider holds the buckle of the reins.

Riding with long reins means the rider is in contact with the horse's mouth through delicately stretched reins, which allows the horse's neck to adopt a series of comfortable positions.

One of these methods should be adopted most of the time the horse is walked. It does not, of course, include those instances when the reins need to be shortened to slow him down, make transitions to another pace, or to have him more in hand if he's too energetic. Why is this mode of walking essential?

The first and most important reason is it encourages him to relax and lower his neck. There is a correlation between a horse's mental state and his physical posture. For example, an excited horse hardly ever has his neck lowered and stretched. The opposite is the case: his neck is arched and raised. But when he is tired or very relaxed, his neck nearly always droops.

We usually think of a physical state as being a product of a mental or emotional state. Even with humans, we describe their mental or emotional state in terms that portray its physical equivalent. If someone is sad or worried we say that he is "down in the mouth" or carrying "the world on his shoulders." That fellow is being physically affected by his mood. His mouth and shoulders droop. His muscles and breathing pattern are in a different state compared to when he is happy, smiling and energetic. In short, a person's mood dictates how his body behaves.

What is less well known is that by adopting a particular physical state his mood can be changed. This is as true for horses as for humans. If the horse is excited (a mental state), we can alter this by encouraging him to change his physical state. If we can get him to lower and stretch his neck, it's almost impossible for him to remain excited for long.

Since the first rule of training is calmness, especially if he is to learn well, encouraging him to lower and stretch his head and neck is instrumental and essential. In a moment we will look at some of the simpler ways to do this.

The second and equally important reason for walking on a long or loose rein is that it allows full play of the horse's musculature. Notice how gracefully a horse walks when unburdened by the rider's weight or constricting tack. His body undulates; different parts moving elastically and in concert.

Then compare his movement when he is boxed up by short reins, held by unfeeling hands. His body quickly loses that catlike suppleness and appears locked. Only his legs seem to move. If his head and neck are allowed to move as naturally as possible, he will be much more at ease. Let's remember that mental tension is often created by physical discomfort.

A third reason is that the trot and canter of a young horse can be fairly energetic paces which often require the rein contact to be quite firm or even strong. Walking on a long or loose rein is a respite from this, and an opportunity for the rider's hands to renew their friendship with the horse's mouth.

In addition, the walk is a sedate pace compared to the trot and canter; it's least likely to wind a horse up. It is, therefore, the pace at which the rider is most confident about yielding the reins to the horse, without the feeling that his mount might take advantage by running away.

The walk is the hardest of the gaits to ride well. It requires the horse to be on the aids, something for which he is not ready yet. It doesn't take much to spoil the walk, hence the importance of leaving his head and neck to move undisturbed as much as possible. The trot and canter, on the other hand, are more resilient to stronger actions and occasional mismanagement of the reins.

Riding on a Loose Rein

One might think that loose rein riding is simply a matter of relinquishing the contact. Not so.

First, a horse is acutely aware of how much slack there is in the reins. He will often stretch his neck only to the extent that it leaves a slight sag in the reins. This is especially the case with a young horse. If the rider yields them even more, the horse will lower his head further but, again, only to the extent that leaves a slight sag in the reins. The horse leaves himself this slack in case he gets jabbed in the mouth, either because of his own fault or that of the rider.

Why isn't the horse frightened of stretching his neck while the hands are in contact with his mouth?

Well, he is, until he learns to trust the rider's hands. Once the horse is confident of the contact, a resistance or pull, created either by the horse or the rider, on slackened reins becomes a jab. That identical pull made on reins that are already stretched results in a slight increase in tension; the severity is cushioned by the existing contact. The rider should either ride with a contact or, if on loose reins, sufficiently slack so if the horse startles or stumbles the bit doesn't punish him.

The rider's hands should go back and forth, following the movements of the head and neck. The arms should almost instinctively follow the movement of the head and neck, as precisely as if the reins were stretched. This forms an invisible link between hand and mouth which, once established can be effective in communicating with the horse just as if the reins were stretched.

Riding on a loose rein is something many riders are wary of doing when a horse is on his mettle, since they feel that by abandoning the contact their mount might take advantage of this liberty and run off. Their fears are not unfounded; on occasion horses will do just that! However, there is a simple and efficient way to put the horse "on parole," on loose reins while allowing us to regain control should the horse suddenly violate this privilege.

For the sake of clarity, I'll describe the right and left hands of the rider as having specific tasks.

While the horse is standing or moving on loose reins, the right hand holds the buckle and is carried close to the pommel of the saddle. The fingers of the left hand are curled loosely around both reins as to form a "tube;" this hand is held four or five inches in front of the right hand *(Fig. 19A)*.

If the horse takes off, it is easy to take the slack in the reins by raising the right hand, which draws the reins through the "tube" of the left hand. The left hand keeps its position near the withers *(Fig. 19B)*.

(Fig. 19A)   *(Fig. 19B)*

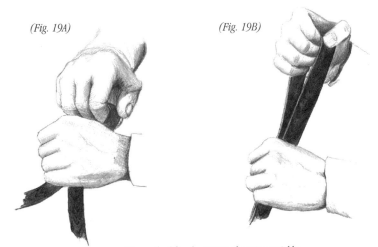

The method for shortening the reins quickly.

If the reins are drawn abruptly, the horse will toss his head because of the jolt he receives from the bit. If the take-up is smooth and done with feeling, the slack will be taken out of the reins more gently, resulting in progressively increased contact instead of a punishing jolt. This smooth take up can only be done on plain reins. Reins that are braided, have hand stops, or rubber coated cannot run smoothly through the tubed hand, especially if one is wearing gloves. Using such reins results in a series of jolts as one takes up the slack.

If the reins are shortened without a complementary closing of the rider's legs, the horse's head and neck will be raised and retracted as the action of the signal influences him from front to back. Even at this stage of training prior to the "meshing" of hand and leg aids, the rider's legs should gently push the horse's forward energy to counteract the action of the reins being picked up swiftly.

The stick should be held in the tubed hand. If it's held in the hand that holds the buckle when it is raised to draw the reins, the stick will wave threateningly, startling the horse into running forward.

Riding on Long Reins

Riding on long reins can be tricky on a green horse because his balance isn't yet steady and he frequently needs to use his head and neck to recover it. This makes it more difficult to maintain a steady contact.

To do this the rider takes a light contact and with elastic elbows and flexible wrists maintains it throughout. To obtain a more sensitive feel, the reins can be held between the first two fingers and thumb. If the horse shows fear or discomfort by avoiding the contact because the hands may have been careless, the rider should temporarily revert to riding on the buckle once more.

A horse who has been habitually ridden on short reins will initially take the rider's hands politely as he stretches his neck forward and down. Then, after a while, he will show signs of being more enthusiastic in this exercise. Not long after that, he can sometimes become belligerent, trying to yank the rider's hands forward.

A horse may behave this way when he has been allowed to repeatedly stretch his neck forward and down and then becomes impatient when the rider's hands ask for a more measured and polite descent of the neck. Whether through expectation of his new-found freedom or because of resentment due to the curtailment of it, the horse will sometimes try to dive past the rider's hands.

There are several possible solutions to this. The one most commonly seen (which is the least effective and most damaging), is to pull or jerk the horse's head up. This degenerates into a tug of war, the horse retaliating by pulling the rider forward again and the cycle repeated until one or other gives up.

After making certain this behavior does not relate to bitting or dental problems, the following solutions should be effective. One is to yield the reins so rapidly the horse cannot lean on or pull at the rider's hands. The rider must be alert and cultivate fast reflexes, because the horse may dive down and raise his head several times in quick succession.

Why not just ride on a loose rein and let the horse work it out on his own?

Well, it's possible to do just that. In some instances, it's the appropriate thing to do. However, what usually happens is the horse starts to blackmail the rider, as if to say "If you touch those reins, I'll pull at you again!" If the rider gives up for the sake of peace, he will make his horse phobic about having his mouth touched.

The real solution is to yield the reins faster than the horse's head goes down. This way the horse's needs are met, after which the contact is quickly but carefully taken up again and maintained when his head and neck are raised. If and when his head dives down again the reins are rapidly yielded as before.

In this fashion the rider acknowledges the horse's need for liberty as if to say, "See, I'm not hanging on to your mouth, so you may as well quit pulling at nothing!" However at the completion of the horse's complaint, when his head and neck stop descending any further, the rider has *his* say by resuming the contact. If the rider clumsily whacks the horse's mouth when he resumes contact, he shouldn't be surprised to see his pupil complain even more bitterly.

If this solution is not effective, the rider can allow the horse to reprimand himself in the following way. The rider's hands are used in the way just described but instead of allowing the horse to lower his head and neck all the way down, he now yields less than the "guesstimated" extension. The hands abruptly stop. They must not pull—only block. When the horse's head meets the limit of the extended reins he will jolt *himself* in the mouth. One or two such experiences will convince a horse that belligerent behavior results in an unpleasant experience.

Another ploy is to tap the stick smartly on his shoulder or correct him with the legs, ranging from a sharp pinch to a kick. The effectiveness of this correction is due partly to the element of surprise and partly to the ability of the legs and stick to suddenly send the horse forward. An unexpected acceleration with the horse's head down would run the risk of pitching him forward. So naturally and instinctively, the horse takes immediate action to redress this imbalance by bringing his head and neck up and backwards, rocking his center of gravity in that direction. This is especially the case the faster the horse is traveling.

Note that these solutions cannot be used indiscriminately; they are not interchangeable for solving various ills. For example, if the horse is trying to rid himself of a suffocating hold on his mouth, any solution that creates a punishing jolt is hardly likely to foster trust in the rider's hands! Instead, rapid yielding is the obvious solution here.

Encouraging the Horse to Contact the Hands

At this stage, the rider must frequently check that there is no unproductive tension in his arms and shoulders. Even if the rider isn't pulling or resisting, the horse still feels tension. He holds himself in, so to speak, and avoids stretching his neck forward and down to take the rider's hands. Riding with stiff, straight arms held almost vertically instead of bent softly at the elbow also provokes tension in the horse. If the contact is unkind and relentlessly resistant, the horse will try to evade it by flipping his nose or diving down with his head and neck, with progressively stronger snatches or pulls.

The contact should have an elusive quality. That is to say, once it has been made, the fingers soften to decrease the contact. With encouragement from legs and voice, coupled with a "pushing forward" feeling of the arms, the horse is lured forward to meet the receiving hands. Their action is similar to baiting the horse with a carrot which, just as he's about to nibble it, is inched forward barely out of reach.

In this manner, the horse is encouraged to stretch his head and neck. This not only develops the musculature of the horse's topline so he can carry us more easily, but also places his head in a position which allows the action of the bit to be more effective.

However, although all yielding is generally beneficial, when the hands are merely yielded, they do so in the hope that the horse will stretch and meet them once more. It's effective but leaves a lot to chance. Instead, what we need is an approach that is almost irresistible to the horse and, that once he understands it, will quickly and willingly reply correctly. What follows is such a way.

This exercise can be taught at all three paces, but with the green horse it's a little trickier at the walk and quite difficult at canter. The energy, symmetry of footfalls, and steadiness of neck characteristic of the trot make this the ideal gait to introduce the exercise.

First, we ride at a steady trot and establish the contact. The horse is then ridden onto a large circle and, without pulling the inside rein, the outside one is

Circling right at posting trot.

slightly yielded. As the horse is gently urged forward, he will meet the resistance of the inside rein and bend to it. By doing so he takes up the slack of the outside rein, thereby establishing contact with both the hands once more.

We may have to bait him with the outside rein by slightly yielding and then retrieving it, so that his attention is drawn to it. He will likely start to give one or two exploratory stretchings before becoming more confident about meeting and taking hold of the outside rein.

With practice, this exercise will develop the horse's ability to seek contact with the bit.

Riding in Straight Lines

This may be difficult at first because all the mounted lunge work has been done on a circle; suddenly the horse is asked to carry weight and go on a straight line.

Early on, he is helped to keep his balance and a reasonably steady course by the walls of the ring. Even more beneficial is riding forward on longer straight lines in an open field, but this is impractical initially until the young horse is more under control.

The primary gait for this work is the horse's natural trot. Deviations are corrected by using a slight opening rein, while keeping the neck straight by not yielding the opposite rein. At this stage, the rider's legs can do little to steer him in a compelling way. They can, however, play a more suggestive role by acting as the banks between which the horse flows. However, their effectiveness is limited by the fact that the horse has not yet been taught to move sideways from the single leg; this is a prerequisite if he's to respect that leg acting as a barrier.

Nevertheless, until that stage has been reached, the rider's legs can still play a useful supportive role, especially if the calves are toned by the heels being lowered. Slackened calf muscles have little influence in this instance.

While it's important to channel the horse's body between the rider's legs, it is equally essential to ride forward. This is not to imply that the walk or trot must necessarily be energetically accelerated, although at times it may be useful to do so. Instead, the rider's legs "shepherd" the horse forward. This isn't easy at this stage because the horse isn't yet sensitized to delicate leg signals. The arms and hands should generate a "pushing" feeling as if the reins were rigid so they persuade the horse to go forward, coupled with the legs.

Equally important, the rider's will should be more focused on directing the horse straight forward, instead of being overly preoccupied with the lateral deviations of the horse's progress. If the rider isn't "thinking forward," the horse ends up snaking as his deviations are corrected first by one leg and then the other.

In addition, the way the rider uses his eyes can help. To this end, pick a target and draw an imaginary line to that point. If you focus your attention towards riding precisely on that line—while looking well ahead—then very soon the horse will travel along it with barely a hint of deviation. This is a fine exercise for both horse and rider but, alas, all too often neglected.

Maintaining an Even Rhythm

This is one of the cornerstones of correct training. Without an even rhythm the horse's balance will always be questionable.

Picture for a moment a small child learning to take his first unaided steps across the room, from one adult to another. The first two or three steps are slow and hesitant. These are followed by a pitter-patter of fast and slow steps, which combine to making the child unstable enough so he eventually keels over. This pattern is repeated over and over, but with one difference. The child is able to walk progressively steadily for longer distances before he loses his balance again. Some weeks later, he walks quite well without falling. How does he do it?

Apart from encouragement, confidence, and so on as long as his steps are rhythmic (which in turn promotes evenly spaced footfalls), he can maintain his balance. When his steps falter, his balance becomes precarious or is lost. The horse behaves in a similar way.

The rhythm should be regular and the speed steady, but without the rider attempting to animate the horse anymore than is needed to maintain it. Once a steady speed with rhythmic footfalls has been obtained, the horse's muscles expend only as much energy as is needed to maintain the pace. To understand this, imagine you are jogging, allowing your body to become floppy, with arms dangling. As you jog rhythmically along, your feet smack the ground in a flatfooted way from heel to toe and roll forward to the next footfall instead of springing off towards it. If you continue in this way for a few minutes, your muscles will relax even more. It feels as if the only expenditure of energy is to put one foot in front of the other. Something similar happens to the horse.

This state of "laziness" is a prerequisite for developing the horse's musculature through thrust; the rider's leg aids are instrumental in soliciting it. The horse must be in a state of sufficient laziness to allow the rider's legs to drive him forward. If the horse is so hot that the rider is leery of using his legs for fear of aggravating the situation, the animal will be difficult to control and train. Unless the situation is altered, the rider is lured into coping by "hand riding."

This highlights an important principle. Put simply: it's a lot easier to make a horse go than stop. Only when the rider is able to use his legs without fearing his mount will overreact can the horse be effectively controlled in keeping his body straight and activating the hind legs to rebalance him. Hand riding can help keep the horse straight, but if performed without great sensitivity, it cramps the action of the hind legs.

Stretching the Neck so It Develops a Certain Rigidity

Without stability in the neck, especially in horses with long, unmuscled ones or where the neck is set on poorly to the body, the action of the reins will be imprecise. The young horse's neck can be bent too easily both laterally and longitudinally. Riding him is like driving a car with a steering wheel with an exaggerated amount of play.

The horse's neck needs to develop stability so that the base of the neck is firmly attached to the shoulders without bending at that point. In addition, the rest of the neck must not be overly pliable laterally. Remember that when the neck is bent more than the body, we lose control of the horse's steering. The more we bend his neck in one direction, the more the horse will tend to drift in the opposite direction. And, the development of stability makes the neck less pliable in the longitudinal plane. Without this rigidity, we run the risk of overbending the horse longitudinally, bringing him behind the bit—something which is dangerous at this stage and not easy to correct.

The young horse is encouraged to stretch by first riding on the buckle, allowing full play of the movements of the head and neck. This will allow him to be bold enough to stretch, without the fear of jabbing himself on the reins. Although this in itself does not stiffen a horse's neck, it will help tone it a bit. Next, the rider's hands *tactfully* support his mouth while he's at the bottom of the stretch. Then, we take up contact when his head and neck are in a natural position, whereupon he is encouraged to stretch again from this position.

Obviously this isn't all done in one session, or even one week. The best approach is to confirm the horse's confidence at the walk before going on to the trot.

How else can we encourage him to stretch?

If he isn't tense, walking and later trotting over poles will encourage him to stretch his topline. The same approach and sensitivity regarding the rider's posture and rein handling mentioned earlier should be observed in this exercise.

Sometimes, when the poles are configured in the conventional way, i.e. parallel to each other, they may not offer enough incentive for certain horses to stretch and use their backs. In this case, laying poles at different angles and close together will focus their attention on where to put their feet, and develop their judgement and self-reliance. It is best not to trot the poles and only walk over them. Cantering over such a configuration can be disastrous.

Later when the horse is ready to be ridden on trails, letting him pick his way over rough ground will promote this stretching, almost like a hound trying to pick up a scent. When he begins jumping, this stretching can be encouraged by putting him over hogsback-type obstacles where he has to peer over them, looking at the ground on the landing side.

Another good way to solicit this stretching forward and down is by a somewhat exaggerated version of the yielding the outside rein technique. However, it's wise to tone the muscles of the neck first; if done unskillfully there is a risk that the horse will quickly learn how to become rubbernecked. This holds less danger for horses with short stiff necks.

Avoiding Misuse of the Rider's Legs

Many horses at all levels of training are cold to their riders' leg aids for several reasons. First, the rider is often unaware of how heavily he allows his calves to rest on the horse's barrel. Consequently, when an aid is given the horse will only react to an even stronger pressure. After a while, even that stronger pressure will become less effective and the rider has to escalate the signals.

Then, since the rider's legs don't have unlimited strength, at some point he has to be helped by the whip or spurs. But even these will eventually fail because the rider has not removed the root of the problem: his legs have yelled so loudly that his mount has "switched off." The rider should cultivate the habit of letting the boot lie softly on the horse's coat so his mount feels the slightest increase in pressure.

Sometimes, the rider initiates a conversation with a tap or even a kick, instead of a squeeze. The horse is not given the chance to answer a quiet signal instead of one that is yelling at him. If he can feel a fly landing on his sides and react to it by swishing his tail, kicking or biting it, why then shouldn't he be able to feel a squeeze from our legs?

Of course, if this signal is ignored it must be escalated. The problem many riders experience is that on finding a squeeze doesn't solicit a response, it's assumed that this "whispering" signal will not work in the future. Subsequently each conversation is started with a tap or a kick. With this approach, how can the rider know if on a command to walk, trot or to increase speed, the horse might have responded to the quieter signal of a squeeze? Clearly he cannot—unless he gives his horse a chance to prove it! If we repeat this pattern, the level of communication between the two parties will degenerate fairly quickly.

It should be noted that although green horses may require firmer leg aids initially, a good deal of their coldness to the legs is due to the reins not being yielded sufficiently. This is analogous to using the gas peddle in a car while the hand brake has not been fully released. In this instance the gas peddle would need to be further depressed in order for the vehicle to move at the desired speed.

In addition, the rider often allows his legs to chatter incessantly in two ways. The legs are not kept quiet against the horse's sides due to the instability of the rider's seat, and thus bombard the horse with a profusion of false signals which he learns to ignore alongside the real ones. In the other instance, the rider incessantly taps or urges his horse forward at each stride in his zeal to maintain a certain speed and rhythm. This all too common practice encourages the horse's indifference to the legs. The aids currently used will be ineffective a short while later when more frequent or stronger aids will be needed to solicit the same level of response.

This last point is one of the most difficult to master because it requires the rider to curb his impatience, to feel when the next aid should be given, and in what measure. With patience, attentiveness, tact and consistency, in a relatively short time one can teach the horse to listen to what will, for the most part, be *hints* from the legs.

Tuning the Horse to the Legs

For the time being we are only interested in the horse's response to both legs applied simultaneously on the girth to solicit a prompt, energetic forward motion. The use of the rider's leg to tell the horse to track sideways is not appropriate at this time, because the horse must first learn to go unequivocally forward. If this point is ignored, whenever we want him to pass or cross something of which he is wary, the horse will use his new found ability to go sideways as a substitute for going forward.

Another example of the horse's penchant for evasion is when the trainer indiscriminately teaches him to rein back. Make it an inviolable rule *never* to teach him to rein back until he has learned to go forward at the slightest solicitation of the leg and click of the tongue. If this rule is not followed, the horse will use this exercise when he doesn't want to go forward. The consequences of prematurely teaching him this seemingly innocuous exercise are far reaching.

For example, at first he may simply refuse to move. Then he will graduate to stepping or running backward. Once he tires of this or is prevented from doing so, his next ploy is to overcollect himself. It is this situation that becomes more serious because it can lead to half rears, spinning around on his haunches, and bucking on the spot—which if vigorous and repetitive soon dislodges most riders from the saddle.

The forward response to the legs can be taught both in a schooling arena and later on the trail.

We teach him to respond to our legs in the following way. First, walk on with the conventional aids and let your legs rest quietly on his sides. After a few steps the speed will wane. Shortly after, the speed decreases further until the horse may even halt unless urged on. As an experiment, allow this whole sequence to materialize a few times. This way you obtain an idea of how long he can stay at the initial speed and how quickly it decreases before he starts creeping along or halting.

Now start over. On long reins, let the horse's speed decrease. Your instincts will urge you to kick him on but do no such thing. When he is almost creeping along, give a soft squeeze with both legs. If no immediate reply is forthcoming, increase the aid to a pinch with both legs and, if necessary, supplemented by a tap of the whip behind your leg. His reaction will be to instantly step out at a walk. He may even give a small hop and jog on or trot. Allow him to do this for a few yards before gently applying the reins to ask for a walk. Whenever he goes energetically forward, praise him immediately with a caress or a kind word. On the other hand, avoid praising him when he is asked to walk again from a jog or a trot. It is illogical (in this exercise, at least) to praise the horse for a decrease in speed—the very thing you've been trying to discourage.

Once the horse respects this pinching of the legs coupled with, if necessary, the whip, these signals should be slightly modified. Why? Because although they had the effect of waking the horse up to the commands of the legs and sent him forward, they likely did so with a spurt. This suited our purposes as an introductory explanation and may be used as a corrective ploy in the future, but we subsequently need the horse to *surge* forward as opposed to leaping forward.

To this end, the legs give the conventional squeeze. If the horse doesn't react, the pressure of the squeeze (instead of a pinch) is increased progressively coupled with a tap of the stick.

This approach should be used for all further training. This does not invalidate the use of the pinch, tap or kick. These should be used as attention-getters, coercive signals, and if the need arises, as reprimands. However, bear in mind that the horse is not a mechanical machine, so he will naturally become tired or lazy and sooner or later lose speed, especially at the walk. You are not penalizing him for that, but instead (apart from when he is tired) are taking advantage of these natural trends since they give you a legitimate excuse to correct him.

These corrections are given with two purposes in mind. First, to teach him to go forward instantly and energetically from a small aid. And second, to encourage him to progressively sustain for increasingly longer periods the initial speed you asked for, before it wanes once again. This being the case, the rider's legs will be used less and less frequently within a given time span. What is the result? Your horse will go forward without incessant reminders. Furthermore, since there will be increasingly longer periods of silence before the rider's legs speak to the horse again, the contrast between action and inaction will be so apparent that the horse cannot help but notice.

Cultivating a horse's responsiveness to this, and further degrees of sensitivity, is governed principally by the rider's measure of attentiveness, consistency, patience, and feel for the situation.

The Purpose of Transitions

As the horse gains confidence in the contact with the hand, and becomes even more confident by taking it through stretching, the time has come to improve the quality of the transitions.

At first, transitions were used more as a change of pace to accustom the horse to carrying the rider at different gaits. They also allowed him to take a rest at walk or halt. Finally, they were used to confirm the obedience he had learned thus far.

Moreover, the legs and hands were used primarily to keep the horse maintaining the gaits of walk and trot or to change gait. Their purpose was somewhat crude and functional. Now they will be used for other tasks.

They still ask the horse to make transitions as before, but not entirely for the purpose of confirming his obedience. This was mostly done so we could stop and start without getting run away with! Rather, when requested frequently, these transitions are instrumental in developing his musculature. They do this because the horse has to go from one state of balance at the walk to another state at the trot. This requires a good deal of muscle control which, in time, develops the young horse's strength to carry his rider without fatigue and to do his own work with controlled energy.

So, the purpose of these transitions is twofold: to flex the joints of the hind legs during downward transitions, and to develop thrust through upward transitions.

The downward transitions should not be too exacting at first. Through a series of slowing-down signals, we allow the pace to wind down gradually as opposed to "slamming on the brakes." Abrupt downward transitions at this stage won't be accepted kindly because the horse is not elastic enough in his joints, back, neck and jaw to absorb a rein action that is too commanding. He will resist it by stiffening his hocks, locking his back, twisting his neck, crossing his jaw, or coming above and possibly behind the bit. When any of these symptoms arise, the rider is alerted that the transition was too abrupt, usually because the rein action was either too strong or even harsh.

It might help to picture the horse going from the normal trot, to a slowed down version of the same, to a jog and eventually to walk. If this is done with the softest rein signals one can get away with, (but without taking all day to make the transition) then the horse's mechanism for slowing down remains relatively undisturbed. In this instance the voice can be a useful supplement.

After all, it's the horse who must figure out how to best use his body to achieve any objective. All we have to do is to tell him when and where— making allowances for the difficulties he may have.

As the horse becomes stronger and able to flex his joints more without hurting him, he will be more willing to rock his weight back onto those flexed joints. In turn, he can make smoother, more elastic, and quicker transitions. However, as long as the horse is weak in his back and hind legs, the rider should be very careful not to force the joints to flex by abrupt transitions and unsympathetic aids.

The horse's only defense against such discomfort is to stiffen the hind legs and back. That is why when sitting the trot on a green horse, the rider feels as if he is sitting on a piece of wood, and bouncing around on this unyielding surface. Until the horse's back becomes stronger, it's wise to continue posting until the horse completes the transition into the walk.

Then, little by little we introduce two or three strides of sitting trot prior to the transition.

Introducing sitting trot.

In addition, as long as his back is stiff or hollow, his hind legs cannot reach forward elastically to relieve the fore legs of some of their load. The result is that the hind legs have less weight-bearing ability but an excessive amount of pushing ability. In this state they push his body even more on the forehand. Any attempt to rectify this matter by adopting unnecessarily strong signals or making the transitions abrupt immediately calls to action the horse's defenses as described above.

The same principles apply when making transitions from walk to halt. During the halt the horse should be encouraged to stand still on loose reins, which has become like a cue for him to wind down. Only when he has learned this lesson should the rider maintain a continuous light contact.

The upward transitions develop the thrust of the hind legs and, if the rider is skillful, the transitions help stretch the legs as well. This last point may appear obvious and redundant since, after all, unless the horse is crowhopping around with stiffened flexed joints, obviously his hind legs will stretch! That's true. However, the question is: how much?

The horse can develop some thrust even with flexed hind legs that hardly stretch at all. However, he ends up being muscle bound: having quite a bit of strength but with little elasticity. The rider feels this stiffness, which is manifested by an unyielding back and a stiff jaw. In fact, if we want to build strength in a muscle, we can get better results if that muscle is stretched because all muscles can only do their job by contraction. The more they are stretched, carefully and within reasonable limits, the stronger their contraction becomes. This way we achieve both objectives, elasticity and strength.

When we eventually take our young horse on trail rides over undulating or hilly ground, the terrain will encourage him to use himself naturally. But the rider must interfere as little as possible with the mechanism that his horse uses so instinctively. In the meantime, we only have recourse to more artificial methods to develop the ability of the hind legs to flex and stretch while thrusting more energetically.

Walking and trotting over ground poles is an excellent way, but it is best to delay trotting over these until the horse carries the rider more steadily. However, since he is already familiar with this trot work on the lunge, we can use it to improve him until he is ready for ridden trot work over poles.

At first, the ridden trot work over the poles should be done in moderation: less than the number of passes over the grid during his lunge work. The rider's weight and the initial instability of the horse during this exercise puts a strain on his legs. This is particularly so when, a little later, the horse springs elastically from stride to stride. This should not be taken as an indication that the horse "can take it." A "hovering" at each stride can be artificially and unwittingly induced by going over the grid too slowly or by the poles being raised, even by a small amount.

On the flat, we can work on transitions in the following way. While using half of the arena, go from trot to walk in the usual way. Walk about ten strides and resume trotting. Continue trotting once around the ring (your half) and repeat the process in the same spot. This will help associate in the horse's mind that in a certain sector of the ring those two transitions will be made.

Continue like this for a while and then diminish the number of walk steps until the point is reached when the horse goes from trot to walk and walks two or three steps before trotting on again.

The trainer must pay attention to the following points. First, a reminder of a point made earlier, that one must guard against making the horse anxious by "machine-gunning" him with closely spaced transitions. He must be mentally ready for them. Second, once the transition from trot to walk is completed, calmness in the walk must be reestablished before trotting on again. If this needs more than ten steps, continue walking until calmness is obtained. This point is particularly important because as the number of walk steps diminish, the horse will begin to anticipate the request to trot and will be tempted to do so without waiting for the rider to tell him. This initiative often encourages the "smart" horse to precipitate the walk steps. We certainly want the horse to use his memory to anticipate trotting after the required number of walk steps, but only to the extent that he prepares his body for it. He must patiently wait for the rider's signal "to go." Impatience or disregard for the "go signal" will be manifested by hurried walk steps.

Third, the horse must be given time at the walk to regain his balance before trotting. If he is leaning on the reins he is not in balance.

These pointers are also applicable to walk-halt-walk transitions. And, this exercise, correctly executed, is the foundation to what at a later date will be the half-halt.

Improved Steering

The principles of efficient steering (or lack of) can be illustrated and better understood by an incident I witnessed recently. It's not without a certain humor because I'm sure that most of us have at one time or another been able to identify with a similar situation.

Visiting a riding stable, my attention was drawn towards a woman who had clearly never ridden before. Her husband was flamboyantly cantering his horse around in circles to show her there was nothing to it. Under pressure, she was eventually shamed into clambering on board a weedy looking Appaloosa.

The stable hand then gave the lady the most cryptic riding lesson I've ever heard: "kick to make him go," "pull the reins to stop," "pull the left or right rein to turn either left or right," and "hang on to the saddle if you feel you're going to fall off!" Away she went, bravely but tentatively kicking her horse who, true to form, barely acknowledged these commands and just crept forward.

About fifteen seconds later, (I'm not making this up) her husband deemed his spouse to be in control of the situation and called her over to go out on the trail.

The lady pulled the right rein to turn but discovered it had no effect since her horse continued creeping in the original direction. So, naturally thinking that more is better, she pulled the right rein harder and, on finding that the horse simply bent his neck instead of turning, she dropped the left rein and reeled in the right rein with both hands. A look of helplessness spread across her face as she realized that in spite of having cranked the horse's neck around to the point where he was all but facing his own tail, the animal simply would not turn.

Finally, to add insult to injury, the horse got tired of this relentless pulling on one rein and slowly began to gyrate on the spot. The poor lady had to be rescued by one of the staff.

What, we may ask, has this bizarre incident concerning a beginner rider have to do with steering our green horse? Everything!

It illustrates the two most important principles of efficient steering, which in this example were not used. First, we should avoid bending the horse's neck more than we can bend his body. And, second, the reins have little effect unless the horse is urged forward. It's worth studying these closely because they pertain to all levels of training.

While the horse's body is relatively bulky and hardly bendable, the neck is relatively thin. On most horses, the neck can be easily bent. Since the reins are attached to the thin end of this pliable unit, when they are applied incorrectly can be guilty of overbending the neck sideways, into "rubbernecking." When the reins are used correctly they keep the neck and body aligned, without allowing kinking at the shoulder or further up the neck. The rein signals turn the whole horse and not just his neck.

The lady in our story didn't have a hope because her horse had a long, weedy, and unmuscled neck that bent easily on the slightest provocation from the reins. If his neck had been short and stubby, the rider would have had an easier time of it. To avoid overbending the neck, the outside rein must barely be yielded while avoiding pulling the inside one backwards. Instead, the inside rein should be opened slightly with both hands moving sideways in the direction of the turn. This sideways action of the hands creates a neck-rein action with the outside rein and a leading rein action with the inside rein.

The outside rein should be suggestive rather than coercive. One must avoid pulling it or applying it with such strength that it makes the horse's nose cock to the outside, away from the direction of the turn. The rein merely touches the neck, applied with a slight but distinct increase in pressure and invites the horse to move away from it.

At first the horse will most likely ignore its action since it's not coercive. But little by little, if it is used at the same time that the inside rein asks for the turn, by association he will learn its meaning. The rider must guard against taking the outside fist across the crest to the other side of the horse.

Later on, when our horse is familiarized with the rider's leg moving him sideways, the action of the outside leg can be an additional incentive to obey the indication of the outside neck rein to turn to the opposite side. Until that time arrives the rider must make do with the tools at hand, which include the fence line of the schooling ring to help turn his mount.

This work is best introduced at the walk and repeatedly reaffirmed at this gait. It is a point to remember because during the early stages of trot work, the horse may have difficulty in answering the turning signals. Until he finds his "sea legs," he will be on his forehand and "running" at the trot. Since his momentum is directed in a general forward direction and he is not in very good control of it, when the rider asks for a deviation from that line of travel the horse finds it difficult. Once he masters this initial clumsiness, his ability to turn smoothly and promptly at the trot will improve.

And, again, remember that the reins have little effect unless the horse is urged forward.

Let's take this step by step because it's an important point, but frequently overlooked. It causes frustration to the rider and annoyance to the horse. First, we must appreciate that whenever the reins are applied, however delicately, they will have a slowing down effect. This is because the reins come backwards from the horse's mouth and act in direct opposition to his forward movement.

Second, at this elementary stage of training the level of energy increases with speed, so when that energy and speed is curtailed by the turning action of the reins their effectiveness will be lessened. The slower the speed and energy, the harder it is for the reins to turn him. Also, the slower the speed the more slack the horse's musculature becomes. For the reins to be effective, they need to act upon a firm unit instead of soft one. The rider's legs must solicit a rise in the energy level and/or the speed of his mount for the reins to be efficient.

This principle is an important one because it embodies the same principles that will be used later on in the horse's training to make correct downward transitions: you must go *forward* into a down transition.

It doesn't matter for what purposes the reins are used, they will always tend to slow the horse down, and curtail or dissipate his energy. If this occurs, their effect will be diminished. The rider's legs, stick and voice are instrumental in maintaining the energy level which tones the horse's body sufficiently for the reins to act effectively upon it.

Work Outside the School

Once the young horse is familiar with the commands to walk, trot, and halt and able to make obedient transitions into these gaits, education can be furthered outside the arena. We start by taking him on a quiet trail ride.

This new experience should be as uneventful as possible, so it's best if certain considerations are met. It is helpful to use a quiet horse as a companion and mentor to your youngster. The quieter the other "schoolmaster" horse, the better, since your horse will watch and mimic the other.

You should plan your first trail ride so that it doesn't take you across traffic, streams, etc., and avoid passing farms or houses where dogs may jump out at you or bark aggressively. Pick a route that requires little intervention to control your horse's speed. For example, avoid going down steep slopes; the terrain will unbalance the horse and lure the rider into using the reins more strongly than is wise at this stage. This results in the horse becoming deaf to the aids, if not rebellious.

These trail rides are better conducted at a walk, on relatively flat ground, and with long reins. This gives the horse confidence in carrying a rider. Every thoughtless request by his rider and each frightening incident will put a dent in his sense of trust.

The Trail Ride

Ride a length or so behind the schoolmaster, trailing him for the ride. You should avoid getting left behind, since your horse will likely want to rush off after his friend. If you have to nag him to keep up, the schoolmaster should slow down; your horse should be ridden with a minimum of intervention from his rider.

Remember to periodically reassure him and acknowledge his good behavior. However, never do so if he shies or suddenly accelerates for you would be condoning such behavior with praise. Instead, regroup and ride forward on a long rein, if circumstances permit, with the attitude that the incident is a small hiccup during an otherwise uneventful and successful outing. If you make an issue of it by riding with shorter reins and a stronger contact your concern will be transmitted to the horse.

During these first trail rides, it's a good idea to dismount every so often and let him stand calmly beside you for a brief spell. If there are gates along your routes, volunteer to handle them so you can take the opportunity to practice mounting.

Even on this first outing, let him graze at the halfway point (the whole trail ride should not last longer than 30 to 40 minutes). During this intermission you should remain mounted. On later trail rides, you can periodically allow your horse to graze, but not at every halt. Though many oppose this practice, I believe it is wonderfully therapeutic, especially for horses that are nervous or on edge.

During the first few outings, you will likely come across situations or objects that will attract your horse's interest. He may stop as if rooted to the spot, going forward only reluctantly from your aids. Be patient, drop the reins, and sit quietly until his curiosity is satisfied. Once it is, his responsiveness to your aids will return to normal. During these investigations you should avoid using the whip or he may associate the object of his curiosity with discomfort or pain. However, it's not advisable to let him stop every time something new crops up since he must gradually learn indifference to distractions. Small wildlife, paper bags, and so on may pique his interest or spook him momentarily. Walk on without stopping to show you attach little importance to these incidents; presumably that's what he should do, too.

Find Out What Your Horse Wants to Do

This next example gives a hint of another training "secret:" find out what your horse wants to do, and then ask him to do it. This way there is little or no conflict of interests.

Let's suppose he wants to stop to look at deer and you allow him. Then you ask him to move on and he refuses; you have shown him how to disobey you. However, if you do nothing but drop the reins and sit it out, he will think that's what you wanted to do in the first place!

Only a well trained horse will unquestioningly obey his rider's aids when his self-preservation instincts are screaming at him to go no further, or perhaps even to turn and run. Your youngster is not at that level of obedience, so avoid provoking a rebellion when one is unnecessary. You are not being weak-willed by taking this approach. On the contrary, it shows equestrian tact. If your young horse is truly frightened, discretion is the better part of valor;

Introducing the horse to an unfamiliar object.

turn away before he does so of his own accord. Then return to the object another time when you have more effective influence over him.

You horse will have a tendency to walk more keenly when turned towards his barn. This homing instinct can be used to help him pass by obstacles which otherwise might prove difficult to negotiate. When you are a quarter of a mile or so from home, dismount, run the irons up, and loosen the girth. Lead him the rest of the way; this is a minor consideration but one your youngster will appreciate. It gives him a chance to walk and loosen up without the burden of your weight before being returned to his stall. This will be the youngster's last impression of his first trail ride. For the first four of five trail rides, stick closely to this basic routine.

To increase your youngster's confidence, follow the same route for a couple of outings. He will recognize the scenery and settle down more quickly. After that, you can vary the routes. You should still be accompanied by the schoolmaster, though now periodically ride beside him instead of following.

Acting Independently of the Schoolmaster

These first outings were designed to accustom the youngster to carrying you with a minimum of intervention; the schoolmaster was instrumental in pulling him along. Now that your horse has settled on these rides, he should learn to listen to your aids. It's time for him to act independently of the schoolmaster.

At first, invite him to go ahead of his companion, turn left or right for a short distance, or even go in the opposite direction. You can ask him to go forward while the schoolmaster is halted, and vice versa. These exercises should not be demanded in a haphazard sequence, or one can provoke the horse's resistance and make him anxious. The following are some thoughts on how to develop this independence.

You can begin with both horses walking side by side: a low bush or other minor object lies ahead of you. With an opening rein, ask your horse to skirt it so the object separates the horses. Your whip should be held in the hand nearest the schoolmaster so, if necessary, a gentle tap or two on the shoulder will discourage your horse from drifting in the direction of his friend. Once past the object guide your horse back alongside the other. Practice this half a dozen times on one ride and increase the number on future occasions. Avoid straying far, and never out of eyeshot; few yards deviation is sufficient.

When your horse is unperturbed by these separations, increase the distance to twenty or thirty yards. In doing so, "stray" from the schoolmaster so they are walking parallel to each other, but be careful not to turn your horse's back on the schoolmaster. Then drift back alongside the other horse for a few minutes before repeating the exercise.

Stop frequently, let him graze, or dismount. These respites break up the new lessons. With this approach, he will feel little pressure and take the new requirements in stride.

Next, you can have the schoolmaster stand while you ride around him on a 30 or 40 meter circle. Then change places *(Fig. 20)*. Your horse may be curious about his friend as he circles behind him; reassure him if he becomes edgy. Then walk the horses side by side, and halt the schoolmaster while your horse keeps going. Walk on for 30 or 40 yards, ride a half circle, and halt; your horse is now facing his friend. Have the schoolmaster walk towards you until the horses have joined up.

You can repeat this exercise as frequently as needed, until your horse can walk away from the other without being cajoled or becoming excited.

Then he can be halted while he watches his friend walking directly away from him. If you reverse the order of the exercises your horse may become upset at being left behind. He may start to fidget and have to be restrained.

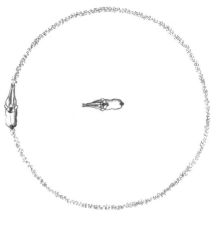

(Fig. 20)
Using the schoolmaster
to teach independence.

Later on you can use these same exercises at the trot and canter. They teach your horse to be less gregarious and to willingly leave a line of horses when asked by his rider. Such occasions occur at shows, while out hunting, or when parting company with friends who have been trail riding with you. Little by little you wean the horse from being a slave to his natural instincts in preference to your wishes.

Introducing Further Experiences

As your youngster acquires better knowledge and respect for your aids, he can be introduced to situations which may not initially be to his liking. However, he is unlikely to offer more than a token resistance to these new requests. These include crossing over difficult terrain and passing different objects.

It's better if you first expose him to difficult terrain because it will encourage him to lower his neck to look where he is putting his feet. Its value as a means of taking up gentle contact on the reins with a long neck is both natural and easily obtained, even if the rider is not accomplished. New objects will invariably cue the horse to raise his head and neck in the posture of alertness and excitement. He is likely also to hollow his back and go above the bit, the positions that make it difficult to control him.

The different terrain to which we expose him includes gentle slopes up and down, shorter but steeper uphill slopes, obstacles such as deadwood and blowdowns, waterlogged fields and marshes by rivers (an excellent introduction to crossing deep or running water) and shallow ditches, preferably without water. If the ditches have water, choose one which is wide enough for him to wade; otherwise he will jump it.

The rider suggests through position and rein contact that the horse needs to find her own way.

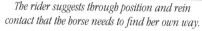

The rider encourages the horse to round her back and stretch her neck.

If the horse is calm, the terrain mentioned, with the possible exception of steep downhill slopes and, at first, the waterlogged fields, should be negotiated on long reins. On steeper downhill slopes, he may need more support from shorter reins. They remind him, through give and take actions, that he must not run downhill.

Crossing waterlogged fields can be upsetting to horses as the water splashing their thighs and bellies is frightening or uncomfortable. With a firmer contact, walk slowly and steadily until your horse settles, then resume moving at the normal speed, eventually reestablishing the softer contact.

If obstacles such as logs, water, and ditches make him uncertain, do not just kick him on, or he may be more determined not to cross them. Wait calmly. He may shake in fright, prance, or stay rooted to the spot with spread legs. Sit quietly without urging him until he is ready to cross or jump the obstacle; be prepared to wait for several minutes or longer. If you sense he is bored with waiting and his will ebbing, give an exploratory squeeze with your legs to see if he goes forward. If he does so, loosen the reins and go with him, ready to hang on to the mane or breastplate. Since your horse is on the verge of jumping from a standstill or scampering across the obstacle, you do not want to jab him in the mouth. The resulting pain would give him a legitimate excuse for balking when a similar obstacle is presented to him.

Riding Alone

Once your horse is at the point where he is quiet, doesn't fret, and is obedient in most difficult circumstances, even if he has to be gently persuaded, you can take him on simple hacks by himself. Don't be misled however by his equanimity thus far. Once he is on his own, he may react in unexpected ways, usually due to insecurity or fear.

If on these initial solo excursions you are struggling to control him, it indicates one of two things. First, your influence over him is not sufficiently established. In this case you should thoroughly recap all the exercises he learned with the schoolmaster. His responses to your verbal aids are especially important: the click of the tongue to urge him forward and the down commands to walk and halt. Second, you may not have used enough tact and ingenuity to avoid provoking his resistance.

For example, if you ride a new route on this first solo outing, you will contend with at least two factors. One is the horse's insecurity of being out on his own; the other is the strangeness of new surroundings. A better plan would be to ride where he already knows, and preferably not too far from home. A short, 30 to 35 minute, hack is sufficient for the first trip. He will not tire and will feel less apprehensive about his short excursion from home.

The first outings should be simple: no complicated crossings of ditches, water or the like. When, after these initial forays, he feels lazy, then will be the time to interest him in other things. Ride him over the obstacles and terrain he was used to crossing when accompanied by the schoolmaster. The pace should be primarily a brisk walk, interspersed with short, 300 or 400 yard, stretches of trotting. This distance is long enough to settle into a trot, yet short enough so he does not get excited and remains calm.

The transitions from trot to walk should be smooth and unhurried, but don't be surprised if it takes longer than usual to make the transition. The horse may still be on his mettle and a little deaf to the aids. Avoid giving strong rein aids; the aids should be more frequent, rewarding him by easing the rein contact for each diminution of speed. Remember to be generous with your praise, especially when he makes downward transitions obediently. Also, keep in mind the old dictum, "it is harder to slow a horse down correctly than it is to speed him up!"

Little by little, the periods of trotting are extended. These serve a useful purpose on two counts. First, the trainer is given the opportunity of riding on long straight lines, an opportunity that wasn't available during ring work. Second, at this pace, the horse has less time to spot things that spook him. He will sometimes shy more than he would have done at a leisurely walk. It's like making a novice swimmer abandon the security of shallow water and venture to the deeper part of the pool. He thinks "What if I'm in the middle of the pool and I run out of breath or my arms tire and my toes can't touch the bottom so I can recuperate?"

In this instance our horse is being put in a similar situation. We cannot mother him indefinitely nor hope to protect him from every frightening object or experience he will encounter—there are a lifetime of them! He must work through his fears and develop courage. Of course, it's a tall order to throw him in at the "deep end" and tell him he can either "sink or swim." Nor is it prudent to do so. However, we can help him by riding forward when he shies, as if we were unaware of the hiccup in his progress. In this way he sees that, since we were unruffled by whatever frightened him, then perhaps he shouldn't be so bothered about it in the future either. We should use good judgement when exposing him to more frightening situations. For instance, we can hardly expect him to be thrilled at the prospect of passing a cement mixer on a narrow country lane!

Once he shows himself to be steady and attentive in these initial excursions, he can be asked to canter. Trot him up a long gentle slope and, with yielding hands, a few squeezes of the leg and the verbal command, let him fall into canter.

Your hands should be elastically supportive. He can lean on them a bit, without the reins being too short. Adopt a half-seat, but avoid committing your body too far forward; he might give a playful buck. This is nothing to worry about if your legs are kept in a slight "safety seat" position, a little further forward than the normal, neutral position on the girth. However, the knees should be squeezed more firmly to avoid getting left behind the movement, which will unnecessarily increase the rein contact and provoke the horse to lean heavily on the rider's arms. This can lead to him pulling.

Canter on a straight line uphill for about 400 yards and then use your voice and a caress to steady him down to a trot. After a few strides, walk on a long rein, then halt to let him relax. Eventually, if he is unexcited by these transitions into canter, he can be introduced to your outside leg behind the girth to cue him, accompanied by the inside leg on the girth and, if necessary, a light tap with the stick on the inside shoulder.

What is the outside or inside of the horse in these circumstances? Your horse will almost certainly show a preference for cantering on one lead. Let us say it is the left lead. For this exercise you designate his near side as being the inside and his offside to be the outer. Cue him with your right leg behind the girth and your left leg on the girth. Then, when you eventually school him to the canter aids during ring work, he will almost certainly give you a left canter when your right leg moves back. It's a good start; he will then know the aids for canter in at least one direction.

Introducing
Lateral Work

Lateral or "two track" work may be considered the "bread and butter" of developing the young horse's balance, straightness, suppleness and obedience. While fairly simple and basic in the early part of training, it is the refinements in this work that will eventually create the equine athlete.

Before moving into the actual movements, it might be helpful to consider the principles of the rider's aids in lateral work, and how the horse understands them.

The Rider's Legs

The rider's legs teach the horse to shift his body laterally in two progressive phases. The first phase is taught to both sides before progressing to the next one. The two phases are introduced in the following order. First, the horse learns to move away from the leg that *nudges* him sideways. Then, the leg on the side to which the horse moves *receives* the horse, and stops the shift.

We begin by teaching the horse to move his hind end sideways. At this stage we apply one leg behind the girth while the other is held slightly away from his barrel so he feels no contradictory pressure on that side. A nudge or series of nudges, supported by the whip if necessary, encourages the horse to go sideways with his quarters.

One signal may provoke more than one step; we allow the horse to take several steps and at the speed he chooses. While this is not the ideal, it suits our purposes for the moment because he demonstrates a basic understanding of what the rider's leg is asking.

The function of the receiving leg is not only to receive the horse's quarters but also to suggest how fast they move sideways, and to instruct how far each side step should travel. The receiving leg is held slightly behind the girth and lies quietly against the horse's barrel, passively following the sideways movement until it is called to duty. As the action of the nudging leg tapers off, the pressure of the receiving leg increases.

On a green horse the position of the rider's legs can be reversed to that adopted on a more advanced horse. The inside leg (the pushing one) is used farther behind the girth than the outside leg (the receiving one), which is only slightly behind it. If it is positioned at the same spot as the inside leg, even if held passively, even without any pressure it can easily cue a sensitive horse to move away from it. If both legs are drawn back the same amount, the sensitive horse could feel the receiving leg contradicting what the pushing leg is saying to him. The positioning of the rider's legs is a matter for experimentation. Each horse differs in receptivity and each rider's legs differ in feel and energy.

The nudging or inside leg should be drawn back a few inches and, if ignored, is supported by the whip used behind the rider's leg, near the hip, on the upper thigh, or even lower down if the whip is long enough. When touched or tapped, one or more of these places will be found to be more effective than the others.

The reins are used in two ways, either by resisting or by yielding. Resisting means that the rider's hand is neither pulling nor yielding. It remains, in effect, static. In early lateral work, the resistance will be predominantly on a single rein and on the same side as the leg that nudges the horse sideways.

Yielding in lateral work is based on the principle that whenever the rider "takes," he has to give something back. If he doesn't do this, a follow-up "take" signal will be inefficient.

In lateral work, the importance of yielding that should accompany each reply cannot be overestimated because the horse's forward energy is in some measure impeded and diverted sideways. Since the reins are partially responsible for curtailing and diverting his forward movement, their action can all too easily become relentless and suffocating. The horse invariably responds by trying to pull his way free.

These are not fancy theories, or to do with some esoteric part of horsemanship. I venture to say that ignoring these and other principles of yielding creates more problems in training, especially with young or difficult horses, than any other action a rider implements. To this end, the trainer's preoccupation about yielding should become almost an obsession.

Although there are a variety of rein effects, in lateral work we limit ourselves to using only two on our young horse. These are the direct rein and the opening or leading rein.

Other rein effects certainly work. However, with the exception of the soft or suggestive use of the "neck rein," the action required to implement them on a green horse requires a stronger contact which is neither necessary or salutary at this stage. Since one of our primary goals is to invite the horse to accept contact with our hands, beefing him around with rein effects which at first sometimes require a strong contact—is hardly likely to further our objective.

We'll further consider the rein effects in the various movements in lateral work.

Lateral Aids

This means that the aids of the leg and rein are on the same side, left leg and left rein, or right leg and right rein.

Lateral aids are coercive because they act like a barrier on only one side of the horse and thus allow him to escape to the opposite side.

At first this suits us very well because they unequivocally tell the horse what we want him to do. However, since he can escape to the opposite side, something we don't want to happen in the long term, the usefulness of lateral aids as a permanent system of communication is short-lived. However, they can always be called to action if the need arises, to re-explain if necessary.

Diagonal Aids

This means the predominant aids are on opposite sides to each other, left leg and right rein, or "inside" leg to "outside" rein.

Diagonal aids channel the horse in such a way that the rider can more accurately control sideways movement than can the lateral aids. Also, the angle at which the horse travels sideways can more easily be dictated as compared to a similar attempt using lateral aids. In addition, the degree of bend in the neck and body in two track work can only be accurately obtained by diagonal aids.

The Turn on the Forehand

In this exercise the horse turns around his front legs, which mark time in the normal walk sequence, while his hind legs describe a larger arc. You can ask for one or more steps at a time, depending on what you want to accomplish. Traditionally, we ask for multiple steps to turn either 90°, 180°, or even 360°. There is no particular value in turning exactly in those arcs, except that they give the rider a frame of reference.

If our horse is to benefit from this exercise, it must be executed step by step, pausing after each one. This confirms that the aids are containing the horse's progression, without him running through them. The pause should be of sufficient length to allow the aids to be "neutralized" without the horse moving forward or sideways; this demonstrates that he is balanced. Only then should another step be attempted. Once these two criteria are met, the pause can be shortened until each step almost merges with the following one.

To teach the turn on the forehand we position our horse at a right angle to the wall. It should be four or five feet in front of him. Let's say we wish to turn his quarters to the right. First the reins are shortened. The left leg nudges him behind the girth with supporting taps of the whip. The horse should yield his quarters in some fashion to the right, after which he is immediately praised.

If he has taken just one step, he will no longer be at the 90° angle to the wall. So, as we ask for another step we must be ready to resist with the reins if he attempts to walk forward or swerve to the left. He can step slightly forward. The resistance, given with more emphasis on the left rein, should be brief, the time needed to slowly close the fist and unclench it. We then repeat the aids for the turn. If there is no response, we escalate slightly the action of leg and whip aids. When he completes this 90° turn, praise him, lengthen the reins and walk forward at a brisk pace or even trot.

We use a forward pace because when a horse is asked to do two track work, he may be colder to the aids demanding forward movement. As prompt forward movement to the leg aids is essential, he must be reminded regularly.

After a bit, return to the same spot and repeat the exercise to the same side. Only after he performs the turn on the forehand promptly to one direction do we ask for it to be performed in the other.

Of course, this all sounds simple enough on paper and is easy when executed on an experienced horse, but teaching a green horse is something else. If we are not careful, this exercise can deteriorate into a confrontation. So, before looking at the problems that might arise, and considering how to solve them, let's explore how the rider's legs and hands interact with the horse's hind legs. A basic knowledge of this process will help avoid problems.

In general, the rider's left leg and rein influence the horse's left hind leg, while the right leg and rein affect the right hind leg. The leg requesting the quarters to move over cannot, in most instances, obtain this movement by the action of the leg alone; it requires the reins as well.

Suppose we use our left leg behind the girth to move the quarters to the right. The horse reacts by lifting the left hind forward. If the rider does nothing else, this leg will simply take a forward step and touch the ground without a sideways deviation. However, when the left hind meets the resistance of the left rein while in the air, the forward progress will be curtailed. The rider's leg behind the girth is able to nudge the left hind sideways because the hind leg is unburdened and not supporting the horse's weight. In addition, the horse cannot mistake the rider's aid as a "go forward" signal because the left rein is saying to the left hind "you cannot go forward anymore." In that instant, the left hind is malleable to the suggestion of the rider's leg behind the girth telling it to step to the right.

Problems

Apart from a perfectly polished response, the horse may react in one of five ways to the action of the aids.

1. Refusing to move.
2. Moving over, in some haphazard fashion with either only one step or

without one leg crossing in front of its partner.
3. Running rapidly sideways, taking several steps.
4. Pulling forward.
5. Stepping backwards.

1. Refusing to move.

A horse may freeze or refuse to move over for different reasons: confusion, insecurity, or stubbornness. In this situation, any kind of sideways movement we can receive from him furthers his progress.

It may help to prepare him with ground work as we discussed in chapter eight. He may be compelled to shift sideways by using the direct rein on the same side as the active leg. The rein is squeezed and then held in conjunction with the leg and whip until the quarters begin to move over. This stratagem is crude but functional. It might need to be repeated a few times until he moves away only when the leg tells him so (without the whip), coupled with a resisting direct rein.

2. Moving over, in some haphazard fashion with either only one step or without one leg crossing in front of its partner.

Many horses will move over sluggishly and tentatively, one step at a time. However, they may not step over correctly, with the inside hind stepping in front of and across the outside hind. They will sometimes shuffle sideways, with the inside foot sometimes treading onto the coronet of the other hind foot. In the first or second attempt this can be overlooked, but after then the horse must be encouraged to walk slightly forward so his inside leg goes forward and across its partner.

At this early stage, the best ways to solve this problem are those least confusing for the horse. One way is to click with the tongue as the aids to sidestep are given. If he's been conditioned to move forward the instant he hears a click, that aid will now serve us well.

Another way is to step forward from a halt. The instant he does, the sideways aids of leg and whip are given.

3. Running rapidly sideways, taking several steps.

The horse who runs rapidly sideways with his quarters does so for two possible reasons. The first is because he is afraid of the rider's aids. This horse may be a reluctant type but due to his sluggishness may have been overcorrected. The second reason is that he is simply a sensitive horse. His overreactions may be magnified because the rider's aids are not soft, or because the horse does not understand the role of the "receiving" leg of the rider and runs through it. The solution in both cases requires a softening of the aids, especially the pushing leg.

4. *Pulling forward.*

The horse may simply ignore the lateral aids and mistake them for forward aids. This reaction is commonly found in horses that have been ridden by many riders as in a riding school, or when the regular rider is slovenly with his aids. In both scenarios the horse will have had a wide variety of leg signals that are meant to tell him to go forward: one or both legs on the girth, one or both behind the girth, or any variety of positions in between. You name it—he's seen it. He accepts all these as legitimate orders to go forward.

Now we come along, put one leg behind the girth and nudge him. What is he to think? Go forward, of course! He doesn't suddenly say "Ah! This person can ride, so I will give an impeccable reply." Instead, he answers the way he's been conditioned and it's up to us to recondition him.

We do this by giving the same signal each time; the leg is positioned in the same spot behind the girth each request. In addition, he must be immediately corrected for misinterpreting such a request, the reins saying "Stop! You gave me the wrong reply." The aids to walk are given by both legs on the girth simultaneously and with equal pressure. He walked forward when we nudged him with one leg used behind the girth. If he isn't immediately corrected for his misinterpretation, how is he to know he made a mistake?

Another reason why the horse will walk forward is because of the way he is standing at the halt prior to the exercise. This is important to note because it will spare him from unjust corrections.

Ideally, we want the exercise to begin with the horse standing "square," with front and hind legs side by side. At this stage of training he won't do this consistently of his own accord, though he can be corrected each time he's halted. Depending on the trainer's skill and equestrian tact, and the temperament of the horse, the trainer may leave this issue for a later date when the horse is stronger, straighter, more obedient to the aids and halts consistently square.

For the moment let's assume that we opt for the second choice; perhaps we feel that at this stage of his training our horse will get upset if we are too pedantic in our demands. If he is standing square and we apply our left leg behind the girth, he will reach forward with his left hind. Once it is ahead of its partner, it will be able to step across.

A more typical scenario would be where the left hind has come to rest at the halt ahead of the right hind. The horse has halted with the left hind in the "supporting" phase of the stride.

When our left leg subsequently asks for a side step, the left hind cannot do so because as the horse moves forward, even slightly, it's still bearing weight. It can only cross its partner if it is airborne, and not in a "supporting" phase. To be airborne, it must wait until the right hind takes its turn supporting the horse's weight. Then the left hind will be unburdened and free to reply to the rider's request.

Between the point when it is burdened and the moment when the left hind can comply with our request, the horse may have travelled several feet. He cannot do otherwise even with the best will; he must be given the chance of answering correctly.

If the rider doesn't understand this point and insists on barring all forward movement, the poor horse will be confused. If he's sensitive, he will become fretful. If he's more stoic, he will try and please the rider; but, effort on the horse's part can only result in a faulty exercise.

5. Stepping backwards.

The horse will step backward because he has not been allowed to go forward! Remember, he must be allowed to do so for the left hind to clear the obstructing right hind before crossing it. In this faulty movement, the action of the hands preceded that of the leg. The horse was asked to go forward into an immovable barrier, the blocking hands, or worse, hands that were pulling.

The solution is clear: reverse the sequence of the aids. First the leg acts to send the horse forward, after which the hands elastically curtail the movement, allowing the rider's leg to nudge the quarters sideways. When the exercise is first introduced, the wall is the barrier that helps the hands prevent him from walking on instead of moving *slightly* forward. That's why we suggested halting the horse four or five feet in front of the wall; the distance gives him enough space to step forward but not enough to barrel away. If the horse is halted with his nose almost touching the wall, he cannot move forward.

Sometimes, if the horse is very generous, he will attempt to cross the left hind behind the right hind. This must be corrected immediately, because stepping backwards is an evasion that can turn into a troublesome habit. Moreover, crossing one hind leg behind its partner has no gymnastic merit and could even lame the horse.

Leg-yielding

Once the horse is competent in executing the turn on the forehand, we can ask him to step forward and sideways with his whole body through leg-yielding. The front and hind legs both cross in front of their partners. The horse's body remains straight except for a slight bend in the upper end of his neck, away from the direction of the movement.

To teach this exercise we use the wall as we did with the turn on the forehand. The wall suggests to the horse that he cannot escape directly forwards, so his only other option is to travel forward and to the side. The wall makes it more difficult for him to misunderstand the aids or to cheat by simply going straight forward. At worst, if we don't obtain this in the first attempt or two, the horse will nearly always offer a turn on the forehand instead. This is acceptable; the horse is trying and partly succeeding because he's correctly doing the first element of leg-yielding.

As in the turn on the forehand we ask for the exercise in one direction until the horse has a working knowledge of what we want of him. With many horses it's easier to begin by asking him to sidestep away from our leg on his "hard" or "convex" side. Let's assume (although it may not be true for your horse) this is the left side.

To ask our horse to side step from left to right, ride counter clockwise on the track at a purposeful but unhurried walk. At the end of the long side, ride a half circle and a diagonal line back to the long side at about a 40° angle.

As you approach the wall, slow the horse. When his nose is within eight or nine feet, stop and *without interruption* ask him for one step of a turn on the forehand, with his quarters going to the right. If you've practiced these turns, he should give you the correct response right away. Immediately reward him and continue the turn on the forehand, step by step, until he is on the outside track on the left rein, where he started *(Fig. 21)*.

Originally the horse was halted at the wall, made to stand quietly, and then asked to step sideways with his quarters. Now he is asked to do so the moment he halts, so that the slow walk of the approach's last few feet merges into the first step of the turn on the forehand. The horse may be confused by being given the signals to stop and to step over in quick succession.

If this happens, the solution is to stop, wait three seconds or so before asking him to step over. When this is done satisfactorily, decrease the time to two seconds between the two signals, and continue to curtail the time until the horse is comfortable with the signals to stop and go over given in quick succession.

Next we want the entire horse's body to travel to the right instead of just his quarters. We approach the wall in the same way as before, but this time the signals are modified so he steps to the right with his forehand as well as his quarters. These modifications relate to the rider's left leg and the angle of the right rein.

The leg is used a little more forward than for the turn on the forehand. Give a squeeze or, if the horse is hesitant, tap his side with the inside welt of the riding boot. The right rein, is opened slightly towards the right to invite him in that direction. The rein should be suggestive. If it's pulled, the neck will bend to the right, forcing the horse to abandon his 40° angle to the wall and ending up parallel to it instead.

Once he has completed one step to the side, halt and praise him so he knows he responded correctly. Then ride a turn on the forehand with his quarters moving to the right until he is on the outer track on the left rein *(Fig. 22)*. Repeat the exercise two or three more times before quitting for the day.

When he can execute one side step correctly, ask for two consecutive steps. The horse is again halted after the second step, praised, and asked for a turn on the forehand to change direction.

This last point is important because it reinforces in the horse's mind that the 40° angle of approach must be maintained until otherwise instructed. Since he is inclined to the wall on the approach, it is easy for him to swerve to the right with his forehand while swinging his quarters to the left. This positions him parallel to the wall, evading our efforts to maintain the 40° angle. If we have maintained the angle through the side stepping, we don't want to sow the seeds of evasion by terminating the exercise as he would like to do and which the wall tempts him to do: by swinging his quarters leftward until he is parallel to the wall once again. To the horse, this appears to be the most logical way to resume single track work, but it's incorrect.

(Fig. 21)
Preliminary exercise for leg-yielding.

(Fig. 22)
First stage of leg-yielding.

The forehand should be brought inwards, in front of his quarters, instead of aligning his quarters to the forehand. This requires adeptness at executing a few small steps of turning *around* the haunches. Our horse is not yet conversant with the meaning of the rider's leg pushing his forehand rightward, while both reins instruct him to do the same, so it is important to not allow him to fudge it by swerving and swinging his way onto the outside single track.

The turn on the forehand becomes a useful ally in avoiding this problem, because it moves the quarters to the right, opposite to the leftward swing the horse wants to make. Also, it opens the angle the horse makes with the wall. The closer to 90° it becomes, the harder it becomes for him to swerve to the right.

This makes an impression on the horse because it is contrary to what he wanted to do. After a few corrections, he will listen to the rider's aids instead of taking the initiative on how to terminate the exercise. This also reinforces his obedience to move away from the rider's left leg which is all important in the leg-yielding exercise *(Fig. 23)*.

Once the wall has outlived its usefulness and the exercise can be done "tail to the wall," the rider no longer needs to terminate it with the few steps of the turn around the forehand. He can simply ride straight ahead

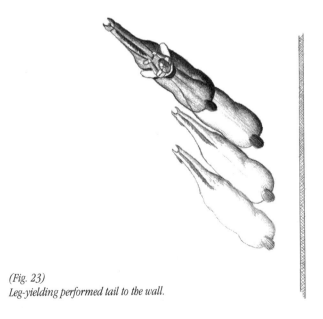

(Fig. 23)
Leg-yielding performed tail to the wall.

into the free space.

At this stage I do not recommend sidestepping endlessly down the track or in the open free space. This achieves little since the multiple steps tend to be hurried and unbalance the horse laterally. Instead, we are interested in promoting effective, prompt response to the rider's legs, one which solicits the sideways movement while the other receives it in a controlled manner. One or two consecutive side steps are all that are required to confirm our horse's obedience to the legs. It will be sufficient to balance him laterally or to help him maintain his balance if it seems he might lose it. If one or two steps are not as effective as we would like, they can be repeated at brief intervals, say, every three steps of straight line travel. We'll discuss this more later.

Problems in Leg-yielding

Most problems in leg-yielding occur when the angle the horse's body makes with the wall is too small or too large. If the angle is too narrow, his body will be almost parallel to the wall, and his travel devoid of sideways movement. The more the angle approaches 90°, the less forward movement there can be. In this instance his ability to move sideways diminishes rapidly so he becomes locked and cannot move.

Sideways movement without forward movement is not impossible for the green horse, just very difficult. Besides, although a step or two of such an exercise may have some disciplinary value in reinforcing the obedience to the pushing leg, it has no merit as a gymnastic exercise for the young horse. Indeed, repetitive use can lame him.

We'll look at how the angle is most commonly lost. Again, we will assume the horse is yielding to the left leg and traveling to the right: he is leg-yielding with his head to the wall.

The Neck is Overbent

When the neck is bent more than the body, the angle with the wall will decrease or disappear. The trainer must guard against overbending to the "soft," or naturally concave, side of the horse *(Fig. 24A)*.

The rider's leg that pushes the horse sideways becomes ineffective when the rein on that side is pulled and the other yielded. This results in a bent neck with the shoulders escaping away from the wall. In their movement to the right the rider has the illusion that the horse is going forwards from the left leg instead of moving sideways from it. This is due to the loss of the initial angle with the wall to the point where the horse travels parallel to it. If the rider does not remedy the situation, the horse will continue to drift into a gradual movement similar to a turn around the haunches, ending up well away from the wall. The quarters will face the wall, while the forehand is turned away from it, a reversal of the initial position *(Fig. 24B)*.

During this process the rider may desperately pull the left rein in hopes of stemming the ever-increasing drift to the right but without success. The more the neck is bent left towards the wall, the more the horse will drift to the right.

The solution is to straighten the neck. In doing so, the straightening action of the right rein will temporarily make matters worse by luring the horse to sweep even more to the right with his shoulders. But once the neck is straightened, it is simple to regain control of the situation. Halt the horse and from that

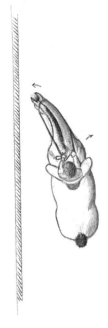

(Fig. 24A)
Incorrect leg-yielding.

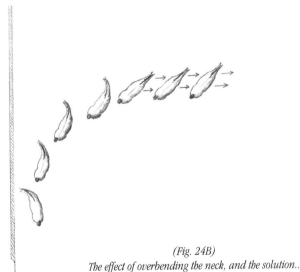

(Fig. 24B)
The effect of overbending the neck, and the solution..

position walk forward slowly and then ask for some sideways movement. Clearly this can be done only if the horse has been "weaned" from the wall (shortly to be described). If he has not, he should be returned to the outside track in the original manner and the exercise begun again *(Fig. 25)*.

(Fig. 25) Leg-yielding.
The horse's neck and body are correctly aligned. The angle of the horse's body to the wall is ideal.

The Angle is Incorrect

Frequently, the rider's leg position is incorrect. The pushing leg is used too far back and the receiving leg not far back enough. This results in the quarters swinging out of control away from the wall, opening the angle to almost 90°, hampering the horse's forward and sideways movement *(Fig. 26)*. The same result will occur when the pushing leg is used in the correct place but too strongly, without the receiving leg tempering its action.

Once the horse has been positioned at such an open angle and the forward movement is impeded or stopped, the angle may be closed in one of two ways. The first is by asking for one or two steps of a turn on the forehand with quarters moving towards the wall *(Fig. 27A)*. From here, the

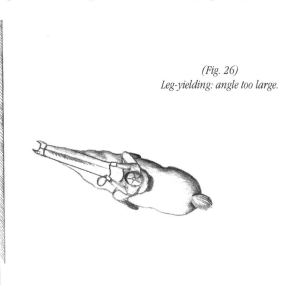

(Fig. 26)
Leg-yielding: angle too large.

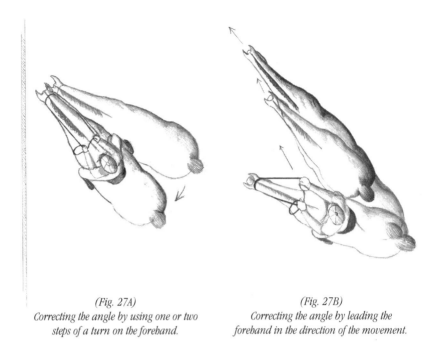

(Fig. 27A)
Correcting the angle by using one or two
steps of a turn on the forehand.

(Fig. 27B)
Correcting the angle by leading the
forehand in the direction of the movement.

exercise can be resumed with relative ease when he is further along in his training. Until he is more malleable to the leg, and his balance improved, this approach will be less successful. At this stage of training, he is more likely to remain rooted to the spot when asked to step sideways from "a standing start." The second way is by the forehand being lead in the direction of the movement *(Fig. 27B)*.

It is possible to make both of these corrections closely together, especially if the horse has some forward movement. However, on a green horse it may not be prudent or even possible to do so because trying to move the haunches in one direction and, a moment later, the forehand in the other can lead to confusion. The horse will lose the angle through over correction. It is safer to alter either the position of the quarters or that of the forehand independently of each other and separated by a reasonable time period.

It's important to note that to obtain the best results these two corrections should not be used interchangeably; each is more appropriate to differing circumstances. If the angle is too open, say just over 40°, and assuming the horse is still moving obliquely at the original pace, the angle can be closed by leading the forehand in the direction of travel by both hands moving that way. In our example, the right rein would act as an opening or leading rein used suggestively, so that it in no way pulls the forehand over nor bends the neck to that side. The other rein acts as a lightly touching neck rein, again suggestively pushing the forehand to the right. The rider must guard against pulling and from bringing the rein across the crest. Otherwise, the crest acts as a fulcrum and extinguishes direct communication from the hand to the horse's mouth.

With a green horse when the angle is even larger it's best to close it by readjusting the quarters with one or two steps of the turn on the forehand. As mentioned earlier, it may not be possible to restart the sideways movement once the angle has been corrected. In this case, it's best to close the angle even further so the horse is positioned parallel to the wall where single track work can be resumed. The exercise is then reattempted.

When the angle is large, readjusting it by attempting to sweep the forehand over such a wide arc is beyond the ability of such an inexperienced horse, or would tempt the rider into using strong rein aids.

Leading the Forehand in the Direction of Travel

In most two-track work, the forehand is lead in the direction of travel with the suggestive help of the reins as described earlier. The trained horse is sensitized to the various positions of the pushing leg that pushes and angles him in the desired direction with the merest hint of help from the reins. Not so with our youngster. The reins, specifically the opening rein, need to be more obvious. This contrast is not made by escalating the strength of the rein signals, but by slightly increasing the range of action of the leading rein helped by the pushing leg positioned a little more forward.

Another way that the forehand can be lead in the direction of travel is by the correct use of one's gaze. Most of the time the rider's fixation is on the horse's head. Since in this exercise the head is pointing towards the wall, the rider's focus also tends to be in that direction. Since the wall is a barrier which the horse cannot broach, it will tend to capture his forehand while his hindquarters move unfettered in the direction of travel, hence the opening of the angle with the wall.

If the rider's fixation is not on riding into the wall but instead looking where he wants to go, the horse will follow his gaze. To this end, the rider needs to look along the outside track, without twisting his torso *(Fig. 28)*. By doing so, the rider has a panoramic view of what is going on and what needs to be done. For instance, maintaining the straightness of the neck will be easy compared to previous efforts. The slightest fluctuation of angle

(Fig. 28)
Leg-yielding.

will be immediately apparent, yet its correction will feel effortless because the rider does not focus on one problem to the exclusion of everything else. His gaze along the track ensures that the whole "show" keeps going.

The result is that the rider is much more aware of impending problems and consequently needs only to hint at an adjustment here or there. In turn, these more suggestive corrections do not upset the functioning of the "whole," and the horse will flow along.

Importance of Rhythm

One other ingredient is essential to good balance in two-track work and that is a steady rhythm of foot falls. At first, when the horse is introduced in piecemeal fashion to the exercise a loss of rhythm is inevitable. However, once beyond that stage, even if we ask for only two or three consecutive sidesteps, the more we take care in maintaining the same rhythm before, during, and after the sidestepping, the fewer "hiccups" or jerkiness there will be.

The idea of maintaining a steady rhythm to influence the angle as opposed to the angle influencing the rhythm may seem a strange concept. But the rhythm, its maintenance or loss, is intimately bound with the angle of travel because the two affect the horse's balance and movement. The perceptive rider cannot help being aware that the loss of one flags him as to the loss of the other.

Improving Two Track Work without a Wall

So far the turn on the forehand and leg-yielding were performed with the help of the wall in front of our horse. The time has now come to wean him from this prop. The successful execution of both exercises in a free area will be a measure of how skillfully we've taught our horse to obey our hands and legs.

Why is this so? Because when asked to go sideways the green horse naturally but mistakenly tends to react to the rider's single leg almost in the same way as if both legs were applied simultaneously. In other words, he goes forward. Now when we ask him to step sideways without the wall in front of him, if all he does is lean on the reins and strains to go forward, he hasn't yet understood that the single leg behind the girth means "go sideways." He needs more practice in the original version of these exercises.

If the trainer cannot tell how the horse will react once the wall is not in front of him, the trainer needs to take the precaution of weaning his pupil off it progressively. For example, both exercises will be started when the wall is five or six feet ahead of the horse. This way, if he should forge ahead in spite of the containing rein signals, he will only be able to do so for a step or two, after which time the wall comes to the rider's aid *(Fig. 29)*. If he meets this new challenge successfully, the exercises are begun progressively further away from the wall until it is so distant that it no longer influences the horse.

The turn on the forehand in a free space shouldn't present a problem because the horse has very little forward movement to begin with. Not so with leg-yielding. At first our horse may enter the buffer space and arrive with his nose to the wall within two or three side steps. This is normal and forgivable. Within a few attempts, if the rider is patient and doesn't start

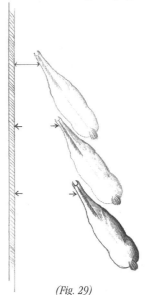

(Fig. 29)
The buffer space from the wall gradually decreases.

pulling with the expectation of obtaining perfection all at once, the young horse will soon understand that he must not go barreling forward. If the horse still does so, it is due to one or more of the following reasons.

First, he needs further practice in obeying the slowing down signals of the reins. Plenty of transitions is the solution. Second, in conjunction with the aforementioned, obedience to the unilateral leg should be confirmed, signalling that a shift of the body to the side is required. Third, he could be starting the exercise with too much forward speed, thus putting him on his forehand. At first he should be walking very slowly. When this happens, the horse's balance is somewhat vulnerable. Exploiting this state helps us to "tip" him in the direction we want, instead of kicking and pulling him over.

If this concept sounds strange, think of a cyclist trying to balance his bike at the red traffic lights without putting his feet on the ground. Since the bike is barely moving forward, it is so finely balanced that it can easily be tipped sideways. The same cannot be said if the bike is going fast because speed improves the lateral stability. Likewise our horse's lateral stability is governed by these same principles and can be influenced in a similar way.

Fourth, the rhythm of footfalls must be kept as even as possible. Uneven footfalls entice the horse to stagger laterally which in turn provokes a loss of longitudinal balance, characterized by an increase in speed or in increased contact with the rider's hands.

An additional consideration is that up till now most of the walk work has been done on long or even loose reins, and so allowing the horse freedom of stride. To maintain an even rhythm at slower speeds requires our horse to be very obedient to the interplay between hand and leg. This is tricky to do because it can all too easily degenerate into "hand riding" which spoils the walk, as well as provoking head tossing and pulling.

How do we get around this? There is no instant perfect solution. One of the most practical ones is to encourage the horse to walk slowly for a short distance, say six or seven meters. His balance, both lateral and longitudinal, will be more favorably susceptible to the influence of small intermittent signals.

If this type of walk for the suggested distance is hard for the horse to maintain, begin by introducing it for three meters or so before stepping out to a normal walk. Then, if he is comfortable with this, return to the slowed walk. In this fashion increase the distance, little by little, until he can walk those six or seven meters slowly, in reasonable balance with hinting signals to help him, not with crass ones.

Fifth, the rider may not be sitting with the horse which can make the arms and hands too unstable to give the subtle signals needed at the slowed walk. It helps to "mentally" settle into the horse, as well as expanding the front of the torso, thus giving the rider a firmer seat. The elbows kept lightly to the sides and dropped give stability to the arms which helps to give the rein aids in a measured way.

Nor should the rider's legs be forgotten. In an effort to deepen the active inside leg, the rider can easily start bracing onto the stirrup in such a way that the body stiffens and is not part of the horse any more. If this is the case, the ankles must be more relaxed and the legs allowed to gently cling to the horse's sides.

Looking at these five points, you may have noticed how no one solution in its entirety resolves the problem satisfactorily. For the best result, one or more other factors must dovetail into the one we've diagnosed as the primary solution. By keeping this thought foremost in our mind when problems arise we avoid the serious error of "tunnel vision" in our diagnosis.

Frequently, more than one factor makes up the correct solution. Also, that exact solution may not be appropriate for another horse. Each solution must be tailored to the circumstances and to the individuality of each animal.

This is not to imply that troubleshooting must become a complicated intellectual exercise. However, if the trainer gets in the habit of looking for a broader view as to why the horse has a particular problem, he unconsciously begins to pay attention to the telltale signs of these impending factors during the training, instead of spotting their magnified form only after things have gone wrong.

Crookedness, Bending & Straightening

When our horse has attained stability in his neck so the neck and the body can act as one unit, we can begin more deliberate work on straightening him, through bending.

The horse is straight when the hind feet travel in the trace of the front feet. The curvature of his spine corresponds to the line of travel. If that path is a straight line, the horse's spine should be straight. If the path is a curved line, the spine should be bent along the line's arc.

In theory, this seems easy enough to do but in practice it is much less so because the horse's tendency is to be crooked. It may be likened to being right or left handed, or in swimmers, having one leg that kicks more effectively than the other. This "one-sidedness" is manifested in the way the horse's body is shaped and by the way he moves.

From a bird's-eye view, the crooked horse has a shape somewhat like a banana lying on a flat surface. It is either concave or hollow on one side while the other is convex and bulging.

In an open space, such as when our horse is not in proximity to the wall, and without the rider's intervention, the horse adopts this curved shape. He almost always does so to the same side. He is said to be hollow or soft on the concave side, and bulging or hard on the convex side. This bulging is due to the contraction of the muscles on the hollow side, as those on the convex side are overstretched. If the muscles on both sides are equally stretched as the horse travels forward on a straight line, he will take equal contact on both reins and is deemed to be straight.

The terms soft or hard refer to the *feel* registered by the rider's hands and legs and are the most obvious indications to the rider that his mount is crooked. An observer on the ground lacks this input, and has only a visual confirmation of the horse's crookedness. When the horse is moving directly towards or away from him, the hind legs will travel slightly to the side of the trace made by the forelegs. Although there are other signs of a horse's crookedness, these are the most obvious.

Why is straightness so important? If the horse has been crooked up till now and still coped with the duties asked of him, why should we meddle and change the situation?

Because he is moving inefficiently. It will do the job but not without a cost: flawed and unsatisfactory results. If we want to train our horse beyond the crudest stage of functionality, we must understand crookedness and how it affects his movement.

When the horse is crooked, his forehand is not directly in front of his hindquarters but is to one side *(Fig. 30)*. Consequently, the hindquarters push his mass forward and *sideways*. This is because one of the hind legs evades bearing its share of the horse's weight. Instead of stepping straight forward, it steps to the side. When it is this leg's turn to push the body forward, it does so forward and sideways, propelling the body in the direction of the opposite shoulder. The rider feels this as an increase in the rein contact on the same side as that shoulder.

The remedy to this situation is to *bring the forehand in front of the hindquarters*. The hindquarters are held in place while the forehand is

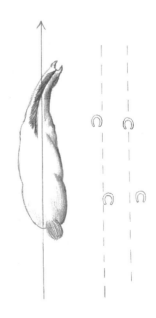

(Fig. 30)
The crooked horse.

shifted in front of them *(Fig. 31)*. This way the horse's body is brought in front of the sideways-evading hind leg, which is then compelled to push the horse straight forward.

We can now appreciate the usefulness of having taught our horse the turn on the forehand. He can yield his quarters to the rider's leg; this is the prerequisite for the horse to understand the meaning of the rider's other leg, which receives and holds the quarters. The turn on the forehand, however, will not be the complete answer because it is an almost stationary exercise. Our horse's crookedness must be corrected while he is moving. The turn around the forehand (which will

(Fig. 31)
*Bringing the forehand
in front of the hindquarters.*

be addressed in the next chapter) will better fulfill this need. In addition, the time spent teaching him to leg yield will now pay dividends.

The following example will clarify this process. Let's assume we are riding on the right rein and our horse's quarters deviate to the right of the track. Our objective is to straighten him by bringing his forehand in front of his quarters.

If we first hold the quarters with the right leg behind the girth, when the rider's left leg (slightly behind the girth) asks the horse to yield to it, with the help of both reins displaced to the right only the forehand will travel to the right. The horse's hind legs will travel in the same path of their corresponding forelegs. In the process, the horse will have made one or two small steps of a *turn around the haunches.*

Initially, the effect of this correction will be short lived, as brief as three or four strides. The horse will then attempt to regain his crooked position and he must be corrected each time he does so. This procedure will help to make the horse straight but it has one flaw: even though his hind feet track in the trace of the forefeet, it doesn't make the horse's body straight. He will revert to travelling in the banana shape previously described, albeit to a lesser degree, in addition to drifting to the bulging side. This is because the contracted muscles on the hollow side pull the hind leg on that side out of alignment, and to the side.

To make our "realignment" more enduring, we take remedial action to eliminate the bulge from the horse's side which in turn helps stretch the muscles on the hollow side.

When a horse's body curves naturally to one side, the task of producing lasting straightness is not going to be achieved by simply making his body straight. It must be bent in the opposite direction in varying degrees.

It's like trying to straighten a flat strip of wood. If we put ten volumes of the Encyclopedia Britannica flat on the strip overnight, it will not be straight the next morning, merely bent less. On the other hand, if it is bent the way opposite to its curvature, when the pressure creating the new bend is released the wood will ease to being straight.

It is this principle that suggests the value of working on a circle for straightening the horse. This is not to imply that a horse with a natural bend to the right will miraculously change his bend when ridden on a left hand circle. Not at all. The usefulness of riding this figure lies in how we use our aids and how we make the size of the circle work for us.

The Horse's Reaction to the Rein Used on the Hard & Soft Sides

Let's consider first how we use our rein aids. When we begin to straighten the horse by bringing his forehand in front of his quarters (to the right in our example) the horse will sometimes bend his neck even more to the right. If allowed to do so, he may drift to the left. This illustrates an important principle of straightening: when the neck is overbent in one direction, the body will drift in the opposite direction.

Before going any further, it's as well to make the distinction between bending and turning. Bending is a change in *posture or shape.* Turning is a change of *direction.*

The rein used on the soft side will bend the horse's neck but will not turn him correctly, unless his neck is kept straight in alignment with the curvature of his body. On the hard side, since the neck and body are stiff, the rein will have trouble in bending him. He can, however, turn promptly to that side *(Fig. 32).* And, due to the forehand's tendency to drift toward the hard side, he will turn in that direction on the slightest excuse. The rein on that side gives him that opportunity—one which he will take all too eagerly.

Having said this, it's all too easy for the trainer to get caught up with the mechanics of straightening while forgetting the two most important points. These are to channel the horse with reins and legs and to ride him forward. These points seem obvious enough but are so often overlooked that they require further explanation.

The reins and the rider's legs act as the sides of a channel through which the horse flows. With steady hands and a soft contact, the reins indicate that he must stay straight. A slight yielding of the outside rein may at times help the bending towards his "hard" side if he is circled to that side.

Whenever the horse slackens the contact, the hands remain quietly where they are while the legs "shepherd" him forward so he moves into the receiving reins again. If the horse slackens the reins more exaggeratedly, the rider's arms retract elastically but softly to take up the slack. As the legs "shepherd" the horse forward to stretch his outline once more, the arms gently yield to accommodate this change. The role of the legs should be one of firm passivity. Firmness means that with depressed heels (which tighten the calves) the horse feels the legs as two barriers through which he cannot push.

The significance of this, in contrast with the rider's single leg correcting an unscheduled sideways drift, is that when the horse is channeled between reins and legs which give him

(Fig. 32)
The horse at the bottom is bent towards his "soft" side, but does not turn promptly. The horse at the top does not easily bend to his "hard" side, yet is quick to turn to that side.

clear boundaries, this becomes a preventive measure.

In addition, the use of the single corrective leg in the early stages may create a snaking effect as the horse bounces off one leg towards the opposite side, only to be corrected by the other leg. But when he is encased between two firm boundaries this is less likely to happen.

However, this in itself will produce only diluted results unless the horse is ridden forward. Riding forward doesn't always mean that he should be sent forwards energetically, although that may be necessary on occasion. Riding forwards is as much a matter of the rider's mental attitude as increasing the horse's energy or speed. If the rider *thinks forward* when riding on a circle, instead of being overly concerned with bending, the horse will often begin to offer the bend almost on his own.

The reason for this is that he is sensitive to the suggestion that the aids which straighten and bend him are coercive. Consequently, he mentally and physically stiffens himself against their demands. When the rider puts less emphasis on these aids, and instead concentrates mentally on riding forward while thinking of equalizing the contact on both sides, the horse relaxes mentally and physically. In this state he is more malleable to the rider's suggestions, mental or tactile, to bend or straighten.

Other benefits will accrue. For example, as the horse begins to bend laterally, little by little he will make exploratory stretches of his head and neck in a forward and downward direction. At first these tentative stretches will be short lived. Then, as the stretches become more prolonged, the horse will arch and swing his back. His trot strides will show the first signs of springiness instead of the flat stomping character they have shown thus far. All these conditions are facilitated by riding forward on an accurate circle.

The demands of bending should initially be very brief to avoid provoking a rebellious attitude due to discomfort. We ask the horse to bend for just a few steps, after which the aids are released for a short while. Then the sequence is repeated. Little by little, the horse will willingly bend for longer and longer periods without discomfort.

Another important point in this regard is to avoid the temptation of riding the horse in one direction for too long, especially on his "stiff," unbending side. Later in his training, more emphasis can be placed to working on his stiff side. Again, this is interspersed with frequent changes of direction to avoid soreness which will provoke the horse into using evasive tactics to relieve himself of strain.

We should offer encouragement to our horse when he finds it difficult to bend. Simply giving the appropriate leg and rein aids is not enough; it's too cold and clinical. This approach will get results, but something is lost in the process. It's like saying to him "If you follow my instructions you will be able to bend." The horse would probably reply by saying "That's all very well, but this is uncomfortable—it hurts." To which the retort would seem be "You'll get over it!"

Instead, the trainer encourages his horse with his voice while his hand strokes the crest and gives light slaps on the neck to the side where the muscles are contracted. He puts feeling into his voice and touch. What does this say to the horse? It says something like this. "I know it's uncomfortable, but I'm confident you can do it. Here, let me help you and we'll get through this together."

What it does not mean is that we should treat our horse as if he's incapable of coping with physical or mental stress. We shouldn't treat him as if he's about to fall to pieces. Much of the time there is merit in presenting a problem in a fair way and letting the horse solve it. However, if a horse is really struggling either physically or mentally, we are not going to further our relationship with him or our objectives by saying "Hey buddy, don't look at me. I've told you what to do. Now it's your problem!"

Bearing in mind the dictum that "If you don't ask, you don't get," we must also be conscious of not becoming greedy when we do "get!" In other words, the horse isn't going to improve his ability to bend unless we push him a little bit, just as a coach pushes an athlete a little bit more each time. This is essential if the horse is to show improvement. However, there is the risk that once the horse gives us what we want, then, instead of us saying "well done, take a breather" either by changing direction or temporarily abandoning that exercise, we are tempted to say "great, this is obviously very easy for you, so give me more—now!"

So, if in doubt, leave it out! Push him, yes, but err on the side of caution. When the horse becomes sore and disgruntled, he won't want to work for us anymore. He might because he is forced, but he won't do it because he wants to please us. At that point he regards the trainer as his taskmaster instead of his teacher.

There will be plenty of times when the trainer asks too much. This is an inevitable and regrettably common process unless one has a mentor constantly at hand. How is one to learn, if not by mistakes? The trick is to learn from each situation from a minimum number of mistakes. In this way, the horse will hopefully be more indulgent towards our faults and the damage can be more easily repaired.

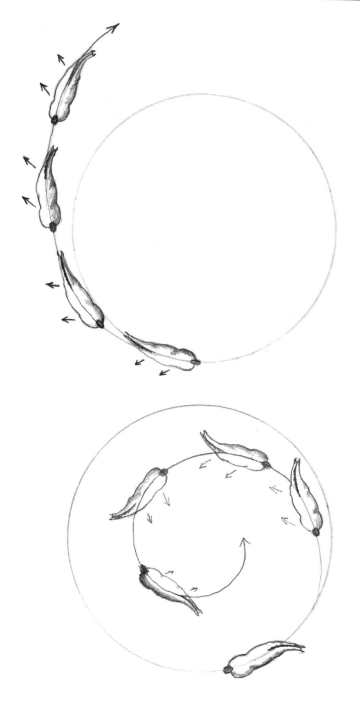

(Fig. 33)
The horse will drift in the direction of his hard, or bulging side.

Using Circles to Straighten the Horse

The process is easier to understand if we remember that our horse will nearly always tend to drift in the direction of his hard or bulging side. This occurs when going both clockwise and anti-clockwise. If his bulge is on the outside of the circle, he will drift outwards. If it is on the inside of the circle, he will drift in *(Fig. 33)*.

This drifting is made worse if the horse is overbent towards his soft or hollow side, by a pulling rein on that side. Instead he is asked to accept its contact which, over time becomes more positive. Guiding the horse's forehand with an opening rein (instead of a direct one) makes the contact more inviting.

Riding large circles, whose shallow arcs require little bend, are the ones least likely to worsen the drifting. The smaller circles provoke the rider to bend the horse more, which in turn incite further drifting.

Since our objectives are firstly to contain the drifting, and secondly to progressively get the horse's bulging side to bend, we mainly use lateral aids on that side. The passive but firm rein contains the shoulders, while the leg helps it, and little by little asks the horse's body to yield to it.

In this way we are able to bring the horse's body in front of the evading hind leg on the hollow side. As we do so, it will try to evade its job of carrying its fair share of the load by stepping sideways away from the burden. The rider's leg behind the girth on this hollow side will prevent this.

The Turn Around the Forehand

Before describing this exercise and its purpose, let us reexamine the turn *on* the forehand and consider why the latter's limitations require it to be replaced by the turn *around* the forehand.

The turn *on* the forehand was the ideal exercise to teach the horse the concept of moving sideways from the rider's leg. However, it has now outlived its usefulness from a gymnastic standpoint. The reason is that at this stage of the horse's training any two track exercise without forward movement stifles the crossing hind leg's ability to convert this engagement into thrusting the body forward.

Another disadvantage is that because of the static nature of the turn *on* the forehand, the inside foreleg around which the horse pivots can easily lock to the ground, instead of being lifted at each step. This can result in the foreleg twisting, and only discomfort induces the horse to lift it in relief. This cannot happen when the horse performs a turn *around* the forehand because it is a turn *on* the forehand with forward motion.

In the turn *around* the forehand the horse travels on two concentric circles with the forelegs on the inner circle and the hind legs on the outer one *(Fig. 34)*.

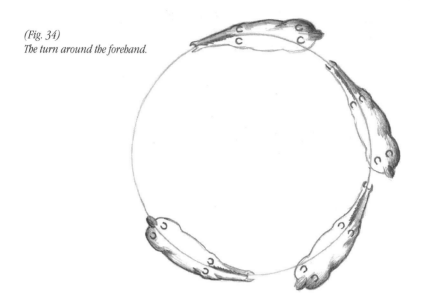

(Fig. 34)
The turn around the forehand.

The front and hind legs travel on their respective circles differently. The front legs travel as if on a single track. The hind legs travel so that the inside hind steps forward and in front of, or even across, the outside hind. The farther apart the circles, the more exaggerated the sideways movement of the inside hind leg will be. And, the more exaggerated the side step, the more the horse's back will have a tendency to hollow. If the sidestepping is more conservative, this problem can be diminished.

We begin by riding a circle on a single track with a walk that is purposeful, rhythmic, in good lateral balance. Our horse should maintain a positive but not leaning contact with our hands. Then, as with the introduction to leg-yielding, the walk is slowed down. The rider's inside leg, slightly behind the girth, moves his quarters to the outside while the outside leg and outside rein receive them.

The benefits of this seemingly simple exercise are considerable when done correctly. The circular element promotes bending to the inside and pushes the horse outwards while going forward. This develops his understanding of diagonal aids, specifically riding him from the inside leg towards the outside rein. Riding the horse into the outside rein during this exercise creates advantages which are applicable and necessary for further training. One of these is the horse's initiation in being ridden from rear to front.

Due to the slight curvature in the horse's body created by the rider's inside leg towards the outside rein, that outside rein has the elasticity taken

(Fig. 35)
The turn around the forehand.
Bending the neck more than the
body causes the horse to drift
outward, especially in the
shoulders.

out of it. Consequently a signal given with that rein has an immediate effect on the horse. The fixed outside rein also helps contain the outward drift of the shoulder, and maintains the uniform bend by defining the extent of bending and, if needed, the straightness of the entire horse.

A common error in the turn around the forehand is when the horse tracks sideways with his forelegs as well as his hind legs, producing a leg-yielding type movement. This is deceptively similar to what we requested, so we must be careful to correct it.

One of the causes is the rider not guarding against the outward drift of the shoulders. There is an excessive inside bend of the neck and insufficient emphasis on the forward movement *(Fig. 35)*. The aids must be precise, especially the position of the rider's legs. The turn around the forehand demands control over two specific parts of the horse's body: the front legs traveling on a single track side by side and the inside hind leg stepping in front of or across its partner.

Going forward—on a single track if necessary—is the top priority, even if it takes two or three circles on a single track to yield a single correct step. Going forward means traveling accurately on the chosen circle with even, rhythmic steps, and with the horse sensitive to the channeling action of the rider's legs and hands. When these criteria are met, obtaining a correct sidestep of the quarters will be easier.

Again, the rider must not get caught up in obtaining the sideways movement at the expense of the forward movement. That was the job of the turn on the forehand, to clarify the meaning of and respect for the rider's leg requesting a sideways movement. Now that our horse understands this, sideways without forward motion has little place in further training, except as an occasional reminder to obey the action of the leg.

The trainer must also guard against using the reins in a suffocating way, which curtails or stops the forward movement. This often comes about when the rider's leg is ineffective in shifting the quarters to the outer circle. Kicking and pulling are common bedfellows.

The trainer needs to be sensitive to the size of circle his horse can follow with relative ease with his front legs. For instance, a small circle has a tight arc and makes it difficult for the young horse's stiff body to follow its path. A larger circle is more akin to a straight line of travel, and is consequently easier for him to trace because he is going more forward, instead of turning. What this usually means is that the inner circle should be relatively large while the outer circle should not be much bigger. Start off with a 8 meter circle and see how he copes.

Also, the horse's body and neck must be aligned with each other. Once the neck bends more than the body, it becomes as if one is riding two horses, as the head and neck do one thing and the body does something else. We have all had the experience of riding a horse where we pulled the right rein so the head and neck were pointing in that direction, while the horse's body mysteriously and frustratingly drifted the opposite way.

The neck and body are kept straight in alignment by three actions. First, the inside rein should have a slightly lighter contact compared to the outside rein.

Using the inside rein in an exaggerated way to stop drifting in the opposite direction (the outside) should be avoided.

Do not get into the habit of pulling the inside rein to reinforce the action of the inside leg when this leg is being ignored by the horse. While it may work and we may sometimes find ourselves in situations where we need to do this, habitually using the inside rein in this way can create more problems than it solves. The better solution is to remind the horse of the meaning of the inside leg behind the girth with the turn on the forehand. This, coupled with an elastically resisting inside rein, will minimize the lateral bending.

Second, the outside rein must be firm enough to keep the neck straight. This is one of the hardest things to do from the riding aspect because the natural tendency of every rider when turning a horse is to do what I call "the bicycle handlebar trick:" when the left handlebar is pulled back towards the cyclist, the right one goes forward.

This may work with a bicycle but not when riding the horse. In fact, the opposite is usually the case: the more the outside rein is yielded, allowing the neck to bend exaggeratedly to the inside, the more likely the horse is to drift to the outside. We must be vigilant to keep the neck straight by yielding the outside rein only a small amount.

Third, the action of the rider's outside leg (on the side towards which the quarters move) helps the horse's shoulders to stay on the turn and not drift outward. The leg's action is slightly behind the girth, to support the function of the outside rein in preventing an outward drift of the forehand.

This is not always easy when riding a green horse. However, if the two track exercises have been practiced, this action of the rider's outside leg should be effective. However, let's assume for a moment that our horse reacts to the outside leg in less than exemplary fashion.

Let's say we are circling to the right and the horse's shoulders are drifting out. He is simply curling around the rider's right leg instead of moving his quarters to the left as was intended. At this stage of the horse's training we can only use tactics he already understands (with a more experienced and trained horse other solutions would be at our disposal).

First, the horse must be kept straight through the action of the outside rein and leg. He must respond promptly to the outside leg and we get him to do this by leg-yielding him away from it. We earlier noted that before a leg can be used effectively as a barrier to stop further progress to the side, the horse must first respect it by yielding away from it. And so it is here.

We begin by asking the horse to leg yield a step or two to the right on a straight line. Go forward four or five steps and then leg yield again a couple of steps. Repeat this until you feel your horse is keen to move away from the left leg.

Now, ride clockwise on a 15 meter circle and ask the horse to yield one or two steps toward the center of the circle. Remember, we bend him slightly away from the direction of travel. In this example, he will bend to the outside (the left). When this is done to your satisfaction without the horse fading off your left leg, repeat the exercise on a 10 meter circle. This exercise will help him be more respectful of the left leg.

We can then again attempt the turn around the forehand while paying attention to any signs of outward drifting of the shoulders, with our left leg ever-ready to come into action. You need to experiment to see exactly where along the horse's side, the leg solicits the response you want.

This exercise requires skillful riding. The benefit, when correctly executed, is that it will develop a greater attunement and response to the aids by our young horse.

Cantering

Thus far our horse has cantered on the lunge and while out hacking. On the lunge he was taught to canter on the correct lead. This was achieved by using the basic figure of the lungeing circle with help from the corners of the ring. However, while hacking, our demands for quality in the canter work were more modest. He was allowed to canter on the lead of *his* choice and on long straight lines since our primary objective was to encourage him to settle without the imposition of turns. If we had requested the lead of *our* choice, he would probably have been unsuccessful unless it happened to coincide with his favorite lead. At this stage, the request for a specific lead would have two drawbacks.

The first is that the horse doesn't yet know the aids for a strike-off on a specific lead. Also, teaching him to canter on the lead of *our* choice is facilitated by prefixing the canter with work on circles or corners of a ring. It isn't absolutely essential but it helps. As these facilities generally aren't available to us when hacking, this part of his education can be taught more easily and quickly in our riding arena.

The Basic Requirements of Good Canter Work

- A balanced trot prior to cantering.
- A calm strike-off, with controlled impulsion.
- Sustaining the canter in calm, even, energetic bounds.
- Maintaining a steady rhythm on straight lines and circles.

These criteria take time to master because they require the development of muscle control. Transitions from one pace to another help develop this muscle control. Also, the green horse experiences difficulty in maintaining his balance with a rider while cantering between straight lines and circles such as when changing direction; this too improves with time.

Nor are these requirements a complete inventory for a good canter. We didn't list keeping the horse straight as a priority for this stage. Not that it is an unimportant point—quite the contrary. In fact, references will be made to it indirectly, not as to uncompromisingly maintain his straightness but rather to minimize his crookedness. At this stage, we don't want to demand unrealistic expectations of a horse. We temporarily guard against overindulgence in a poor habit, crookedness, which can more easily be improved at a later date. However, this latitude should only be allowed during the initial canter transitions. Thereafter we take a more active role in making the horse straight.

Another reason for this temporary indulgence is that the signals to make the horse straight could be confused with those for cantering. This can result in hesitation while he tries to decipher our intentions, especially if his crookedness needs frequent corrections prior to cantering.

The patient trainer will address the problem of crookedness to the point where only occasional reminders to stay straight are needed. Only then should the canter strike-offs be attempted. This is an important consideration because it allows the horse to focus his attention on learning the new signals with a minimum of distractions from peripheral instructions.

Difficulties

The difficulties below give us an idea why training the horse to canter correctly is a time-consuming project. Again, it's made easier if we postpone formal ridden training at this gait until he is well balanced in his other work and responds willingly and promptly to the basic aids.

1. The canter's energy tends to erode the calmness we have been at pains to cultivate so far. In view of this, the canter work must be moderated and, if necessary, integrated with more calming work. We must dissociate in his mind the thought that cantering and excitement go together. Cantering quietly on the lunge will go a long way in quelling these tendencies.

2. Since canter work requires energy, the horse usually needs more grain. If the grain ration is increased before he is easily controlled at walk and trot, he may become difficult to handle at canter. But handling a lively horse is not the real problem; it's the strong rein signals the rider is tempted to use to control this excessive energy which erode his trust of the rider's hands, and result in negative repercussions in this and other work.

3. It is difficult for the green horse to canter at the working speed that one would expect from a more experienced animal because his hind legs at this stage have more ability to propel rather than to share the burden of the front legs. Because of this, he is constantly being pushed on his forehand. Also, he has a tendency to "fall" into the canter, which leads to a canter that is faster than we would like to see. His muscles take time to develop the strength to canter with rhythmic, energetic, but controlled bounds. And, the canter is the most difficult gait for the horse to learn how to balance himself while burdened by the rider.

Understanding the Objectives

To satisfy the four requirements for good canter work we have six objectives. The first four constitute the first phase of his canter lessons and the last two the second phase. These objectives are:

1. Striking off into the canter, using a simple method that helps the horse concentrate on the new signals.
2. Accustoming the horse to carrying the rider at the canter.
3. Taking care of typical problems that arise during the initial canters.
4. Down transitions.
5. Improving the strike-offs and the canter itself by using the skills the horse has learned up to this point.
6. Maintaining an energetic but balanced pace on straight lines and circles.

Before elaborating on these six objectives, the reader is reminded that canter work on the lunge greatly helps the ridden work. Lungeing should still be a part of the training program along with the ridden work. Specifically, the horse must be well tuned to our verbal signals for cantering and trotting. His familiarity with the verbal signal to canter will help him understand the meaning of the new tactile signals. Once he is conversant with these aids, the verbal signals take a back seat role and are eventually held in reserve.

On the lunge, the horse should be tuned so he replies smoothly but promptly. This will improve his balance so that the accelerated trot strides during the canter transition will not appear or, as the horse is better trained, will be only a short-lived habit. If he isn't prepped by the lunge work, this problem is likely to be a bigger problem.

Along with the lunge work, the horse should also be similarly prepared under saddle, with the transitions between halt, walk, and trot made in fairly quick succession. Again, as in lungeing, these should be prompt but smooth, without making the signals—especially those with the reins—tough, or the horse will become tense.

First Objective: Strike-offs using simplified aids.

The task here is to get our horse into the canter calmly, without coercion, and to encourage him to focus on our legs. We shouldn't be deterred if the first transitions are somewhat ragged. They can be polished as the horse comes to better understand the aids and his balance improves.

The best time to introduce this schooling is towards the end of his lesson when the horse is a little tired. This way we don't have the additional difficulty of coping with a horse that's too fresh.

To begin, we ride the long side of the ring and ask for the canter a few yards before reaching the first corner on the short side. It's important to ask for the canter before the corner because the horse will likely be confused by our new aids, even if they are given with the familiar verbal one. We must allow for some delay as he deciphers what we mean. Then, the bend of the corner will help to unbalance him slightly inwards so that he breaks into the canter on the inside lead. If the aids are given as he enters the corner, he will likely pass through it and be on the short side of the ring before he figures out what we want. At this point, the straight track gives him little incentive to canter along and with the opportunity to trot faster.

I'd like to bury a misconception often touted, that if the strike-off is unsuccessful in the first corner, one gets another chance at the second one. This can be done with a horse that is further along in its training . However, with a green horse this is impractical and will produce poor results.

Since an unsuccessful strike-off in the first corner nearly always results in an accelerated trot, he will arrive at this speed at the second corner of the short side all too soon. Giving a fresh canter signal here, while he is wound up, is hardly likely to create the reasonably calm strike-off we desire.

Also, when teaching the horse something new, the lesson should be conducted in the same spot each time so he associates that place with the demand. It makes it easier for him to learn what we mean.

Having said that, it is also true that horses who are either very smart or nervous often won't tolerate this procedure for more than two or three attempts. They anticipate the request to canter in a certain spot and make the rider's job of preparing them for the transition more difficult. The trainer must be sensitive to this and solve the problem in a non-confrontational way. One approach is to distract the horse by temporarily doing something else, such as circling, transitions to walk, and so on. These should be done on a large circle in the corner or away from the original trouble spot. Then, taking care not to make a big fuss about the preparation for the canter, the trainer almost casually asks for the transition. The horse will either pick up the canter relatively quietly or he might do the opposite, where he suddenly wakes up to the fact he has been tricked and takes off. For a horse that is not so easily duped, we simply ask for the canter in another corner. This way he is less likely to know what's coming.

Sometimes this may not work because a smart horse will associate the preparatory signals for shortening the trot, bending, and so on with the canter that follows. To foil his anticipation, we give these preparatory signals but then change our minds about cantering. When this ruse is repeated several times, the horse will find it difficult to tell whether these instructions will be followed by a canter or not. He has little choice but to learn patience and wait.

With a sensitive horse who is "all ears," the trainer must avoid betraying his intention to canter by stiffening his body, or holding his breath since the horse will easily read these telltale signs. The signals should be given in a casual way, almost as if the trainer doesn't care whether his horse canters or not. This is where the voice aid can help. Instead of being commandingly crisp, it should be laconic.

The Aids

While there are many ways one can get a horse to canter, most of them require him to be well schooled for the aids to be understood. In view of this, the less we restrict the movements of his head and neck and the less we upset his balance by not shifting our seat, the better will be his chances of success. Later on when he understands the meaning of the initial simpler aids, our conversation can become more sophisticated.

Each of the rider's legs has a specific task. The outside one is applied behind the girth with a uniform pressure as opposed to a more intermittent pressure. With a green horse the backward placement of this leg may need to be more obvious so that he clearly recognizes a shift of position. Keep in mind, though, that if retracted further it might make the horse ticklish or take him by surprise. In any case, an exaggerated shift will destabilize the rider's seat.

The inside leg on the girth gives a series of rapid squeezes, or if necessary, taps. Kicking is impractical because such signals can't be given rapidly without destabilizing the rider's position. While a kick can be an attention-getter for a cold horse or a habitually inattentive one, kicking should be used sparingly since it's the equivalent of yelling. It's effectiveness rests on the element of surprise. If we are constantly yelling, horses—just like people—switch off.

The reins are best used as little as possible. Their primary function is to prepare the horse by slowing his trot slightly during the last few yards prior to giving the canter aids. Thereafter, they should be passive and in an elastically supportive role.

During these first attempts we are not interested in positioning or bending him to ensure a canter on the correct lead every time. The corner will help him in this regard, with a fairly good success rate. Our objective here is to make him pay attention to what our legs are telling him.

The whip may be tapped on the inside shoulder if we feel that it can salvage an successful situation. It should be used if we feel that a tap of the stick is the one remaining ingredient to encourage the horse to canter.

The voice is essential. It acts as a bridge between what he has already learned about cantering on the lunge and the strange sequence of leg and whip aids he now feels with a rider on his back.

One other aid should precede all of these: the rider's mind. If we calmly focus on the outcome and try to project that idea to our horse, the chances of a successful transition are increased. The rider's will is also important but it must be transmitted calmly. It's easy to misuse by converting it into disruptive physical actions such as "scrubbing" the reins (like a jockey at the end of a race) or by trying to "lift" the horse into the canter with the reins or seat. While these tactics can on occasion be successful, the interference that accompanies them, especially hampering the freedom of the head and neck, are contrary to our objectives. In short, we explain to the horse what we want, after having adjusted the speed of trot before arriving at the corner, then allow him to figure out how to do it. We cannot do it for him.

To continue, we trot the long side and as we approach the last section, slow the trot with the outside rein. A stride or two later, we sit lightly for a moment then give the aids to canter before the horse has reached the corner. Once he passes through the corner and canters, the rider should remain in a half-seat so that his buttocks are not heavy in the saddle but are just grazing it.

During the first canter transitions, it's good to reward our horse with a cheery voice to show we are pleased with him. A more soothing tone runs the risk of inviting him to break into a trot.

Note that "sitting" need not be taken literally, unless our horse has a strong back. A half-seat, without posting, will suffice until he becomes used to the rider's deeper seat.

This interruption of posting will soon be understood by the young horse as a cue that something other than trotting is impending. After all, we don't post at the halt, walk or canter! We do so only at the trot.

Second Objective: Accustoming the horse to carrying the rider at canter.

The canter sections need to be lengthy enough that he gets the practice during any one canter session. This requires some judgement because it poses two options. One is whether to prolong the canter to give the horse the practice, but perhaps at the expense of him progressively losing his balance. This will be signaled by an increase in speed and a stronger contact with the rider's hands.

The other is whether to remain cantering as long as his balance is fairly good, and to resume trotting when the deteriorating balance cannot be salvaged. This option means that although for the most part the horse canters in good balance, he won't get much "mileage" out of each canter.

Neither option is right or wrong. The trainer must decide during the canter what latitude he thinks is healthy for the situation. For instance, he might deem that a particular degree of increase in contact is acceptable but no more than that, or it causes more problems, with shrinking advantages.

Again, it's worth bearing in mind that although good training should follow a broad but logical set of steps, we cannot make these ideals into a rigid formula. Each horse is unique in his behavior and the way he moves, so we must tailor his training to his individuality. If there was a formula which explained to the last detail what to do, anyone could train a horse. One of the essentials of good training is the ability to weigh one option against the other, the advantages versus the disadvantages, and all at a moment's notice. It's a matter of judgement based on knowledge, intuition and feel.

In fulfilling the requirements of this second objective, the rider must sit still. This doesn't mean he should be rigid, but that in the process of being in harmony with the horse, his movements should not be exaggerated or disruptive.

Some examples of these are:

- an exaggerated forward seat.
- leaning to one side, especially during turns.
- a rigid, inelastic posture.
- sitting too deeply so as to hamper the arching of the horse's back.
- fixed hands which lock the natural movements of the head and neck.
- "busy" hands, which dictate what the horse has to do, instead of allowing him to find his own balance, aided by quiet and elastically supportive hands.

Third Objective: Typical problems that can arise during the initial canters.

Rushing in the canter

The horse at this early stage will frequently increase his speed due to his being on the forehand. The reason is that his hind legs mostly push him forward with flat unenergetic strides instead of propelling him upward and forward in well-defined leaps or bounds.

The rider feels this imbalance as the horse leaning on his hands for support. All too often the rider's reaction is to pull, instead of elastically resisting him, which in turn provokes the horse into leaning even more. Unless the horse rushes off into a dangerous gallop the rider should instead try to "go with the flow." He should sit quietly, with supportive hands and try to calm the horse with a soothingly authoritative voice.

The reins can be used intermittently, preferably the outside one, in a suggestive action. The fist closes more tightly. If the horse is strongly pulling away, this can be with a hint of a "knocking," a slight staccato action. This action should not be a tug or a jab, as would happen if the rider's arm was pulled back. The voice can be synchronized with the rein signals. If the rider avoids reacting in a hasty and belligerent manner the horse will come to recognize that the hands are authoritative but not unfriendly.

It can happen that the horse becomes so unbalanced or excited that he "switches off" to the point where these tactics have little effect. In this case, the rider should circle or spiral using an opening rein (instead of the direct rein which might provoke more pulling), while giving slowdown signals. Bear in mind that although circling or spiraling will slow the horse down, they are useless as a means of teaching him unless used in conjunction with the rein aids that ask for the same. Since it is the rein aids the horse is ignoring, they should go to work with the help of the school figures since the latter compels the horse to listen to and obey the aids by association.

If the horse is repeatedly excited at canter, it should be abandoned and substituted by ridden work in the other two gaits until he settles and becomes more balanced. Excitability at the canter is often due to physical weakness. By giving the young horse frequent, long slow hacks out in the country, preferably with some hilly terrain, he will become stronger. If he is overfed or is naturally high spirited, these rides will help settle him.

In addition to hacking, cantering should be continued on the lunge. Frequent transitions in the form of walk–trot–canter–trot–walk will promote balance and strength. How these transitions are done on the lunge is important. The walk must be unhurried before he starts to trot, as must the trot before he starts to canter. This way, he will not use the momentum of an accelerated walk or trot to fall into the next pace up.

Downward transitions on the lunge are also useful, but only if the horse doesn't saunter his way down the scale. When they are executed with some rapidity, he is encouraged to bring his hind legs more underneath him.

However, this is tricky work. We don't want to be harsh with the lunge line just for the purpose of obtaining prompter replies, or it will result in mental and physical tension. It is his obedience to our voice, backed up by diplomatic use of the lunge, that produces the best results.

Bucking

With a young horse, this occurrence must be carefully considered, or it will create problems if the rider's reaction is inappropriate. For example, repetitive or unjust punishment may sour a sensitive horse, whereas ignoring it could encourage his more opportunistic peers to make bucking a habit. So what is one to do?

First, we must ascertain why the horse is bucking. It could be any one of the following reasons:

- The girth is too tight.
- The saddle is pinching at the front end. This may only become obvious when the rider adopts two-point position, especially if he's in the habit of letting the stirrups take most of his weight without letting his knees and thighs share the load. This results in his weight being concentrated at a point very close to the stirrup bars.
- The horse has a "cold back" but hasn't had sufficient warm-up work.
- He may have a medical problem that becomes more evident when cantering and jumping.
- He is being fed too much grain and is too high.
- The reins are too short or locked, so he tries to free his cramped neck and back by bucking.
- He reacts against the whip which is used near his flanks—a ticklish spot.
- The whip was used too strongly and startled him.
- If the rider is wearing spurs (a practice that has been advised against so far), the horse may react to their incorrect use.
- He hasn't had enough practice in carrying the rider's weight; he is hurting and wants to get rid of it.
- He bucks because he's enjoying himself.

- He bucks because he has been previously spoiled; he's mean; he's ungenerous.

From this list of 12 commonplace reasons, we observe that 10 or even 11 of these do not merit a reprimand or punishment since it's not the horse's fault. He's reacting to discomfort or pain in one form or another. In these cases the solution is self-evident. However, the last two deserve a closer look.

What do we do when the horse bucks because he's enjoying himself? The first option is to ignore it. The more the rider makes a big deal out of it, the more the horse is likely to repeat it at some point, even making a game of it. Ride forward, keeping an elastically supportive contact with his mouth. The rider's seat can be a little deeper than normal but only on the condition that he is supple in his waist. Alternatively, he can stand on his stirrups so he's more out of the saddle. If the knees are kept springy instead of being locked, his body will be relatively unaffected by the horse's movement below. The main disadvantage to this option is that the rider's center of gravity is raised, leaving him perched on top of his mount. This position decreases the rider's stability and lures him to hang on to the reins as lifelines.

The next option is determined by whether the bucking are just "baby capers," i.e. innocuous small leaps, or if they are the full blown version. The former can easily be ridden out by urging him forward, but the latter is dependent on other considerations.

For example, if he has given one or two bucks at the beginning of the day's canter work, I would be indulgent for the first few times and thereafter tell him to quit. We don't need to be harsh but he must get the message. An authoritative "No" with the voice may be a sufficient rebuke with some horses, while others may require a more tactile reproof. A slap on the shoulder with the stick, or a kick coupled with the verbal correction is generally all that is needed.

Nevertheless, it's possible that with these tactile corrections the horse may respond by bucking even more! This can be prevented by raising our hands so the forearms are parallel to the ground while keeping the elbows close to our sides. The fists must be closed to stiffen the arms. The horse will find it very difficult to yank the rider's arms forward so he can drop his head and neck, a posture without which he finds it difficult to buck.

The last reason listed, the horse that is either spoiled, mean or ungenerous is a special case. At first glance it may appear that all three of these traits are best dealt with by punishment but that is not necessarily the case.

Although retraining the spoiled or mean horse is not the primary purpose of this book, it's worth a brief investigation to provide food for thought which may be helpful in of training the young or green horse.

Let's take the spoiled horse first. It's true that a couple of smart strokes of the whip may convince him to quit bucking—but what if it doesn't? The trainer must try and figure out why the horse persists with this habit. For example, if a rider has antagonized the horse repeatedly through bad riding, it would be wrong to adopt punishment as the only choice of correction or the primary correction. I use the word "primary" because even if the rider rides better, the horse often retains a residue of his defensive habit. It may be difficult to encourage him to abandon it simply because he is ridden better, and he may still need to be physically (though not sharply) reproached for his conduct.

An analogy to illustrate this in human terms would be a scene where you were commiserating with a friend on his misfortune. The person may be crying or sobbing but at some point, seeing that your sympathy isn't making him feel any better (indeed, it may encourage self pity and perhaps make matters worse) you say to him "Snap out of it and pull yourself together!" Although this won't cure him of his misery (at least not at that moment) it does interrupt his current pattern of emotions, thoughts or actions, at least enough to make him reconsider. This may need to be repeated several times at various intervals. So it is with our horse.

It's rare to come across truly mean horses. The so-called mean ones are usually intelligent, sensitive horses who object to being treated roughly. They don't thrive in just being a "number" in a busy and often understaffed barn. They require extra personal attention to keep them sweet. When they don't slavishly and instantly cooperate like their more docile peers, they often get punished. If this is a frequent occurrence, they build up a resentment that can turn into aggressiveness.

This would be displayed by pacing in the stall, cribbing, kicking, biting, and lungeing threateningly at passers-by or anyone entering their stall.

In work outside of the stall, their aggression may manifest in barging over the handler, lungeing threateningly, biting and kicking, or rearing. Bucking may be one of the ways he expresses resentment. It's a sad state of affairs when a horse has been driven to such desperation. This horse needs a cool but sympathetic trainer who has the experience and tact to know when and if to punish him.

Sometimes, the so-called "mean" horse that bucks may benefit by getting as much as he gives. The problem is that the trainer must win—and quickly—to make an indelible impression on his recalcitrant pupil. There is a risk of unleashing the horse's powers against the rider—a difficult proposition on a green horse who hasn't sufficient conditioning in obeying his rider. It's like driving a car that's out of control on a slippery road while having to cope with a faulty steering, brakes, and gas peddle!

For the ungenerous horse, using the stick may well be the only remedy to dissuade him from bucking. He is a "nine to five" worker and a grudging one at that. He gives back no more than what you can cajole out of him, which makes him a difficult subject to work with. He may buck simply to evade working, which usually means he doesn't want to go forward. However, there's a ray of hope even with him; sometimes such a horse can be encouraged to view life more interestingly instead of regarding it as drudgery. His interest can be piqued by changing his living quarters to where he can poke his head outside the stall and see what's going on around him. Another ploy is to stimulate his interest by frequent trail rides, varying the routes. Cantering or galloping alongside other horses will often encourage him to give of himself in a natural way, without being goaded into doing so by his rider.

However, it's quite likely that one can never achieve an entirely satisfactory result. The trainer must be imaginative and see what works best.

Veering

Veering manifests in different ways, but is often made worse by the rider overcorrecting with the reins while omitting to channel the horse between hands and legs and to ride him forward. Having said this, the rider is not altogether to blame. You will notice that when the young horse is cantered on a straight line in an open space, he is generally undisturbed by this problem. It's true that he may drift off the original course to one side, but he generally won't snake left and right.

When we ride him in the ring, especially if it's a small arena, the corners come all too quickly, and we have to slow down. The very ingredient that kept him relatively straight out of doors, the energetic uninterrupted forward motion, is now curtailed. Such a canter would be too lively in a restricted space. And, because his balance is disturbed as he turns across the short sides of the arena, the slowing and turning action of the reins encourage him to twist his body and veer.

He will also veer if he is made to slow the canter more quickly than his level of training can comfortably cope with. Again, we must channel the horse as best we can between hands and legs while restraining the horse's natural canter speed as little and tactfully as possible. To this end the corners on the end of the long side of the ring must be generously rounded.

Also, if the arena is too short, consider cantering outside on straight lines as an option until he becomes more balanced and can canter more comfortably at the slower pace.

Fourth Objective: Down Transitions.

Once our horse has settled in the canter, the chances are that in a short while he will trot of his own accord since initially it's tiring for young horses to canter with a rider. When we feel he is on the verge of breaking into the trot that is the most propitious moment to use the voice and reins to tell him to do so. At first, this may seem an odd tactic: one where the horse indicates to us when to give the trot signals instead of us deciding when to do so. But if we give the signals a little before he is about to trot, because he feels like it, we have the advantage of being obeyed. Our horse doesn't know we were being opportunistic!

If we repeat this process a few more times, we will have conditioned the horse to obey the slowdown or trot signals so he will unquestioningly respond correctly, even at those times when he isn't predisposed to break into a trot.

Again, the voice signal which he knows from his lunge work will be an effective addition to the tactile signals. And, it goes without saying that we must reward our horse for the correct response.

Two more points are noteworthy, especially since their essence is applicable to further stages of training. One is that since a young or green horse canters on his forehand, it's difficult for him to readjust his balance at short notice to make a prompt transition to trot. Thus we shouldn't be hasty about implementing contingency plans until the horse has been given a chance to carry out our original request. His response time will improve as he becomes more practiced. At this stage we must exercise patience, while being alert to the possibility that our horse either had not heard us or perhaps had misunderstood our request.

Two, since he is on the forehand, when we ask for a down transition he will tend to spill into it and end up trotting fast. If his "formal" canter training is started before he's had a chance to develop a good balance at walk and trot, this fast trot is inevitable.

The good trainer is careful to avoid confusing the horse by asking him to go from the forward, rolling canter of the green horse to the working speed of his trot work. He avoids giving one signal for two completely different requests. The first request is to change gait from the canter to trot, not from canter to trot at x miles per hour. Any speed of trot the horse initially offers is legitimate, since we are only interested in the transition.

Once the horse is in the process of giving us the transition, we immediately yield as if to say "That's correct. Thank you." Only when he's trotting, usually fast, do our next set of signals say "Now I want you to moderate the trot you just gave me." These signals are yielded with each diminution of speed and reapplied until the desired speed is attained. When the green horse is ridden this way, he feels unconstricted in the first few strides of trot and is more than willing to comply with the rider's new requests to slow down. On a psychological level, it's essential not to give one continuous signal for the two tasks.

We may liken the forward energy of the young horse's canter to the kind displayed by an excited horse. Although it's true that with some horses a locked, unyielding contact can steady and slow them down, a horse with spirit will not be quite so compliant. He will fret and become more excited. Only yielding will help restore his composure.

Thus, every time we restrict or take, it must be followed by giving something back to the horse. When we do so, in that moment, we allow the horse to be temporarily in charge. He feels he can express himself after having been patient and self-controlled enough to listen to and carry out his rider's needs. Now that it's his turn, he feels liberated—a natural feeling that even domesticated horses long to express. The astute trainer never forgets this. He doesn't fight nature.

It's true that as time goes on, the trainer will habituate his horse to tolerate shorter time-spans of freedom. However, the *frequency* of freedom he gives to his mount will *increase*. This way the horse doesn't feel suffocated and will remain fresh in spirit. This point is very important. Ignoring its principles during the canter–trot transitions invariably results in the horse characteristically tugging at the reins and stiffening himself for several strides once he is trotting.

Lastly, for the first few times, it's a good idea to walk the horse on loose reins after each canter. If he is also excited at this gait, he should be halted and encouraged to stand on loose reins. This way he comes to understand that canters will immediately be followed by quieter exercise, which mentally conditions him to maintain or regain his composure.

Fifth Objective: Improving the strike-offs, and the canter itself,
by using the skills the horse has learned up to this point.

The information in this fifth objective (phase two) can be used as an improvement on the first objective for strike-offs with simplified aids (in phase one). If the horse's balance and strength have been sufficiently developed with the work at walk and trot, canter work can profitably begin with this fifth objective.

At first glance, the difference between the first and fifth objectives may not seem so far apart. However, on closer inspection it will be found that with this fifth objective the horse will be better balanced prior to striking off. He will have a much better chance of picking up the correct lead, and once he is cantering, will need little support from the rider's hands. In addition he will be calmer and more attentive to our instructions.

If we study these advantages carefully, we can avoid many of the problems that have been numerated so far. If they do confront us, they will be in a diluted form and easier to deal with.

One of the main differences between the strike-offs in the first objective and those in this fifth objective is the energy level of our horse. In the first objective, due to the horse's inexperience it was prudent to make the trot that preceded the canter a quiet one with relatively little energy. However, this generated disadvantages such as "falling" into the new gait and, once there, the canter leaps were so flat the pace couldn't be sustained for very long. These setbacks were traded for the advantage of keeping the horse calm with this lower energy level. As a temporary measure, it served its purpose.

Now, however, if the horse's aptitude in cantering is to be improved beyond the level where calmness is the only criteria, he must have the ability to generate and accept certain conditions. These are:

- A controlled energetic trot.
- The ability to obediently and smoothly shorten the trot.
- Willingness to accept the aids to bend.
- The ability to stay balanced during the strike-off, without continuous support from the hands.
- The ability to maintain his balance for a short while once he is cantering.
- Obedience to the aids to return to the trot.

These criteria are listed in a progressive order to more easily explain our interaction with the horse and what is expected of him. Moreover, the purpose of this section is not to explain the basic aids (which we already know), but to highlight the main principles that govern each step. If we are clear about the mechanics of the process, an informed attempt can be made at troubleshooting should the need arise.

A controlled energetic trot.

The horse must be energized before the exercise is begun, especially because the trot will be also somewhat shortened. If this shortened trot isn't preceded by a more energetic one, the horse will likely make it a jog, devoid of the energy that we require. The transition into canter would then be little better than the one offered in the first objective. This energy doesn't mean that the horse must do an extended trot or move forward as if he was high. On the contrary, the working trot must be a controlled energetic trot.

How do we do this without exciting him? Transitions up and down the scale, in quick succession help, but should not be at the expense of creating tension. Riding progressively smaller circles while maintaining the same speed and rhythm will make his hind legs (especially the inside one) reach forward, flex more, and thrust forward more energetically.

If the horse is phlegmatic we can use ground poles or low cavaletti to encourage him to energize his trot. Take care that he's not on the forehand or it will create problems in the next step.

The ability to obediently and smoothly shorten the trot.

The reason why this shortened trot needs to have energy has already been addressed.

The slightly shortened trot makes it easier for the horse to spring into canter while helping him to be less on his forehand.

The horse must shorten the trot obediently and smoothly; the transition into it should be done with some dispatch, to retain the energy of the working trot that preceded it.

This is not done while sacrificing the smoothness of the transition. The rider must avoid giving the signals so they disrupt the horse's posture and cause him to raise his neck, come above the bit, or hollow his back. If the horse is incapable of making a correct transition within the trot, more practice is needed before reattempting the canter.

Willingness to accept the aids to bend.

So far we allowed our horse to strike off into canter without much concern as to how his body was positioned. It is likely that much of the time he leaned his outside shoulder onto the wall and so moved crookedly. We should now be more vigilant about keeping him straight by bringing his forehand inwards so it is in front of his quarters.

Once he is straightened, his ability to bend to the inside leg and rein facilitates a strike off the inside lead. The outside leg and rein, in their turn, guard against the quarters and shoulders from drifting outwards.

His ability to stay balanced during the strike-off without continuous support form the hands.

The rider contains the energy of the shortened trot by a series of soft, elastic but positive reminders. However, he must not lock the energy in the horse with each of these signals. Instead, they are hints to his mount that he should contain this energy dynamically on his own.

The rider's leg aids are given in the conventional way for cantering but the reins are used slightly differently from the way advocated in the first objective. Here, at the moment of strike-off, the inside rein is yielded slightly to avoid restricting the inside lateral pair of legs (the leading ones). This yielding should be smooth, not slackened abruptly so the horse suddenly finds himself leaning on the outside rein; this would bend him to the outside.

If this occurs and if the outside rein is locked, the horse may accelerate. He does so because the abruptly freed inside rein suddenly gives him an escape route to that same side. Also, his nose is probably all but scraping the wall, so he tries to turn away from it by pulling and accelerating.

The correct yielding with the inside rein is gained by the rider looking slightly upwards and outwards at the moment of strike-off. This action helps the inside rein advance.

Another improvement over the original simplified strike-off relates to the way the rider uses his seat. Originally, we made a point of sitting centrally, with no shift of weight, on the principle that a still weight is an easy weight to carry. We wanted to avoid distracting the horse by such shifts to which he would be compelled to adjust and not always successfully.

Now, for the rider's seat to be in harmony with his mount, the rider must alter the way he sits. If our horse is cantering on the left lead, the rider now sits deeper and adopts a posture with his left hip slightly in advance of his right hip. This gives the horse the left lead with both the front and hind leg on that side. When this occurs, the rider's seat must adopt a corresponding posture for his seat to harmoniously follow the movements of his mount. The rider's left seat bone must (like the left lateral pair of legs) be in advance of his right seat bone. If this posture is not adopted, both the horse and the rider will feel that each is not in harmony with the other.

This probably begs the question of why wasn't the horse or rider bothered by this disharmony with the previous canter work, which advocated no change in posture for the rider?

Well, in the original strike-offs during the first objective, we were able to dispense with this change of seat position because the half-seat we had adopted separated us from the horse. In other words the horse could move freely beneath us, so our neutral position was not antagonistic with his change of posture. Now, since we are sitting deeper and we wish to be in harmony with him, our inside seat bone needs to be shifted slightly forward by deepening the knee on the same side.

Maintains his balance for a short while once he is cantering.

Unlike the horse in the first objective, our horse will now maintain his balance for varying lengths of time after the strike-off, depending on the quality of the work that preceded the canter. The more balanced he is in the trot, the better his balance at canter.

If the balance can't be regained, we should quietly return to the trot or even the walk and rebalance him before cantering once more. By explaining to the horse again and again at the easier gaits, what he must do, he will begin to understand how to use his body to maintain a good balance at canter. This is repetitive work and requires patience.

Remember, when the horse finds difficulty in maintaining a balanced canter, he is not being stupid, lazy or ornery—so he shouldn't be punished for his struggles. Instead, it often highlights his difficulty in accepting the aids. Sometimes these may have been so demanding that they stifle the forward reach of the hind legs and the elasticity of his back. The horse is then on the forehand.

The remedy is, of course, to practice transitions between halt, walk and trot. Circling and spiraling can also help. Further approaches are given in the sixth objective.

In all these exercises—valid and necessary though they are—there's the suggestion that we are molding the horse. It's as if we are saying "Do this and you'll get this result. Now do that and you'll get that result." In contrast, another approach that is worth pursuing with some horses (and which distances itself from the above suggestions), is where the horse almost teaches himself to canter in balance. It goes like this.

We ask for the canter and continue for say, sixty yards, after which we carefully bring him down to a walk. We walk him on a long rein for as long as is needed to settle him before trotting and quietly picking up the canter again. This routine is repeated over and over for a while in each schooling session. After some days or even weeks have gone by, the horse will canter with energetic bounds yet quietly and in excellent balance.

What have we done to make this happen? By repeatedly cantering the same distance, followed only by transitions to the trot and walk, the horse begins to understand the routine and anticipates the downward transitions. In order to make life easier for himself, he will quite naturally, of his own accord, begin to use his body in the most effective way to accomplish this task.

Once he can canter in balance for that distance without the rider's help, he will be able to do so for longer distances. This exercise can be done on its own or in addition to the approach we've adopted thus far.

One word of caution: this exercise is like a two-edged sword. Although it is effective in balancing the canter, it can make a horse too quick in his strike-off if the rider isn't careful. For example, a sensitive one will quite soon anticipate the strike-off and quicken the walk or trot. Then he may begin to react too sensitively to the aids, no matter how discreet they are. Next he begins to react to the telltale signs of the impending transition such as the shortening of the reins at the walk. The rider finds himself a prisoner of his own horse, not daring to move or breathe lest he betrays his intentions.

Obviously, this is not what we're after! The rider must take care to disassociate the horse's mind from *up* transitions, and instead mainly interest him in the *down* ones.

To this end, he must be walked until he is completely calm. If that doesn't distract or bluff him, we can *occasionally* ask for the canter from a walk on a long rein, while allowing two or three trot steps. A sharp horse will only be temporarily duped by this approach, so the rider must resort to either walking or trotting while asking for simple figures to distract him before cantering once more.

*Sixth Objective: Maintaining an energetic but
balanced pace on straight lines and circles.*

Bearing in mind that the canter consists of a series of leaps in a combination of upwards and forward energy, if this energy is allowed to dissipate, the canter will be lost. And while it is true that the rider's legs can rekindle the canter's waning energy, inattentiveness to certain factors will erode their effort. These pointers need to be uppermost in the trainer's mind.

- Think ahead.
- Avoid drifting.
- Maintain an even rhythm.
- Maintain his forward energy.

Think ahead.

Due to the sluggish response to turning, especially when doing so away from the rail, the trainer must adjust for this. One way is by turning earlier to allow for a delayed reaction. The other is to make a tighter trajectory than originally planned, give the aids to do so and then abandon the plan.

For example, if a 20 meter circle is planned and the trainer notes his horse expanding the arc to make a larger figure, the trainer goes through the motions of requesting a 15 meter circle. Once the horse is about to begin this smaller arc, the rider changes his mind and rides the original 20 meter figure instead. What happened is the intention to do a 15 meter circle stimulated the rider to ensure his aids were respected. Then he could be certain that his aids would be effective in holding his mount to the larger (and less demanding) trajectory of the 20 meter circle.

Avoid drifting.

At first this is difficult because of the horse's crookedness. Moreover, his rapid approach to the corners invite him to drift or to turn prematurely. Once he has begun to do this, the rider's aids used to return him to the original trajectory are of little use. At best—and with difficulty—they may be able to prevent further drifting.

Sometimes the problem is that the rider has not anticipated these deviations. Or if he has, the aids that suggest that the lateral balance must be maintained are either not being heard or are not effective enough. To be fair to the rider, we should note that although these aids are effective at the slower gaits, their influence often diminish as the speed within the gait increases. Since the canter is the speediest of the three, this is the gait where the rider's influence is most eroded.

The solution is not to increase the strength of the aids, which often degenerates into using strong rein effects, but to return to a lower gait or speed where the balancing aids are more influential. Once there, the horse is reminded to maintain his lateral balance, so that a degree of this influence is carried through when the faster paces are resumed.

This correction is not a one time affair or, for that matter, long lasting in its effect. On the contrary, these corrections are frequent, and the horse's respect for the lateral balancing aids while cantering are at first short lived.

The corrections, first at the walk and then at trot, take the form of leg-yielding away from the side to which the horse shows signs of drifting. We are not interested in making him yield for several consecutive steps, but as to how promptly and willingly he responds to the aids; we ask for one or maybe two sidesteps at a time.

I use the word "willingly" to describe how malleable his body is to our leg. He could move away from our leg promptly enough, but his body may feel resistant. It's as if he is following orders, but under duress. Instead, he should feel more supple to our leg, bending around it and demonstrating a measure of mental and physical acceptance.

These tactics are designed to minimize the horse's sideways drifting and at best are a stopgap measure. The main problem is that the horse is crooked, and so must be straightened. However, at this stage it may be difficult to remedy this as effectively as one can at walk or trot. Little by little, as the canter work becomes more settled and the horse more responsive, we will be able to straighten him with polite aids. In addition he will remain straight for longer spells.

A steady rhythm.

Maintaining a steady rhythm while cantering does not require strong or abrupt corrections with the reins or an exaggerated shifting of the rider's weight.

These corrections are best done in a more suggestive way, while thinking forward. The trainer has several tools to do this: rocking his body faster or slower, "polishing" the saddle with his seat, and using the reins in various ways; these are all useful when given skillfully and tailored to the appropriateness of the situation.

However, a solution that is more suggestive and particularly suited to a green horse, is for the rider to verbally cue himself to maintain an even rhythm. Once the horse is in canter, the rider verbally utters a word of his choice every time the leading leg strikes the ground. A good one to use is the word "now!" The word must be audible to the rider's ear because it automatically cues his body to instinctively, yet in a subtle way, do what is needed to maintain the rhythm.

If the rider is not very fit, he can run out of breath quickly and subsequently is tempted to say the word mentally instead of audibly. In this case, it's very easy for the horse to seduce the rider into adopting the rhythm the horse has chosen, instead of the other way around. However, if the rider is musically inclined, has a good sense of rhythm, and a disciplined mind, he can save his breath!

Maintain his forward energy.

Bearing in mind that the canter consists of a series of leaps in a combination of upward and forward energy, if this energy is allowed to dissipate, the canter will be lost. And, the more strongly the reins are used to turn or to control the horse's speed, the less energy will be available to propel him upward and forward.

One can use the legs more vigorously or frequently, but that would run the risk of either contradicting what the reins are saying or send the horse forward in a way that would make him deaf to them. This violates one of the basic rules of training: to avoid soliciting more energy with the legs than one can control with the hands.

How then do we accomplish this juggling act?

At first the rider ensures the horse has enough energy to get through the turn before starting it.

Secondly, he carefully chooses how much to turn so that the horse's energy remains more or less intact throughout the procedure. For instance, a simple quarter turn such as rounding a corner, would satisfy the above conditions, whereas an attempt to do a half circle and reverse might "kill the engine." Clearly, no single action from the rider will satisfactorily solve the problem, whereas a combination of two or more almost certainly will improve the situation. This may seem obvious, but as we well know, it's all too easy to get wrapped up in taking care of one thing to the exclusion of everything else. Doing so can lead to complications.

For instance, taking care of the lateral balance is just as important as how much contact he is allowed, how fast he is going, the energy level within that pace, how attentive he is to the aids, or the quality of his reaction time.

Teaching to Load into a Trailer

As the land is increasingly segmented by roads and fence lines, trailering horses to places unrestricted by these boundaries becomes increasingly important. The days when we could hack to a meet or a local show, easily and safely, are all but over. In this day and age, a horse that won't load onto a trailer is seriously handicapped.

The horse that's difficult to load is at least able to travel, but invariably spoils the occasion by his behavior, bringing punishment on himself as well as angering his handlers. This needn't be the case if he is taught progressively, logically, with patience and, if the need arises, with firmness. Brutality has no place in this exercise since it only reinforces the horse's will to avoid getting into that strange and cramped-looking box on wheels.

Although there are countless small things that make a horse hesitate about loading (all of which can be fairly easily overcome), there are three major reasons why he won't load willingly. The first is the trainer's negative attitude. The next is trying to load an inexperienced horse without any preparation. And then there is the horse that has had a bad experience while travelling, such as a trailer accident or being thrown about because of inconsiderate driving.

Let's look briefly at each of these because without understanding their implication, loading a green horse will be a hit or miss affair, and a frustrating one.

Except for maybe trying to get a horse across a stretch of water, there is no other obstacle that invokes as negative an attitude in many people as trying to load an inexperienced horse into a trailer. The first and probably only question running through the minds of all present is "Will he go on?!"

We think this way because we have witnessed countless occasions where horses didn't want to load. The fights that ensued are indelibly registered in our minds. When it's our turn to get a green horse to load, these memories prey on us. But the question "Will he go on?" shouldn't even cross our minds. Instead, we should have the conviction that "of course he will load."

It's true that some horses will need more schooling, while others climb on as if they've done it all their lives, but the trainer should have unshakable faith in a successful outcome. It might take minutes with an unspoilt green horse, or several hours over a period of days with an older, frightened one. However, the trainer should never doubt that his pupil will overcome his aversion to being loaded. If the trainer harbors doubts, the horse will pick up on them and lose confidence in his handler.

If a horse is being taught to load, it's not very smart or fair to lead him straight to the back of the trailer in the hope that he'll just climb in.

He might, in which case it's your lucky day, but there's an equally good chance that before he is within twenty feet of it he will refuse to advance any further. That's not good because we have taught him not only how to disobey us, but how to be prey to his own fear as well.

The horse that has had bad experiences in a trailer has every right to be frightened of being loaded. The problem here is not that he must overcome his fear of going into the trailer, as much as it is that he must develop confidence in his handler.

Just because such a horse is familiar with his trainer doesn't necessarily guarantee that he will immediately follow him into the trailer! In that moment, the horse's instinct for self-preservation overrides any other consideration—including love or loyalty to a person. He understands nothing except his fear. Because of that, any attempt to force such a horse into *approaching* the vehicle against his own will is doomed to fail.

When he goes forward because he is ready to do so, even for only a single step, and the trainer skillfully asks him at exactly this propitious moment the horse's trust in his handler will be developed. This is because the trainer does not ask the horse to go forward while the horse's instinct for self-preservation is uppermost. There's no conflict of interest. Moreover, with each of these instances, the horse develops more confidence in his trainer's judgement and begins to feel safe, eventually coming to realize that his mentor would not expose him to something harmful.

Once he is on and shut in, the problem is only half solved. If the horse was frequently thrown around by inconsiderate driving, this also must be remedied.

If the horse was loaded into a trailer with a low roof, he may have jerked his head up and smashed his poll on the ceiling. If he was wearing a poll guard it might have cushioned such a blow, but if he was unprotected he might have ended up bruised and bleeding, an incident not easily forgotten.

These solutions are usually obvious but often overlooked. Yet it's true that most accidents or hurtful episodes are due to laziness, lack of caution or too much faith in "divine providence." Divine providence doesn't condone foolishness, however.

The advice that follows is for teaching a green horse to load. While it doesn't cover in depth how to reform a problem horse, the basic principles are the same and will help considerably in retraining.

Setting Up the Trailer

If the trailer doesn't have a solid base of support when unattached to the towing vehicle, it must be stabilized so it won't roll forward or rock. Without the two rear telescopic stands, the rear of a lightweight trailer can sag when the horse steps onto the ramp. In turn, the top of the ramp lowers and the horse, feeling this insecure base, becomes wary of stepping any further.

A second and equally important consideration during the first introductions is the location of the trailer. One way sometimes favored is to place the trailer where the horse is fed hay or grain (outside of course), so he becomes familiar with the vehicle. Food is first left near the tail of the ramp, then on the ramp itself, and finally within the trailer. The idea is that by appealing to the horse's greed, he overcomes his shyness of this strange object.

This method can produce good results but it's also dependent on variable factors such as degree of hunger, and so on. Apart from leaving a lot to chance, it has the disadvantage of robbing the trainer of the opportunity to influence the horse gained by leading the horse into the trailer. At this stage of a horse's training, such opportunities shouldn't be missed.

The trailer is best placed where the footing is grass, dirt, or sand, but not asphalt. If the horse gets upset and there's a scuffle, we don't want him slipping and sliding with possible injury, especially to his knees or hocks. The trailer's right hand side should be parked close against a fence or wall. This way he cannot escape off the ramp to the right, only to the left. Since we lead him on his near side, if we insist that he respects our space and not run us over, he finds himself channeled laterally.

Since the wheels jutting out on the right hand side beyond the shell of the body are hugging the wall or fence, the right hand side of the ramp will not be flush with this barrier. There might be as much as a two foot gap, enough room for the evasive horse to step down into that gap and injure his legs. A simple solution is to tie one end of a jump pole to rear right hand side of the trailer; the locking bolt for the ramp (with the butterfly screw) is convenient for this. The other end of the pole lies on the ground and in line with the right hand edge of the ramp *(Fig. 36)*. The horse is prevented from stepping into the dangerous gap between the ramp and the fence line. If this seems overcautious, remember Murphy's Law!

The center partition should be removed or swung to the right hand side and secured. It's best to remove it because if for some reason as we are leading the horse in, he gets excited enough to barge forward onto the breast bar, or rears up, we will be trapped and could be squashed or kicked. It's true that if we take things steadily we diminish the chances of such accidents, but you never can tell; it's still risky.

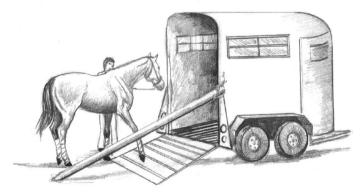

(Fig. 36)
Using the jump pole to guide the horse and to prevent possible injury.

If the partition is fixed at the rear and cannot be swung to one side, don't use this trailer unless you are very experienced. It poses a new set of problems which will become apparent later on in this chapter. Borrow another trailer and teach your horse in that one before returning to your own.

With these conditions met, we minimize the risks of injury to both horse and trainer and can begin to work with the horse.

Equipment

The following list of items is essential for teaching a green horse or reschooling a spoilt one.

1. Lunge cavesson.
2. Lunge line.
3. Protection on legs such as brushing boots.
4. Fairly long but stiff dressage whip.
5. Tidbits.
6. Grain in a bucket.

The lunge cavesson is firmly attached to the horse's head so the horse's nose receives precise signals from the lunge line. A halter is a poor alternative because it twists and is so loose that a signal from the lunge line would have to be given more strongly than with a lunge cavesson.

Attaching the lunge to a bit does nothing to promote the horse's confidence in us since there may be times when we need to use the lunge line very firmly. The horse may run sideways or backwards and punishes himself in the process. Either way the result is the same: he gets jabbed in the mouth.

The lunge line is absolutely indispensable. A lead rope is not appropriate. With its short length, the trainer will end up being dragged, lose his horse, or have to resist in such a way that the animal is on the receiving end of unnecessary punishing signals. The lunge line allows the trainer to play the horse like a fisherman plays a fish: sometimes reeling him in, and a moment later giving him slack. The horse is given latitude to express his fear by running away but at the same time appreciating that it cannot be an "unbridled escape." In other words, he is always conscious that he cannot escape the influence of the trainer. If the trainer is patiently persistent, the horse realizes that he must overcome his fear and trust the trainer.

The need for protection for his legs is because during this type of work there is a high probability that the horse will knock his legs against each other and/or tread on his coronets. The reason is that the horse is likely to go sideways, mostly to the right, because the lunge prevents him from escaping forwards while the trainer's body is a barrier to his left. His only escape before he gets onto the ramp of the trailer is to his right. This will take the form of turns around the forehand since the lunge restricts the nose's sideways movement, while his quarters are able to swing out unchecked. In these instances he is likely to knock his legs so we must protect them. Brushing or galloping boots are a good choice and, even bell boots.

Shipping boots feel strange to a horse that's never worn them and they are inappropriate because of the amount of moving he will undergo. Shipping boots are designed to protect an animal when he is standing still or hardly moving, not for one that might jump sideways, spin around or backs up hurriedly.

If the horse is used to being wrapped with bandages that stretch down to the coronets, these can be a substitute for the brushing boots. Since these are for protection against knocks and scrapes as opposed to being supportive bandages, they must have some material underneath them as a cushioning, cotton wraps or the synthetic equivalent.

A long but stiff dressage whip is needed to tap the horse on different parts of his body. For the most part we walk alongside the horse just as if we were lungeing him, with the lunge line in the left hand and the whip in the right one, held like a fencing foil.

Tidbits are kept on one's person to frequently reward the horse for obeying our signals, especially when he has been brave and overcome his fear. I prefer to feed small pieces of carrot which I bite off for him during each offering. I think it's better than grain that spills out of your hand, which tempts the horse to pull down to glean the leftovers on the ground. He doesn't pay attention since he's more interested in being greedy instead of understanding the relevance of having been fed a tidbit.

Grain in a bucket is kept inside the trailer on the floor or hanging on the forward center post that holds the partition. This food will be the horse's reward for standing quietly when he is fully inside the trailer. He will associate an abundance of food with standing inside the vehicle. Since he will be snacking quite a bit (if he's a particularly suspicious and sensitive horse), it's a good idea to have him hungry prior to the exercise. We don't need to starve him; skipping his previous meal of grain will be sufficient.

Depending on the individual horse, it's sometimes useful to have a hay net hanging inside the trailer in the usual place. However, for the first few entries I prefer to do without it because it can cause problems. Quite often a horse will practically attack the hay. He does so not because he's hungry but because he's excited and edgy. Then when it's time to back him out of the trailer, he refuses to pay attention and nothing short of a firm tug on the lunge will dislodge him from his eating frenzy. This same signal may cause him to throw up his head, as if he had been oblivious to our presence and has been suddenly taken by surprise, and he begins to hurriedly back out of the vehicle.

Also, it's sometimes difficult to secure a hay net at its bottom so it doesn't swing around while the horse greedily rips out the hay. This can cause such a commotion that having a hay net during these initial lessons with an excited horse is counterproductive.

Other Conditions

Contrary to tradition where one or more people become volunteer helpers (or interested bystanders), in most cases it's best to work alone, at least until we get to the part where the ramp is pulled up to shut the horse in.

People distract your horse either by their voices, movement or simply by staring. This may surprise some readers, but the staring of one or more people has a mesmerizing and almost psychic influence on a jittery animal, usually in a negative way. Apart from this, as soon as your horse has stepped completely into the trailer for the first time, there is nearly always one well-meaning soul who opens the side door to see if you and the horse are o.k. in spite of specific instructions to the contrary!

The result is that the horse invariably takes fright and hurriedly backs out of the trailer. This can dent his confidence. Of course, many horses won't care a hoot about such incidents, but why possibly set back his training by finding out if he's bombproof or not? Our motto should be "Do it right the first time." It doesn't make sense to waste time patching up mistakes that were due to laziness or carelessness when we knew better.

The second but no less important point is to give yourself *plenty of time*. If you only have half an hour at your disposal, forget it. Return when you have at least an hour and a half. This is not to say that you will need all this time; but it should be available to you. Why an hour and a half? There's nothing magical about this time span, but if the horse is troublesome, working beyond this becomes nonproductive. The horse becomes physically tired through tension, and mentally inattentive.

If the horse has not been spoiled by previous negative experiences, with skill it's not unreasonable to expect most horses to step fully into the trailer within a few minutes. But if we encounter a problem, it's counterproductive to quit when the clock says so. We need the extra time.

With a difficult horse this extra time may not even get him nearer the trailer or further into it. However, it gives us the opportunity of showing the horse that although we are not interested in forcing him forward, his resistance will be met with resistance. He can resist if he wants—but he has to work for it. If that were not the case, our horse would soon behave like a spoiled child. All he has to do is yell and throw a tantrum to get his own way. The more he's allowed to do that, the more he plays this card for all it's worth. At that point—especially if the horse is smart—this behavior will infiltrate other interactions with his trainer, such as in the ridden work. Before we know it, we have a problem horse on our hands.

Loading

Assuming everything is prepared as outlined, we lead the horse in the direction of the rear of the trailer. If we think we can get him in with one "run," we are risking that he won't like what he sees and will stop without being told.

A better approach is to walk slowly for five or six steps at a time, stopping for a few seconds in between. This reinforces the "go forward" signals and doesn't pressure the horse into relentlessly going towards an object about which he may be uneasy.

During this process of stopping and walking forward, we must be sensitive to the horse's willingness to go forward and to stop him *before* he does so of his own volition. When the horse is reaching the limits of his boldness, we stop and *casually* reassure him. The way we do this is important. If we do it with an attitude of "there, there; I can see that nasty trailer too; don't be frightened, it's o.k.," the chances are we will fuel his doubts and fears.

The better way is not to make a big deal out of it. We should certainly caress him and even use our voice. But it's often better to be completely matter of fact about the whole thing, as if the caresses and sweet words would have been given in any case, even if this stressful circumstance wasn't around.

We stand calmly, preferably unfocusing our gaze from either the trailer or the horse. If he moves—and he will invariably do so with quick short steps in any direction—we calmly resist with the lunge and then *slightly* slacken it and look away again.

This is not to say that by looking away and defocusing from the tense situation, an excited horse will magically and instantly become calm, well behaved, and courageous. That is a utopian way of thinking that will surely get us hurt. Instead, however impervious to the tension of the situation we may appear to the horse all our senses must by fully alert. We should have eyes at the back of our head!

A point worth noting here is to avoid standing too close to the horse, or we risk being stepped on or being pushed off balance. We should stand far enough away to his side by his shoulder (not in front of it, or he can tread on our heels), so that our "whip" hand and arm have enough room to push or prod him with the butt of the whip if he tries to invade our space.

There may be times when this correction is given that he will swivel sideways with his quarters so quickly that we find ourselves in front of the horse. Often, once in this position, he won't hesitate to escape directly forward. The only problem is that we are in his way. If he's not audacious enough to run us over, he will certainly come very close to doing so by passing to either side of us and giving us a glancing blow with his body. This must not be allowed to happen. He must be told in no uncertain manner that our space is ours—not his.

If he tries to charge us, we take immediate action by firmly standing our ground while giving one or more tugs on the lunge, one after the other. Only experience can tell us at what angle those tugs need to be given in the vertical plane. For instance, the lunge line angled sharply downward will have the effect of raising his head against the pull of the lunge. With some horses, although it may postpone their advance for an instant they will continue to charge.

With such horses who are disrespectful of the trainer's space or are so excited they don't understand much, it may be prudent *to advance* while repeatedly throwing the slack of the line in their face and abruptly raising the whip to face level. The whip is held parallel to the ground, at right angles to the fore and aft line of the horse. We are not hitting him on the face with the whip, it's simply raised, in almost a brandishing manner, so he becomes conscious of it as a barrier against which he must not advance.

If this ploy needs to be used, be careful not to stand so close that he can strike out with his front legs or rear and make contact. In practice, as the horse swivels away before charging forward, he will probably have pulled an extra length of line, which automatically places the trainer at a safer distance from the horse's front feet.

Some of these corrections may appear invasive and almost drastic but if given with a cool head and only as much as is needed (and no more), they usually have a salutary effect. It will bring the horse to his senses enough to immobilize him. If the horse was being silly, it will sober him up and dissuade him from playing games. If he was frightened, he will remain so until we soothe him, but at least we will be able to do it with safety to ourselves. Yes, he will be somewhat frightened to move after this, but this immobility is a starting point for improved receptivity on his part. If he's gyrating around, there's little chance he will listen to anything.

When difficult circumstances arise, we must decide what our priorities are. For instance, we may have to frighten or allow the horse to be frightened a little to regain some order in a disorderly situation. It's a trade off. Making the correct decision and with the appropriate mix is a large measure of the trainer's skill. These quirks are best addressed immediately when they are manifested, preferably not too close to the trailer. However, sometimes we won't have that luxury.

Make it a rule when he is acting up never to *deliberately* turn the horse around so he is moving and facing directly away from the trailer. This results in the horse thinking that you are not committed and that he can easily sway you from your purpose by misbehavior.

The only exception to this rule (always there is a caveat!) is if the horse, for whatever reason, is so rooted to the spot that no amount of tact, cajoling or time will make him budge. The most practical solution here is to shift his quarters sideways by first asking for a turn on the forehand. This will unlock hind legs sideways and may do the trick.

I say *may* do the trick because some horses will be so uptight they will turn on the forehand without the slightest inclination or urge to go forward. Their posture will be very stiff and erect. Their legs move mechanically, precisely, and ungenerously. The one advantage is that at least they aren't creating further problems for the trainer by escaping sideways with their shoulders and producing a leg-yielding type of movement. This we want to avoid because we may not have the luxury of a fence line or wall close at hand to curtail this evasion.

Our most practical recourse is to ask for a turn around the forehand. This must be done carefully and precisely because we don't want the horse to escape so he ends up going more sideways than forward. If this occurs and we cannot end the pattern, we should immediately play the line out carefully and lunge the horse. The circle should be about 10 meters diameter. While doing so it may be more practical for the trainer to not stay in the center of the circle, but to walk on a concentric circle. This is done for two reasons. First, the horse needs to be within threatening distance of the dressage whip. Second, the trainer is in a more advantageous state to position himself more towards the horse's tail and thus unequivocally show the horse that he can effectively be chased forward.

Once he goes forward steadily, we do a few halt–walk–trot transitions before returning to our work in hand. We use the whip on his side while ensuring his immediate response to the click of the tongue.

Continuing with our progression, we bring him to within three or four feet of the ramp and halt. He will probably peer inside and sniff the ramp. We wait calmly until he loses interest, often denoted by him giving a sigh. It's at this moment that we lead him on in a matter-of-fact way. It may help (contrary to our normal procedures) to step onto the ramp just ahead of him so that we literally lead and not pull or drag him into the trailer.

During this phase it's very important for the trainer to walk in with almost an attitude of indifference. The trainer must in no way betray any misgivings he may be harboring about his horse's lack of courage. If he displays such doubts, the horse will quickly become aware of them and will gladly oblige by not going any further.

Once the horse is inside or almost so, he can be fed grain from the bucket as a reward. We let him eat for a short time while we stand quietly by his head in a relaxed way. Some horses are tense during this time and the distraction of a caress or even the trainer's voice is often sufficient to break the spell. At this point, the horse usually flings his head up and, if he senses danger and feels trapped, starts to back out of the trailer. With such horses we must stand calmly and with a nonchalant air. If we stand transfixed, not daring to breathe or move, those horses will feel the tension and get panicky.

If all goes well, the partition can be swung over by an assistant. The butt bar or chain is hooked up, and then we can tie the horse while still feeding him grain. The ramp is carefully raised and the horse left inside for a few minutes.

We first untie him before lowering the ramp. The horse must be completely calm before we unhook the butt bar.

This is because a jittery horse will automatically think that once the ramp is down, his escape route is open so he can hurriedly back out. If we leave him in for a minute or so, he might get impatient or think that his handler is waiting for him to back out, and will attempt to do so. That's exactly what we hope he will do, because he will lean into the butt bar and bounce off it. A few attempts will usually convince him that he should stay put, and will teach him not to anticipate exiting the trailer until told by the handler.

Once he is quiet and the butt bar unhinged, we ask him to back out by uttering the word "Back" (*never* the click of the tongue that denotes either more energy or forward movement). At the same time we gently pull the lunge backward while the other hand presses into his chest intermittently until he starts to move.

Most of the above information has been on the assumption that he will not walk up the ramp and enter all the way into the trailer without a problem. If we are fortunate to have a horse that takes it all in stride, there's not a lot more to do except give him more practice in going in and out before he is taken on his first journey.

However, this kind of flawless entry may not come about. The horse may hesitate before going forward again when asked. He may even decide to run back out during any phase of the entry. It is these moments which are the trickiest because the trainer must decide whether to shepherd the horse forward, cajole him, resist backward movement, or to let him go backwards unchallenged. A series of bad decisions can be costly in time and trust.

Especially tricky are the ones concerning whether to resist backward movement (with the risk of provoking the horse into panicking) or decide whether to let him go unhindered. The latter decision is wisest when our instinct tells us that resisting him would be fruitless and counterproductive.

Resisting can be as delicate as the merest hint of a very brief resistance with the lunge, ensuring that its brevity has a soft quality, otherwise it becomes a jerk and consequently is provocative. Or it can mean that the trainer strongly resists by bracing the lunge against hip, using his own body as a snubbing post. This can sometimes provoke the horse into feeling claustrophobic and shouldn't be used unless we sense the horse will feel dominated and quit pulling against us.

Infinite patience is needed, especially when the horse maddeningly steps or runs back time after time. Losing one's temper achieves very little. Instead we should be doggedly persistent. The horse knows he has to enter that trailer. He should be left in no doubt as to our patience or our firmness of purpose.

One last point concerns the position of the partition while loading. Up till now we had it secured to one side. Once the horse was loaded it was pulled back into its central position to box him in. Some horses might object to being disturbed by this procedure, so it's best to load them several times, bringing the partition more and more to the central position before each loading. Only when the horse is willing to go into the narrow bay should he be shut in with the butt bar and ramp.

When the horse is practiced in entering the trailer calmly and willingly, it's easy enough to slide the lead rope across his withers and encourage him to step into the trailer by himself.

Epilogue

The trainer of the young horse is in some ways disadvantaged because the rather questionable control he has over his charge prevents him from implementing the kind of structure seen in a training program for a more experienced horse. When we train the young horse, unless we want to bore him or stultify his physical and mental development, we are compelled to teach him predominantly in a spiral mode instead of a linear one.

In the spiral mode, he learns many things relatively quickly and improves the quality of each one over a period of time. In the linear method, he is taught in a more sequential manner—not literally of course—but leaning towards that trend.

To adopt the latter method in its pure form with a young horse would be the equivalent of telling a two-year-old child she is not allowed to read or flip through the pictures of a story book until she can ready the first line fluently and with good diction. She's never going to buy that idea unless there is some huge incentive. I would like to know what that could be for a two-year old—short of giving her her own candy store!

The predominantly spiral method of learning frequently means taking care of a problem here, then another one there and so on. Often times this can be disruptive to the training plan we had in mind for that day or week and our well meaning intentions are sidelined.

It is in acknowledgment of the probability of this trend, that the work described in this book has not propagated a strict training plan. This does not imply that it is unnecessary to have one.

Instead, we have examined a series of approaches and techniques presented in a way that I hope will stimulate the thought process of the trainer, even if one doesn't agree with all the material.

After all, there are many ways of doing any one thing. Some are better than others, of course but it is by appraising even the not so good ones that we come to appreciate the true worth of the better ones.

The recognition of these can only be gotten by concentration, observation, logic, paying great attention to detail, and the intuitive process. At the end of the day, we may even wonder who has learned and developed the most—the horse or us?!

If the trainer has adhered to the points that have been advocated, with some polish he should have a horse that is polite, quiet, obedient and be able to carry the rider at walk, trot, and canter in an efficient manner.

In spite of the apparent complications of some of the exercises, this in no way suggests that he is a "made" horse. He is still a long way from that. However, he has gotten a very useful start, which is a good springboard for further training.

A famous politician once claimed that "all politics is local politics." The truth of that statement extends even to the equestrian field and may be paraphrased by saying that "all training is really basic training."